NEW HANDBOOK OF
PASTORAL LITURGY

To David Hebblethwaite, Trevor Lloyd,
Jane Sinclair, David Stancliffe
and Kenneth Stevenson,
fellow workers in the Liturgical Commission
from 1986 until the present day,
and to the memory of Michael Vasey,
who worked with us until his death in 1998

NEW HANDBOOK OF PASTORAL LITURGY

Michael Perham

First published in Great Britain in 2000 by
Society for Promoting Christian Knowledge
Holy Trinity Church
Marylebone Road
London NW1 4DU

Acknowledgements
Extracts from *Common Worship: Services and Prayers for the
Church of England* (Church House Publishing) and
Common Worship: Pastoral Services (Church House Publishing)
are copyright © The Archbishops' Council, 2000
and are reproduced by permission.

British Library Cataloguing-in-Publication Data

A catalogue record for this book is
available from the British Library

ISBN 0–281–05252–2

Typeset by Wilmaset Ltd, Birkenhead, Wirral
Printed in Great Britain by
The Cromwell Press, Trowbridge, Wiltshire

Contents

Preface   vii

PART ONE: INTRODUCTION   1

1   Why Liturgy?   3
2   Why Church of England Liturgy?   10

PART TWO: PRINCIPLE AND PRACTICE   17

3   People and Prayer   19
4   Priest and Deacon   30
5   Furnishing and Space   38
6   Symbols and Gestures   47
7   Cycles and Seasons   55
8   Texts and Traditions   62
9   Scripture and Lection   69
10   Sunday and Weekday   77
11   Young People and Children   88
12   Clothing and Colours   92
13   Fellowship and Wonder   97

PART THREE: THE EUCHARIST   101

14   Rites and Orders   103
15   The Gathering   111
16   The Liturgy of the Word   119
17   The Liturgy of the Sacrament   127
18   The Dismissal   139

PART FOUR: WORD SERVICES   141

19   A Service of the Word   143
20   Daily Prayer   149
21   Celebrating the Sunday Office   156

CONTENTS

PART FIVE: INITIATION AND PASTORAL RITES 161

22 Baptism 163
23 Steps along the Baptismal Way 172
24 Marriage 181
25 Healing and Reconciliation in Church 189
26 Funeral Rites 195
27 Welcome, Blessing and Commission 205
28 Liturgy in the Home 209

PART SIX: THE CHRISTIAN YEAR 213

29 Advent 215
30 Christmas to Candlemas 221
31 Lent and Holy Week 228
32 The Great Fifty Days of Easter 236
33 The Kingdom of Christ and of his Saints 242
34 High Points and Holy Days 247

Epilogue: Liturgy for the World 253

Bibliography 255

Index 257

Preface

❧

The publication of the series of new services under the title of *Common Worship*, to replace on 1 January 2001 the provisions of the Alternative Service Book of 1980, means that there will have to be some liturgical change in most parishes across the Church of England. The changes will not be as radical as those experienced a generation ago, partly because we have moved in most church communities into a more evolutionary approach to liturgy, and partly because the central rite of the Church, the eucharist, has been only modestly revised. The greater changes come in relation to initiation and the pastoral offices – in the baptism service, for instance, and the funeral rites – and in preaching controlled by a very different lectionary provision. It would be possible for the transition to happen with very little disturbance to the worshipping life of most of the laity. Even the clergy and others who lead worship could, if they chose, adopt the new services with minimal thought and preparation, make them seem as much like the services of ASB 1980 as possible, and carry on to some extent much as before.

But that would be to miss a huge opportunity at the beginning of a new century to renew the worship of countless parishes and other communities. Liturgical Commissions and General Synods can and do revise the liturgy, but only in the local church community can revision turn into renewal, and a Church of England with its worship renewed would give great glory to God and be a far more effective instrument of Christian mission in today's world. The purpose of this book is to help clergy, worship leaders and whole congregations grasp that opportunity.

I am grateful to SPCK, who have published all my books since I first started writing about liturgy in 1978, for inviting me to take the message and insights of *Liturgy Pastoral and Parochial* (1984) and *Lively Sacrifice* (1992) and to work them, alongside fresh material, into a new volume that would help people to engage with the new *Common Worship* series of services and provide a handbook that those concerned with liturgy in the local church could turn to for some years to come.

So this is not an entirely new book. Parts of it (particularly the section entitled 'Principle and Practice') draw very heavily on *Lively Sacrifice* – the principles at least have not changed in the eight years since that was written. Some other parts represent careful rewriting of material in the two earlier books. There is not much in *Liturgy Pastoral and Parochial* that has survived unaltered, for it was written before all the developments in Church of England liturgy that have come through such publications as *The Promise of His Glory*, *Patterns for Worship*, *Celebrating Common Prayer* and *A Service of the Word*, let alone the rethinking that lies behind *Common Worship*. Some of the writing here is entirely new and takes into account not only those developments, but also the growth of lay leadership of worship in many churches and the ordination of women to the priesthood, making the gender bias of much that was written before inappropriate.

I have written this book for all who have a love of good liturgy and for all who desire that the worship of their church shall be the very best they can offer. It is not intended to be a book for a particular tradition or churchmanship. My own experience has been broad. As a bishop's chaplain and as the chairman of a diocesan liturgical committee I have shared in worship in a whole variety of settings. As the rector of an urban team ministry in Poole, with churches built in the last forty years and with membership of a local ecumenical project, and then as a member of the clergy team of two cathedrals (in Norwich and Derby), I have had to explore how in a whole variety of settings liturgical principle and pastoral practice need to meet and to refine one another. Some will read this book and wish it reflected more unquestioningly the current liturgical practice of the Roman Catholic Church, and others will wish it seemed more aware of charismatic worship. I hope they will make allowances and still find information and ideas here that will help them devise the very best liturgy that is true to their own tradition.

I express my grateful thanks to Joanna Moriarty, Editorial Director at SPCK, who has been unfailingly encouraging, to my colleagues over many years in the Liturgical Commission (to the longest serving of whom this book is dedicated) whose friendship I value much, to Jonathan and Susan Bailey for making available to me the peace and solitude of their cottage in which to write this book in January 2000, to my wife, Alison, for her encouragement and support in this and so much else, and to the congregation of Derby Cathedral, with whom it is a delight to worship, and to my colleagues in the residentiary chapter who kindly gave me leave of absence to undertake this work. To all of them I owe a great debt of gratitude. All of us love the liturgy of the Church, but not as much as we love the Lord to whom the Church offers worship in spirit and in truth.

Michael Perham   Derby, Candlemas 2000

PART ONE

Introduction

1

Why Liturgy?

Grasping the heel of heaven

Worship is the offering to God of praise, glory and honour in reverence and in love. It is something that can be done in community or alone, in church or in a thousand other contexts. But what is this strange thing called 'liturgy' that seems to occupy more of the Church's consciousness than used to be the case? Worship and liturgy are not exactly the same thing.

Liturgy is that subtle blend of word, song, movement, gesture and silence that enables the people of God to worship together. Liturgy is, at a certain level, always about compromise, for it is about finding the forms that will enable people to experience something satisfying collectively. In that sense perhaps heaven will be a divine compromise, for that too will provide a setting where people with their infinite variety of personality and preference can experience something overwhelmingly wonderful that binds and draws together. You can worship without liturgy on your own. You can worship without church on your own. But the moment you engage in worship with others, there has to be a shared form, and that is where liturgy comes in. For that form is likely to be shaped by words, by music, by movement, by gesture and by silence. That is what liturgy is – the way in to the Church's corporate worship of God, the Father of our Lord Jesus Christ.

So what is the purpose of this worship that we so often do through liturgy? What is it for? What are we trying to do? The word 'trying' has its problems, for at a very fundamental level we are not 'trying' to do anything at all. We worship because that is a deep human instinct within us. We worship because the Spirit of God conspires with our human spirit to bring us into a relationship with the Father through Christ. The story of Christian history confirms that the instinct to worship God has never been capable of suppression for long. We are not trying, we are doing what we have to do, we are doing what comes naturally for us. Yet, for all its inadequacy, it is important to press the question: What is it we are trying to do?

To look at different Christian communities as they prepare and celebrate their Sunday worship is to get some strange answers. There are some churches where it looks very much as if the major aim of the Sunday service is to evangelize. The service has been put together with a conscious intention of drawing into faith, maybe by a powerful challenge, those not already committed. There is no doubt that worship at its best is a highly effective means of evangelism. But I doubt very much if it is what we should set out to do each Sunday morning.

Or there are churches where it looks as if the major aim of worship is to teach. Anglicans in the past have been very ready for such an approach, for they have come to 'hear the sermon' more than anything else. Nowadays it may be dividing into groups or looking at the diagrams on the overhead projector, but the intention is the same – to teach. Again this is very important, and there is no doubt that the liturgy itself is a great teacher, but is teaching what we are trying to do?

In a third sort of church the emphasis seems to be on the building up of a sense of community. Here again, there is no doubt that true worship does engender a deep sense of fellowship, but it is not what we set out to achieve. This third sort of church illustrates how the pursuit of a lesser objective may blind that church to what is most needed. What really creates fellowship in a church community is faith deeply held and shared. While busy exhorting the people to be friendly, to share the peace more enthusiastically, and to be sure to come to coffee after the service, the vicar may be missing the point that what is needed in that church is a deep experience of the living God. If they had that, they would have something to talk about after the service, and might even flock to coffee to do so!

The truth is that the deep purpose of worship is not to evangelize, nor to teach, nor to engender fellowship, but to be in touch with the living God. It is important to say that worship is for worship, not primarily for anything else. Worship is to enable us to reach up to grasp the heel of heaven, to glimpse, albeit imperfectly and fleetingly, the life of heaven, to plug in, for a moment, to the worship of the angels and the praises of the saints. However and wherever the 'Holy, holy, holy . . .' found its way into the eucharist, it deserves to stay there for all time, if for no other reason than to remind us, every time we come, that we do not create worship; we simply join ourselves for a while to the perpetual worship around the throne of God.

> Therefore with angels and archangels,
> and with all the company of heaven,
> we proclaim your great and glorious name,
> for ever praising you and saying:

Holy, holy, holy Lord,
God of power and might,
heaven and earth are full of your glory.
Hosanna in the highest.

My worry is not that our worship so often falls short of this. Our sinful human nature makes it inevitable that we shall, most of the time, remain fairly earthbound, and indeed there is a sense in which our feet ought to be firmly grounded on this earth, even though our hearts are up in heaven. No, I am not worried that we fail to find ourselves caught up in the holiness around the throne of God every time we share in the liturgy. My worry is that we appear not to expect it ever to happen. We are not yearning for it. We have lost sight of it as the crown of our worshipping endeavour. I believe that our worship will be of little avail until we have rebuilt that expectation in priest and people, worship leader and congregation, alike. Of course it will not happen to everybody every day. Of course it will rarely be a vision of God in all his beauty, and nearly always grasping the heel is the nearest we shall get. But we must not settle for less than a yearning to be touched by the glory, and to sense the angels and the saints.

The other things follow. Evangelism, teaching, fellowship, and much more, do indeed happen when the people of God are engaged in the liturgy, but not because we set out to do them. They happen because the worship is pure and deep and filled with the Spirit. People are converted, people are taught, people are drawn together, but only if they are touched by the power of the worship, and that depends on the relationship of the community to God. It is a kind of turning on its head that is part of the divine way of things.

It works something like this. We offer to God our worship, as much in Spirit and in truth as we can. In our deluded human way we imagine it to be worthy. In reality it falls far short of what it ought to be, but God accepts it and uses it. We think we are giving something to him and, lo and behold, he turns it round and makes of it a gift to us. We have brought him our worship; he has turned it into a tool of evangelism or teaching or fellowship. That is his activity, not ours. We offer the worship; he does the rest. Supremely of course this is true of the eucharist and perhaps it is not surprising in a sacrament where we bring bread and wine, and here again find them returned to us changed by his touch. He turns our offering into gift. Such is his way.

Experiencing freedom through order

But if worship is essentially about the reality of our relationship with God, is there room for the liturgist, who works by shapes and forms, by set texts and rubrics? Surely in the Spirit we are set free from all that? Indeed we are set free, or should be, from a kind of narrowness that imagines that God can only be worshipped in a certain way or will only receive our prayer in a particular style. Nevertheless the tendency in the Church today to draw a contrast between openness to the Spirit of God and concern with good order is unnecessary and harmful. The matter can be presented in such a way that those who are concerned with order are branded as those who follow the letter of the law, which kills real worship, whereas those who are free of that follow the Spirit who gives life. Undoubtedly there is a legalistic mind that can creep into the ordering of worship, and the Church of England, with its elaborate parliamentary and synodical procedures for authorizing forms of service, is prone to it. But, on the whole, a concern for good order is in reality a concern to create the conditions in which people feel free and open to receive what God is always offering.

The basis of much liturgical thinking today is to provide sufficient shape and structure to worship that people are secure enough to benefit from the spontaneous and the unfamiliar (which is very often the moment when the Spirit of God seems most at work). Where people are lost, perplexed or even (if their traditional landmarks have been removed) angry, there is not likely to be an openness to the Spirit of God. There are occasions, of course, when it is right that liturgy should shape and disturb, but that is not the way that it normally draws people to God. They have their spirituality deepened from the sound basis of a shape and a structure, and even a set of texts, that are familiar, reassuring and well tried. With that sort of security, they can be open, imaginative and bold. Order is, for most people most of the time, the precondition for spontaneity and freedom. The liturgist, with his or her concern for satisfying structures, is in league with the Spirit.

There are many who would recognize some truth in that when it comes to broad principles about shape and structure, but some would be doubtful about a concern for liturgical order that ended up in prescribing details. 'Should the bishop stand or sit during the ordination prayer?' 'Should the *Gloria* be used on a saint's day in Lent?' 'May a lay person give the blessing at Evening Prayer?' Do these questions matter? At one level, of course, the answer has to be No. No fundamental Christian principle is at stake. No one's eternal salvation is under threat for not knowing the answer, if indeed there is one correct answer. Yet there is a sense in which, if some of this detail contributes to the creation of a liturgy that is deeply satisfying, these matters ought not to be despised.

Ordinary churchgoers are not aware of the rules by which the liturgist works. They ought not to be aware of them. If they were, these rules would be an intrusion into worship. In some way that is why clergy and

others who do know these rules find it so much more difficult to worship
– there are so many more things that can irritate them if they are not to
their taste. But ordinary churchgoers can often know by instinct that a
service does not feel quite right, has not come together in a way that
creates deep prayerfulness or a sense of the presence of God. And the
reason that that has not happened is sometimes that those planning it
ignored the rules of satisfying liturgical practice. There was the intrusion
of a text introducing a change of mood when it was not time for it. There
was an imbalance in the way the parts of the service were shared between
the leaders. There were two many verses in the song between the
readings. There were no climaxes or there were too many. Application
of some rule-of-thumb liturgical principles might have ironed those out
and created the kind of worship where everything humanly possible came
together to open up the people to the Spirit of God yearning to come in.
The detail can make its humble contribution to the noble enterprise of
helping Christian people to be in touch with their Creator.

When people go to the theatre or the ballet, they do not want to be
aware of the stage directions. But they know it would be a chaotic and
unsatisfactory experience if there were none. It is strange that we can
sometimes be suspicious about the use of words like 'drama' and 'theatre'
in relation to the worship of the Church. Of course liturgy cannot only be
drama or theatre, of course it must never be only performance, but it
cannot be less than any of those things. The liturgy, especially the liturgy
of baptism and of the eucharist, is the drama that celebrates the story of
our salvation, nothing less, and the attention to detail must be such that
we are all caught up in it, never audience, always participants.

Celebrating redemption

To be caught up in the action, to participate in it fully, is to 'celebrate'. It
is not only the presiding minister who 'celebrates' when the people of
God are at worship. 'Celebration' is the characteristic activity of the whole
worshipping community. We use the word in two senses. In the more
limited sense, we mean that praise, thankfulness and joy will never be far
below the surface, and often will burst into song, in Christian worship. In
a wider sense, we know that even when worship appears to be chiefly
concerned with some other aspect of Christian experience – confession,
reflection, intercession – it is all within the context of a trusting joyful
faith, founded on the good news of salvation. There is the celebration of
the party for the prodigal son behind every act of sorrowful confession
and search for forgiveness. There is an *alleluia* deep down in every

reflection or meditation, however anxious, perplexed or uncertain it may be.

And so it is that Christian celebration, for all its liveliness – and how much we need that liveliness which all too often seems absent from our pew-bound worship! – must never degenerate into superficiality, a kind of surface bubble without much depth. Celebration need not be like that. The liveliness that Christian worship needs comes from a serious waiting upon the Holy Spirit and being open to his influence which renews and deepens, and from engaging in every act of worship with the central truths of the faith – with the birth and death and resurrection of Jesus Christ. The service we most often describe as a 'celebration' is the one that takes us deepest into the mystery of the cross. It is right that it should be so, for we can celebrate only because we are adopted as God's children, loved and redeemed.

Yet the danger in the majority of churches today is not, to be honest, that the celebration will be superficial, too much of a party and the cross not in sight. The danger is that, despite the good news there is for which to give thanks, the liturgy will not feel like a celebration at all. It may be reverent, it may be well ordered, it may be serious. Or it may be lifeless, condescending, unconvincing. The young are not always wrong when they say it is 'boring'. Some of the adults look fairly unengaged too. What the Church needs today is worshippers, and especially worship leaders, who have taken the trouble to engage with liturgy and to understand its underlying principles and who see its potential to deepen the love of every Christian for the Lord, and who will then, confidently and prayerfully, set about helping to bring the worship of the Church to life, to do old things much better and new things well, to explore fresh paths, to look for alternatives, determined that the liturgy shall deserve the title 'celebration'. King David danced before the Lord with exuberance gone a little wild. Jesus himself radiated a thankful joy in life, in people, in his Father. The liturgy does need the beauty of holiness. It does need to engage with the cross and with the suffering of the world. But it also needs to sparkle with a hint of heaven.

Making connections

What will stop the descent from sparkle, that has about it a hint of heaven, to superficiality is engagement with the cross and its outworking in the lives of those who suffer. The Church's worship is never an escape from the realities of the world. People come to a service weighed down (or sometimes uplifted) by the world's concerns, and the Church must be able to respond to this. The enthusiasm a generation ago with which the new freedom for intercession about the issues of the day was greeted illustrated how people responded to the opportunity to spell out their daily concerns within the context of the Church's worship. So did the enthusiasm for 'offertory processions', which, whatever the danger of Pelagianism, enabled people to symbolize the bringing to God of the ordinary things of daily life.

But the fundamental point lies in the transformation of the gifts we bring. What we bring, God uses, God touches, and we receive back what we have brought, but it has been transformed. The concern and anxiety we bring in our heart, as much as the bread and wine that we symbolically set before God in the eucharist, is touched by the hand of God and given back transformed. That is the real point of connection between liturgy and life. It is, as often as not, an argument for time in worship for silence and reflection, as much as for urgent, fervent prayer, time for God to touch and thus to heal. The liturgy may be at its most practical – helping the worshipper to self-understanding or to self-acceptance – when it seems most ethereal.

There is a yet deeper level at which liturgy and life are inextricably bound. Liturgy involves bringing into consciousness deep truths about human nature. The liturgy of Holy Week and Easter, for instance, is not, in the end, an historical exercise, a glance back into the past to discover what happened to Jesus. It is about a remembrance that makes him present, and that makes his experience present, to the extent that I discover it to be my experience; and by entering into the way he lived through his experience, I find the strength to live through mine. Liturgy reflects life that it may inform and transform life. It does not simply teach about a life (though it does that too), but is a dramatic engagement with every human life.

Thus it is that, for all that the liturgy is necessarily corporate, bringing us together that we may worship through shared words and songs and symbols, it needs to interact at a deep level with each individual and their spirituality. In the late twentieth century the Church concentrated too much of its attention on the revision of outward liturgical forms and too little on the revival of spirituality that will give life to those forms. The richness of the liturgy, with its message of the fellowship of all Christian people in prayer and praise, must be joined to the deep hunger and longing of individual souls if liturgy, spirituality and life are really to be experienced as the unity they are. Renewal must follow from revision, and, for all the liturgists can do, renewal must start from the individual and the heart.

9

2

Why Church of England Liturgy?

The path of diversity

A large number of Church of England worshippers do not remember the days when the liturgy all came from one book, the Book of Common Prayer of 1662. This is not surprising, for more than thirty years have passed since then. There is a tendency to imagine a uniformity in those days that is not true to the reality. Anglican churches all had their distinctive ways. The architecture and ordering of the church building helped to create the style. The robes and vestments the ministers wore contributed to it too. The music, even the choice of hymn book, made a huge difference. None of this is surprising if liturgy is about symbol and song as much as it is about words. These same things help to create style in our worship today. But there was, nevertheless, a commonality of text that has been to some extent abandoned. Even then people went to other sources to enrich the authorized texts. Altar missals for the more catholic part of the Church introduced all sorts of additional words, quite a lot of them from what was euphemistically called 'the Western Church', which simply meant Rome. Parishes all over the land, with the goodwill of bishops, used material from the failed Prayer Book of 1928. Indeed many parishes had copies of these for the congregation, even though right through into the reign of Elizabeth II the text continued to pray for 'our gracious sovereign lord, King George' – and it was George V the text had in mind, though Edward VIII and George VI had come and gone. Almost every priest and Reader had a collection of prayers for use 'after the third collect' at Morning and Evening Prayer. There was textual variety.

Nevertheless at the heart of liturgy was a substantial body of common text and order from which deviation was minimal. It was difficult to be creative. It was difficult, if there was to be renewal in a parish, for it to find its focus in worship. Some of us, who love the Prayer Book and Thomas Cranmer's beautiful evocative texts, nevertheless experienced it as spiritually constricting. But it was undoubtedly 'common prayer'. Despite the architecture, the ordering of the building, the vestments, the ceremonial and the singing, when you went into St Mary's, which was 'high', and into St Peter's, which was 'low', and into St George's, which was somewhere in the middle, you knew where you were – very definitely in the Church of England – and you could say much of the service off by heart.

From 1967 for the rest of the century the Church of England seemed to march resolutely away from that commonality. Its first new services – Series One, Series Two and even Series Three – through the late 1960s and the 1970s did not within themselves have great variety or permission to improvise or extemporize. In themselves they were tightly constructed rites, different from the Prayer Book in shape and in language style. But their very existence introduced diversity. If you went to Holy Communion, you had to be ready for three or four different rites and, at least with Series Three, you had to ready for a complete new set of texts. There were too just the beginnings of new freedoms within the rites, a sprinkling of permissive 'may's and 'or's and certainly an encouragement to bring into intercessions the issues of the day and the matters of concern to the local church community. Common prayer was not so uniform.

Then came The Alternative Service Book of 1980. Here the options had grown. In Holy Communion Rite A even the eucharistic prayer itself was in four main forms, though they were remarkably similar and only the presidential texts changed. Local decision making became part of the liturgical picture. Shall we have the prayers of penitence at the beginning or in the middle at the eucharist? Shall we have the vows before or after the Ministry of the Word at a wedding? Shall we have the sign of the cross before or after the dipping in water at baptism? The local minister and, to some extent, the local congregation owned the liturgy in a new way by deciding what was right in that community and on that particular occasion. 'Other suitable words' were often a permitted alternative to a text provided and, though suitable words might be found in anthologies of prayer and liturgical text, or even by borrowing from other Christian Churches, 'suitable words' could also mean that the priest or the worship leader wrote their own or formulated their own as they prayed spontaneously.

Yet the new freedoms did not seem to go far enough. In addition to using authorized services and sometimes pushing the new permissions to the limits, clergy and other worship leaders were devising other services, variously called 'informal', 'non-liturgical', 'all-age', most frequently labelled 'family services' in order to engage new people and to engage existing congregations in a new way. Many of these services were highly

11

creative and imaginative, had real attractiveness to people who found the authorized services unhelpful, and in many parishes the family service, whether on a weekly or a monthly basis, became the best attended, most popular act of worship in the life of that church.

What was happening when the best attended service was officially the one on the fringe, the one that sat lightest to the authorized liturgy of the Church of England?

The Church's response, through its Liturgical Commission, was *Patterns for Worship*, first published in 1989. It was more than a response to the family-service phenomenon; it tried to engage, for instance, with some of the criticisms of the liturgy in *Faith in the City*, the report of the Archbishops' Commission on the Church in Urban Priority Areas. But *Patterns for Worship* did provide encouragement to those who found previous provision constricting. It gave a rich collection of seasonal and thematic texts. But, more importantly, it tried to show that shape and order are crucial to good liturgy and that certain things need to be present if worship is to be recognized as 'Anglican'. In other words it focused 'common prayer' more on shape and outline than on shared text and put more emphasis on 'family likeness' in liturgy than on any sort of textual conformity. It encouraged the less creative to be more so, the very creative to return to some liturgical principles.

It is difficult to see the Anglican liturgical path for thirty years as anything but a resolute march, in response to a variety of pressures, away from the commonality, if not uniformity, that it valued in the past. It is important to say that, although there are those who have regarded this march as an unmitigated disaster, they are a (probably small) minority and for most people the experience of the last thirty years has been one of liturgical renewal. Where a parish is coming alive, the liturgy can be at the heart of it, can indeed be where renewal begins. Where people are finding their prayer life and their spirituality deepened it can be because of the stimulus of liturgy where the Spirit can move among the worshippers. Where the Church has the opportunity to reach out into the community in a special service to mark a great occasion or a national disaster, it is the better equipped to do so because every community and every worship leader has had experience of being liturgically creative. Not everywhere, of course, but in many churches up and down the land, the worship has 'taken off' because of the new climate that gives people choice, that takes the local needs seriously and sees a creative relationship between, on the one hand, order, text and rubric and, on the other, openness to where the Spirit seems to be leading today. Liturgical diversity seems to have replaced common prayer.

Yet the new Church of England services that come into use from the First Sunday of Advent 2000 have the overall title *Common Worship*. At first that may seem extraordinary, unless there is an attempt to reverse the trend of the last generation and march back up the hill to the uniformity of the past. *Common Worship* does indeed mark something of a shift, though not a dramatic reversal, and it is important to explore why this shift seems necessary and exactly what it will mean.

The recovery of commonality

In the last years of the twentieth century, through its Liturgical Commission and its General Synod, but also in discussions in many parishes, the Church was beginning to ask: What will be the loss to the Church if we no longer have a common liturgy? Three distinct losses can be identified.

The first is doctrinal. The Church of England has not been a confessional Church that responds to those who want to know what are its particular emphases by pointing them to a denominational confessional statement. We say, in effect, if you want to know our doctrine, look at our liturgy. When a minister begins a new appointment he or she makes a declaration (included in the new *Common Worship* book) in which the Thirty-nine Articles of Religion, the Book of Common Prayer and the Ordering of Bishops, Priests and Deacons are given as a repository of Anglican belief. Two of those three documents are liturgical ones (and the third bound up within the same covers as the Book of Common Prayer). The Church of England is a Church that reveals what it believes by the way it worships. However much it may have been denied officially, the Alternative Service Book of 1980, for all that it did not have the status for doctrine that the Book of Common Prayer has, was doctrinally significant simply because it was the theological emphases that it contained that informed the people of God in the majority of parishes through twenty years. But if we are to allow a very wide freedom, to pick or choose liturgical texts, or even to compose them, or to accept extempore praying as a liturgical norm, where is doctrine to be found? It is of course quite possible to have a Church that does not look to its liturgy to reveal its doctrine. But a Church of England that did not define its doctrine by the words, and to some extent the actions, of its worship would be a very different sort of Church from the one we have known.

It was this sort of concern that caused the General Synod (and the House of Bishops in particular) to agonize long and hard about whether it was right to allow the proliferation of eucharistic prayers. If, in the eucharistic prayer, which is one of the moments where doctrine is expressed most overtly and where there are historic sensitivities to be respected, there is no norm, where is the common prayer of the Church? It does not help us to answer that the Roman Catholic Church has a large variety of eucharistic prayers, for that Church has its own quite different ways of maintaining doctrinal norms. For all that it is a thoroughly liturgical Church, it does not rely on its liturgy to enunciate its doctrine as clearly as Anglicans do.

The second loss is ecclesiological. It relates to our communion and fellowship one with another. Anglicans have traditionally seen their liturgy as a major source of their unity. This is not just an internal Church of England attitude. Anglicanism worldwide has been a communion held together by a book. Although many provinces of the Church have developed their own liturgical forms, until recently they were all very much 'son or daughter of Book of Common Prayer'. With the emergence, quite rightly, of a new emphasis on liturgical inculturation, and the consequent collapse of liturgical identity, we see the Anglican Communion looking for another focus of unity, and finding it, to some extent at least, in the seat of St Augustine and the person of the Archbishop of Canterbury. But it remains true that a kind of family likeness to Anglican worship, that manages rather remarkably to shine through even our traditional churchmanship styles, has been a crucial element in our sense of identity and unity. If I cannot find from Sunday to Sunday and church to church sufficient of that family likeness to strengthen my sense of belonging to a national and international Church, I am impoverished. When there is so much to divide us, we are foolish to abandon in too carefree a manner something that has long held us together.

I put this case in Anglican terms, with all the dangers that it may seem unecumenical and narrow-minded. I do believe and pray for the coming Church where all will be in communion one with another, but I believe also that distinctive traditions enrich rather than weaken the Church and I see no strong case for the disappearance of a distinctive Anglicanism, any more than, say, a distinctive Methodism or Moravianism. However, for those who would see virtue in the absorption of these traditions into one more obviously single Church, the argument for commonality still applies. The last century saw a remarkable convergence in liturgical shape and text across the denominations. Common liturgy is one of the elements in the growing together of the Churches.

The third loss, which some would count the most significant, is spiritual. It is, very simply, that the human soul needs to be fed and sustained by sufficient common text that the words can go deep down inside, almost subconsciously, and can help form the Christian in the way of Christ and come to the rescue in times of testing, tension and sickness. There is still a generation in the Church that has a kind of memory bank of scripture and liturgical text that sustains in times of crisis and will sustain them until they die. The scripture that is part of it is mainly in the Authorized King James version, the liturgical part mainly, though not exclusively, from the Book of Common Prayer.

For fifty years now we have been making it less likely that the scripture part of this knapsack of text will be retained or even added to. Ever since the daring, as it seemed, use of J. B. Phillips' translations of parts of the Bible in the 1950s, the Church has engaged with new translations, some more official than others, some more accurate, some more lasting. There has been enormous gain in these successive new translations. They have opened up the scriptures to new people, they have given new insights to many readers which older translations had not revealed. But there has been loss. If, every time I hear a passage of scripture read, I hear it in a new version, it may hit me a fresh way, but I do not have the chance to commit it, or at least phrases within it, to memory. It is good that *Common Worship* and the various publications supporting it appear to be giving the New Revised Standard Version a certain priority, not because it is a perfect translation, but because it is the one around which the Church in this generation is most likely to unite so that we can hear key passages from it over and over again until they have become part of our memory bank.

But what of the liturgical element in the knapsack? Among a younger generation, fed principally on the Alternative Service Book, there is still the chance of texts in the memory bank. Some of them are only light revisions of the Book of Common Prayer, for example the prayer at the beginning of the eucharist, 'Almighty God, to whom all hearts are open . . .' and others belonging to our own age, for example both of the prayers after communion. Some of us, with a kind of bilingualism, have these contemporary texts in our knapsack, but also older material from the Book of Common Prayer, the general thanksgiving or the *Magnificat*, for instance. But, if for the future there is little common text in church, what will be in the memory of those now coming to church for the first time?

It needs to be emphasized again that the need for liturgical memory is not in order to be able to worship in church without book, service sheet or overhead projector screen (though more liturgy from memory setting the eyes free to engage in other ways with the action would be no bad thing), but in order to have this immense spiritual resource in crisis times. When I am near to death and the priest comes to minister to me, what will be the texts that he or she will use knowing that I, ill to a point where conversation has gone and my mind is confused, will recognize and even begin to move my lips to join in saying?

The Church needs common prayer. The witness of the early centuries and the wisdom of the present age is that principally we need common shape. But we do also need common words; perhaps not many, just a core, and a core that can change slowly, but words nevertheless. Of course it is a matter of balance. Most of us want to stay somewhere on the path to liturgical diversity that takes occasion, place and culture seriously. But the vital question is: What are the proper limits to that diversity?

15

It is with that question that the *Common Worship* series of services engage. Whereas the Alternative Service Book and the material that followed from it simply opened up the possibilities one by one, so that there was an ever greater sense of freedom. *Common Worship* tries to ask much more clearly at which points this freedom is desirable and helpful – and where it is to encourage it all the more – and at which points commonality is much more desirable and helpful – and where it is to signal its importance. Thus *Common Worship* is stronger, less permissive than the ASB, on order and shape. There is, in almost every case where the ASB gave options of shape, one clear, preferred structure to the service. It is also clear where only authorized texts are permitted, such as prayers of penitence and eucharistic prayers, and where there are almost unlimited freedoms. It is clear at what points in the year the Church is to unite around a common lectionary celebrating the central events of our salvation and at what points local decision making might lead to a different lectionary track. For those ready to follow there is a clear message: common prayer is good, liturgical diversity is good, finding the proper balance is important.

The balance will not of course be the same in every community. For some the arguments for familiarity, security and memorability will have strong appeal and people will go tentatively only a little way down the path of variety and diversity. And that may be right for them. For others freshness, creativity and a suspicion of repetition will mean that every week is an almost new experience, but there will be a recognition that deep underlying structures matter and that some common texts committed to memory enhance the experience of worship. And that may be right for them.

There is a crucial need for the debate that has been implicit nationally in the revision of the liturgy for 2000, about the balance between commonality and diversity, to be taken up in each church community. Each church needs to ask: have we got this balance right? There is also a need for each community to recover a proper sense of law in liturgy. One of the negative results of twenty years of increasing diversity is to create a culture where people not only claim all the freedoms they are given, but assume the same freedom at points where it has not been granted. There will be parishes that will decide that, despite the best efforts of the Liturgical Commission, the House of Bishops and the General Synod, none of the eight authorized eucharistic prayers of Holy Communion Order One quite fits their need. They have written their own and much prefer it. In the end the liturgy of the Church cannot be about congregational preference, for, with all its broad freedoms and encouragement to creativity, the liturgy holds the Church together and safeguards what the Church believes.

PART TWO

Principle and Practice

3

People and Prayer

The congregation

It is easy to say that every Christian liturgy should be a reaching up to heaven to share the worship of the angels. It is more difficult to see how this comes about. I believe that the key lies in understanding the role of the people, the congregation. It is the congregation's participation that is crucial, and we very easily misunderstand what that participation is.

The word 'congregation' needs rescuing before we can go any further. Rightly understood it is a description of the whole assembly gathered for worship, all the lay people together with their ministers. There is nobody participating in the celebration who is not a member of the congregation. It is a wonderfully inclusive term. We have turned it into quite the opposite. We have taken out the ordained ministers, and so we can use a phrase like 'the minister turns to the congregation'. We have, very often, taken out the choir, and thus we can have settings of the eucharist written for 'choir and congregation'. 'Congregation' has become a description of those who have no other role, the passive receivers, those down there in the nave. This is a dreadful debasement.

Perhaps the word is beyond redemption. The Roman Catholic Church speaks instead of the 'assembly' in order to regain the sense of the whole community gathered. But it would be a pity to let 'congregation' go and, if we could recover its meaning, an important lesson would be learnt. The congregation is the whole assembly. The worshippers come, in all their variety, individual people with their own needs and expectations, but as the liturgy begins they become a congregation. They discover their corporate identity as they give glory to God who is the Father of them all. The key to true worship is the participation of the whole congregation.

Yet the word 'participation' also needs rescuing. It was seen as one of the great benefits of the new rites in the 1960s and 1970s that they allowed for far greater participation than the Prayer Book Communion

19

rite or the old Roman Mass, in which the people could seem very passive. It was not just that they remained kneeling for most of the service, in their pews, but that their vocal participation was very limited also. In the Catholic tradition people spoke of 'hearing Mass', and that phrase summed up the problem.

Perhaps it was therefore inevitable that 'participation' should become the watchword, and be understood in a rather superficial way. For many churches it could be described as 'everyone joining in everything possible'. Some worship leaders have missed no opportunity to invite the people to say words with them. The effect can be disastrous. Words written for speaking by a single voice become heavy and turgid when ploughed through together. (There are exceptions to this – 'We do not presume...', 'Father of all, we give you thanks...' – but the generality holds.) Opportunity for slight variation to pick up the mood and season of the day is lost when all are reciting in unison, and so 'set parts' of the service become so set they might as well be in stone.

Vocal participation is at its very best in dialogue. The opening of the eucharistic prayer illustrates this:

> The Lord be with you
> **and also with you.**
> Lift up your hearts.
> **We lift them to the Lord.**
> Let us give thanks to the Lord our God.
> **It is right to give thanks and praise.**

Spoken or sung with clarity and feeling it provides a momentum to the prayer that is carried on through the parts spoken by the president alone, to which the people respond at points in the *Sanctus*, acclamations and 'Amen', and, in Order One Prayer H, in the parts of the prayer designed for speaking by the whole congregation together that move both the logic and the action on. The prayers vary in the amount of text they allocate to the congregation, but the words put into the mouths of the people need to be words written for speaking 'in chorus', not words for a single voice. Some of the shorter prayers in the new *Common Worship* services are written to be said together. It remains true that participation is not about everybody saying everything.

The Notes at the beginning of the *Common Worship* Eucharistic Rites is helpful and applies to some extent to other services too:

> Holy Communion is celebrated by the whole people of God gathered for worship. The ministry of the members of the congregation is expressed through their active participation together in the words and actions of the service.

Notice, it is words, but actions also, and it goes on, 'but also by some of them reading the scripture passages, leading the prayers of intercession, and, if authorized, assisting with the distribution of communion'.

In some church communities participation has been seen mainly in these terms of singling people out for particular ministries that together make up the whole. This is getting closer to the truth, and indeed there is something very important here that will be examined later in this chapter. But even this understanding has its difficulty, for, if participation means coming out of your pew to do something 'up front', whether singing, or reading, or even dancing, there is a danger that those who have none of these gifts, and will always stay within the security of the pew, will feel excluded. Apparently worship means using a liturgical gift, and they are, they fear, liturgically ungifted.

To discover true participation we must look for something in which all can share. It is probably that person in the pew, who is possibly the most reticent member of the congregation, who can provide the clue. For, in the end, I believe that the deepest level of congregational participation is praying the liturgy. The most active and crucial contribution may be the one that, to the outsider, may seem a passive non-role. We may be participating most deeply when we are silent and still.

Praying the liturgy

What is needed is a kind of undercurrent of prayerfulness that sustains the worship from opening greeting to concluding dismissal and which comes to the surface, so to speak, at those moments in the liturgy that are specially labelled 'prayer'.

If we take the eucharist as the model, it is not because this truth applies only there. The liturgy needs praying as much at a wedding or a funeral as at the eucharist and, of course, though we do not usually celebrate either wedding or funeral within the context of the eucharist, the fact that in the new rites their shape and structure is much the same as the eucharist should tell us that many of the same principles apply.

The classic opening stages to eucharistic worship (well signalled in our new rites) are the president's greeting and the invitation 'Let us pray', a time of silent corporate prayer, and then the drawing together of that prayer in the collect. The classic form of the intercession prayers is a repeated sequence consisting of bidding, silent prayer and collect. One of the options for the end of the eucharist is corporate silent prayer emerging, so to speak, from the sharing of communion or singing that accompanies the distribution, and rounded off by the post communion prayer that the president speaks.

In all three of these examples it is clear the prayer is the people's task. The president or another minister may set the agenda for that prayer (or leave it wide open as in the simplest of all biddings 'Let us pray'), and the president may draw the time of prayer to a close in a collect, but the praying is by the whole community and very often it is when all are silent. This is very far removed from much of our liturgical praying in the Church of England, which is the relentless pouring out of words, either by the whole congregation, or more often by a single leader, who proceeds without pause, let alone genuine space for silence, with the people trying to keep up with the leader's thoughts, and responding with an 'Amen' to make it their own.

The first stage towards the recovery of this concept of praying the liturgy is to concentrate on those particular points in the eucharist (and their equivalent in other rites), and to work away at making them moments of deepening prayerfulness by the whole congregation. We need to help people to rediscover the classic 'Let us pray' as an invitation to do just that, to engage with the living God, rather than as an instruction to change posture. The use of 'Let us pray' to mean 'Please kneel down' has deprived this little invitation of its straightforward but crucial meaning and, as with 'congregation' and 'participation', if we can communicate what it really means, we shall teach a valuable lesson.

If we can show people how to pray at these key stages in worship, and to see that prayer as being of the very essence of the liturgy, and if we can show them how to use silence creatively, then I believe that a new attitude of mind will develop that will begin to affect the whole of our liturgy. Prayer may only be on the surface at certain moments, but it goes underground still flowing, through the other activities of the service, so that all of them are carried along in prayer. This prayer may be unconscious, but everything is being approached with prayerfulness.

We hear the scriptures read, but in a way we pray them; and that is why God is able to speak to us through them. We listen to the sermon, but in a way we pray it, and it is partly the prayer that changes it from dry theology into good news for our lives. We sing hymns and psalms, chants and songs, but at another level we pray them. St Augustine is credited with the view that those who sing pray twice. For many people we need to recover the sense that those who sing pray at all, let alone twice. We tend to compartmentalize our worship, and not to see the thread of prayer running through it all. We offer our hands to others at the greeting of peace, but if we want that to be something that expresses and deepens the body of Christ, we have to pray that peacemaking; and if we do, it will no doubt change the way the greeting of peace looks as it is shared among us. We come to the altar table to receive, but we do not leave our prayers behind in our pew, but bring them with us and pray ourselves through the reception of the bread and wine. At every point, whatever is going on at the surface, the liturgy is being prayed. That understanding of prayer shared and practised is a key to the renewal of worship.

I think that part (though only part) of what some people value in the Prayer Book tradition is the ability to submerge oneself in totally familiar and unchanging words, setting one free to pray at another level. It is one of the ironies of the Anglican '8 o'clock' tradition that you habitually took to church your copy of the Prayer Book, though you had no need of it because you knew the service off by heart. You opened it probably at the epistle and the gospel, and followed them, but otherwise you did not use it. It is easy to see how that could and did produce services that were stale and barren. But it did not, and does not, have to be so, and there is an important lesson to be learnt by those who prepare worship. We need to be set free, at least some of the time, from the printed page and reading to keep up, if our praying is not to be a terrible struggle.

I am conscious of the danger that praying the liturgy can easily degenerate into doing one's private thing in worship. Even that cannot always be wrong, and there ought not to be guilt where the worship has set us free to think our own thoughts. Nevertheless praying the liturgy is different from using it as a setting for personal devotion. Some in earlier generations were brought up to take to church, not the Book of Common Prayer, but the particular devotional manual given them at their confirmation. Often it provided them with a prayer for every gap in the service, and that could constitute praying the liturgy, but on the whole the prayers were too formal and also too personal to fulfil that function. They encouraged the worshipper to withdraw into a private world of 'me and God', and did not foster the sense of corporate worship and identity. That style has gone out of fashion, replaced by an emphasis on the worshipper being caught up in the central shared action of the service. That is almost wholly to the good, for a return to an individualistic piety is not what is needed. But something of that spirit of prayer, albeit in a new, more spontaneous form that is always conscious that we pray together, needs rescuing, probably through teaching and trying and reflecting together in the parish, rather than through the issuing of a new wave of little holy books.

The use of silence

Progress down this path to a more prayerful liturgy cannot be made without a new and bold use of silence in our worship. It is not easy, for in many churches it has had no part at all in worship for generations – every gap has been plugged, usually by the organist! We live therefore in a transitional era when it may be necessary to help people rather self-consciously to use the silence well, in a way that would not be necessary when the skill has been acquired. A few ground rules may help.

Silence must be for everyone. If it appears to be simply because the people are waiting for the ministers to finish some task (cleansing the vessels after communion for instance), the conclusion will be drawn that we are silent merely because we are not yet ready to go on. If silence is to be taken seriously, everyone, worship leaders and robed ministers, need to be still and seen to be part of it.

Silences need to be of the right length. One cannot prescribe how long. It will depend on the type of service, the kind of congregation, the experience of silence the people have, and much else. But, as a general rule, a distinction needs to be drawn between the kind of momentary silence of just ten or fifteen seconds, that enables people to focus or to assimilate an idea, and a more extended silence, in which people can develop thoughts and prayers. But a bidding, even the shortest of them – 'Let us pray' – that plunges on into the next set of words without any silence at all is a nonsense. Do not invite people to pray and then give them no time to do it!

There is a question of posture. Those momentary silences can be sustained whether the congregation is standing, kneeling or sitting. But, if the silence is of the longer sort, with real space to reflect and to develop prayer, standing will nearly always be inappropriate, and kneeling a strain for some. Sitting will probably be best, and it needs the ministers to be seated too, and not to be hovering at the altar table or the lectern, looking as if they are about to get on with the next thing.

Silence is good, but too much silence destroys the momentum of the liturgy. A minister and a community need to be selective about the points where they opt for silence, especially of the longer sort. Where a pause becomes a break, people can lose the development of the service. A long tradition recognizes the need to draw people together at the conclusion of silence; sometimes this is done by a collect, sometimes by a song.

There is also the need to distinguish between silence for reflection and silence for prayer, though not too firmly, for the one can lead naturally into the other. But silence before the collect is clearly for corporate prayer, whereas silence after a reading is to reflect upon what has been heard. If people are inexperienced in the use of silence in worship it is helpful to guide them a little: 'Let us pray silently for few moments' or 'Let us reflect in silence on what we have heard.' Simply to be plunged into silence unbidden makes it difficult to know how to use the time.

Silent prayer by the congregation does not necessarily mean no sound in the building. Although it is important to treasure that total silence, when one can hear a pin drop, silent prayer can be offered as music is played or sung. Some of the frustrations of those who complain of choir anthems as 'performances' or, when they go to cathedrals find the words they usually sing restricted to the choir alone, would be eased if people could learn to pray silently through the music, to see it as a stimulus to prayer, and if the musicians could understand what it is they are providing.

All with their ministry

Providing we are clear about the primary expression of participation in the eucharist through this prayerful attentiveness, we can return to look positively at the secondary level of participation, that of being called out of the congregation to exercise a particular skill or ministry.

In most churches we have moved on from the days when one man (and it was always a man, never a woman) dominated the service, reserving the spoken parts of the service entirely to himself, perhaps delegating a reading (almost inevitably to another man). In many churches a wide cross-section of men, women and children take their turn in reading the scriptures, in leading prayers, and in other vocal parts of the service. Indeed the problem in some church communities is that too many people are drawn out to do this in a single service, without much sense of anyone being in charge, and the service loses cohesion.

People are also learning that this move to wider participation at this level is not a purely practical thing, but has a theological base. They are understanding that the passage about gifts in 1 Corinthians 12 and the passage about ministries in Ephesians 4 point to a pattern of church life where this is appropriate. If we want to express and symbolize the nature of the body of Christ, we want to do it in worship, and supremely in the eucharist where we share in a liturgy that is itself a reflection of the meaning of the body of Christ. For liturgy both forms and reflects the Church. In other words, on the one hand, because we organize Christian worship as a co-operative venture in which all contribute their gifts to help build up and sustain the whole, the Church is helped to become that all the more. Yet, on the other hand, because the Church is like that already, it is natural that when we come to worship we should give expression to it ritually.

It is important, I believe, to make a distinction between the gifts we exercise in the liturgy and the gifts we use in daily life both in the Church and in the wider community. It is not that some people have churchy gifts, and exercise their ministry mainly on Sundays and mainly in sanctuaries and sacristies, while others have gifts more appropriate to the world of every day outside. It does look like that sometimes in churches, where some of those keenest to be involved in the liturgy seem least happy to get involved where the Church is most engaged with daily life. The truth is that God gives all of us gifts to use in daily life, whether we exercise them chiefly through the Church's direct work or at work, at home or in wider community concerns. But, additionally, the Church then invites us all to have a share, a particular ministry, in worship, so that we express ritually that mutual dependence that we have in daily life.

Sometimes the ritual ministry we have in church is a natural extension of the gift we are using day by day. A teacher reads the lesson in church. A person whose daily work is keeping a home clean, tidy and welcoming gives an afternoon to making the church building the same. But it need not always be so. The nurse may sing in the choir, the computer programmer may look after the churchyard, the car salesman may serve at the altar. The liturgical ministry is simply revealing something about the way the body of Christ functions, though there is a special appropriateness where it reflects a God-given gift and skill.

We have already noted the difficulty with making too much of the need for everybody to have a ministry. It can exclude. It can make it appear that to be part of the body you need to have a gift, and some feel ungifted. The problem arises if we have too narrow a view of what constitutes a liturgical ministry. If we restrict it to those who distribute Holy Communion, lead prayers and read lessons, we have taken the narrow view. Perhaps people would broaden it very naturally to include those who welcome at the door, those who take up the collection, those who serve, those who sing in the choir and those who, at the eucharist, bring up the bread and wine. That is less exclusive, but still it makes liturgical ministry a minority activity in most churches. We need to broaden it further. Every work that contributes to the spirit, the beauty and the smooth running of worship is a liturgical ministry. Those who at the service sit in their seat, but in the days and hours before have washed the linen, arranged the flowers, typed the service sheet, or rung the bells, have made their contribution too. And, if we may broaden it one stage further, the person whose only gift is to bring a deeper commitment to maintaining that undercurrent of prayer than most can bring has possibly brought the most precious thing of all.

We should not exaggerate the novelty of this. People may not have articulated it quite like this in the past, but the idea was present. In particular the ministry of the organist and the choir has long been recognized. The presence in the chancel and the sanctuary of men (and more recently women) as assistants and servers of different kinds has been a ministry, at least in theory, of representatives of the people, the whole congregation, so that there are lay people, not just clergy, in the drama as it unfolds. Yet in reality choir and servers have often seemed more like a different order altogether than like representatives of the people.

One of the ways in which we exalt some ministries at the expense of others is the way we authorize people for ministries. A lay person needs the bishop's authorization to help with the distribution of Holy Communion, but not to read the scriptures in the liturgy. In many parishes those who are to sing are admitted to the choir during public worship. Those who arrange the flowers are not. Inevitably some ministries are affirmed and some are not. Baptism is the commission to minister within the body of Christ; commissionings should be used sparingly and, when they are used, perhaps they could be related to that baptismal calling.

Some particular ministries

Although there should be no hierarchy of ministers, there are some specific liturgical lay ministries about which a little more needs to be said.

First there are readers. We use that word confusedly in the Church of England to mean both those authorized lay people who may preach and lead worship and also ordinary members of the congregation coming to the lectern to read the scriptures. In the following chapter there is a section on the former. At this point I am referring more broadly to the latter.

There is a tradition, with which some parts of the Church are familiar, that the reading of the gospel at the eucharist is the prerogative of a deacon. But, with that possible exception, the reading of the scriptures is not a ministry reserved to the clergy. Even in the old High Mass of the catholic tradition the epistle was read by the subdeacon, and the subdeacon was a member of a lay, not an ordained, order, and his equivalent in today's church is a lay man or woman. The scriptures should not be usurped by the clergy, however many of them are present.

Similarly the prayers of intercession are 'the prayers of the faithful', the people's prayers. Traditionally the deacon has a hand in them (drawing them into shape and order as part of a ministry of serving the people), but they are the people's prayers, and again should not be taken over entirely by the clergy.

Then there are servers. Some churches do without them. Some have a faithful few – perhaps three, one carrying the cross and two carrying candles, week by week. Some have an army of them and either work on rota or find jobs for them all. The motive for having them is sometimes more pastoral than liturgical. How do we hold the youngsters in the church? Give them a job to do! It is not a bad principle and has nurtured many vocations to ordained ministry.

But there are other considerations as well as the pastoral. The number of servers ought to be dictated at least in part by the liturgical space in which they operate. In a small chancel and sanctuary too many bodies falling over one another can detract from the liturgy. Worship is never served by fussiness. There is in any case an argument for not having a job for everybody every week, for there ought to be the discipline that those who are sometimes in the sanctuary should also sometimes be in the pew. If we cannot hold our young people without a job for them to do every week, we need to look at our church life and liturgy, rather than at our serving rota.

As far as the eucharist is concerned, there is the additional ministry of the man or woman authorized to help with the distribution of Holy Communion. Permission to do this is normally nowadays given to men and women alike, as permission to distribute the consecrated bread as much as to deliver the cup, and, in many places, to do so in the homes of the housebound through 'extended communion' as much as at the communion rail in church. In some ways it is unfortunate that this ministry needs a kind of episcopal permission that makes it different from others. It tends to mean that fewer people share in this ministry than could do so, and that, where the diocese allows permission to be renewed, those who exercise it tend to keep it, almost as a job for life, and can become 'clericalized' through the process. There is nothing priestly about the distribution of the consecrated elements. However much we may hold to ordained presidency of the rite, there is no good theological reason why lay people should not exercise this role and, as with the reading of the scriptures, exercise it even when there is a superfluity of clergy present.

All these ministries need to be exercised competently. This means care in matching people to task and equal care in their training. People do not want to meet in the communion assistants a lack of assurance that intrudes at the moment of communion. Servers are actors in a drama; they need to be sufficiently briefed and trained that what they do looks natural and does not draw undue attention to itself. For both reading and leading prayer, there should be voice training, and for leading prayer careful exploration of the theology and practice of public intercession. People should be asked to undertake particular ministries because, with training and practice, they have been judged capable of doing them in such a way that the body, and its worship, will be edified. There rests on every minister in charge of a church and on every worship committee a responsibility to see that the training is given and the practice monitored sensitively.

There is a final question about the gender balance in the leadership of worship. A generation ago all the leaders – clergy, choir, servers, probably readers too in most churches – were male. We took it for granted. But what do we say about the nature of the Church if the whole team leading worship is male, or female, or old, or young? If the liturgy is a kind of acting out of the life of the Church, should we not, without being doctrinaire or silly about it, try to ensure that there is a good mixture in every celebration? Do we not by so doing affirm in a subtle way some categories of people who have felt excluded – whether it be women, or the young, or, in some churches, the old? We say something also, not only about the nature of the Church, but about the God who has broken down every barrier that divides us.

4

Priest and Deacon

Presidency

Not everybody sees the point of describing the priest at the eucharist as the 'president'. It can sound rather grand. But the concept is important and not just for the eucharist. Perhaps people are uncomfortable with the word because it smacks too much of the secular world. It sounds modern, though Justin Martyr spoke of 'the one who presides over the brethren' in almost the first liturgical material we have outside the New Testament. People still prefer the 'celebrant', despite the truth that we are all celebrants at the eucharist; or the 'minister', though we are all ministers of the gospel and the eucharist has several liturgical ministers; or the 'priest', though that has its theological problems for some.

Whether the term 'president' is used or not, every leader of worship needs to understand the concept that lies behind it. It applies not only to the eucharist, but equally at some services where the president will not be a priest, but a deacon, a Reader or another lay worship leader. At its simplest it is about holding the congregation together.

It has a lot in common with the effective chairing of a meeting. One cannot reduce the leadership of worship, let alone the exercise of Christian priesthood, to being about chairing a meeting, but that element is part of it. Think how a good chairman (or woman) functions at a meeting. When the chairman is in place and calls for order, the meeting comes into being. He (or she) speaks at significant moments. A good chairman does not speak a great deal, but does ensure that the other contributions have balance and move the meeting forward. The chairman's own words include beginning the meeting and ending it, and certain other interventions, often expressed through an established formula: 'I declare the motion carried', 'We will now move to next business.' On the whole these contributions are ones that draw matters under discussion together, and sometimes draw the people together. Often they are contributions that would sound oddly out of place from the 'floor' of the meeting. The good chairman does not stand throughout the meeting, dominating the proceedings, but sits 'in the chair'; yet the chair is always visible, and, if the chairman disappeared from sight, the meeting would be a little unsettled or uncertain. The chairman communicates with people not only through spoken interventions, but even with the smallest gesture of hand or eye to restrain, to encourage or to reassure. The good chairman has a clear idea about how the meeting should go, how it might develop, and even when it might end, but knows he will not have thought of everything.

The leadership of Christian worship will include much more than chairmanship, but it is difficult to see that much of that is irrelevant to good liturgical leadership. Worship can be impaired both by over-strong presidency that dominates, and by a lack of presidency, in which there is little sense that anyone is holding the assembly together or that it is going anywhere.

We need to look to the *Common Worship* provisions for presidency at the eucharist to discover its attitude to the leadership of worship in general. In the opening notes to the eucharistic rites, it moves on from what it has to say about the ministry of the whole people of God (already quoted) to something about the ministry of the deacon (to which we will return) and then states:

> The unity of the liturgy is served by the ministry of the president, who in presiding over the whole service holds word and sacrament together and draws the congregation into a worshipping community.
>
> The president at Holy Communion (who, in accordance with the provisions of Canon B 12 'Of the Ministry of the Holy Communion', must have been episcopally ordained priest), expresses this ministry by saying the opening greeting, the absolution, the collect, the peace and the blessing. The president must say the eucharistic prayer, break the consecrated bread and receive the sacrament on every occasion. When appropriate, the president may, after greeting the people, delegate the leadership of all or parts of the Gathering and the Liturgy of the Word to a deacon, Reader or other authorized lay person.

The issue here is not principally about priesthood (and who may absolve, consecrate, bless, etc.), but about presidency. The particular words and actions that are reserved to the president (either absolutely or normally) are exactly those parts that need to be the prerogative of the representative figure who holds the community together. They are the equivalent of the chairman's words at a meeting which 'include beginning and ending it' and are the contributions 'that draw the matters under discussion together, and sometimes draw people together', the contributions 'that sound out of place from the floor of the meeting'.

If people need a basic sense of security in which to be open to change and surprise, part of that security comes through a good experience of presidency. Like so much else in liturgy, people may not talk in such terms, but they know when a service has been badly led and when there has been no sense of leadership at all. The more people who have a distinctive 'up front' part in the liturgy, reading, leading prayers and so on, the stronger the need for a sense of one who presides.

The kind of profile that such leadership requires will also differ from community to community and service to service. There are services, where everybody knows what they are doing and where the service is going, where there needs to be only the lightest touch from a leader. Morning and Evening Prayer within the life of a residential community would be an extreme example of where the lightest of touch is sufficient. There are other times when, either because there are people present not accustomed to worshipping together, or because there are to be unfamiliar elements in the service, a far higher-profile presidency is needed. A fairly loosely structured family service would be an example of this. So, for different reasons, would be a funeral.

To return for a short while to the *Common Worship* note on eucharistic presidency, it is worth exploring how it understands the president's speaking role. It leaves a good deal to be delegated, and it also allows, as we shall see, for the development of a second, complementary, minister's role. It even allows that there are circumstances where, after greeting the people and thus creating a relationship with them, the president steps back and allows the whole of the first part of the eucharistic liturgy to be in the hands of others; flexibility is very much built in. But the norm assumes a slightly larger role for the president in the first part of the rite, involving the absolution and the collect, but even this is a very light-touch presidency in which there is room for others to play a significant part. Yet what the note is clearly against is the entire delegation of the first part of the service to another minister, for that undermines the overall presidency of the rite and the unity of word and sacrament. Even here, recognizing some pastoral realities, the note adds, 'In the absence of a priest for the first part of the service, a deacon, Reader or other authorized lay person may lead the entire Gathering and Liturgy of the Word;' but what is intended by 'absence' is a priest still finishing a service in another church, not one sitting in the back row until the moment to take over arrives! Instead, where it is desirable to develop a second leader ministry, the model is that of the president/deacon relationship, not a kind of co-presidency or serial presidency as the rite develops.

Of course the leadership of worship is about much besides the words that are spoken. It is about visibility, posture and seating, and it is about even the smallest gesture of hand or eye. Putting all these things alongside one another, presidency can be seen to be about bringing and holding the worshipping community together, providing it with a focus, being a kind of anchor, and thus giving it the security in which to be free.

It has its own danger, which is why some people (clergy included) are suspicious of it, for the focus that the president wants to provide is to draw people to Christ who, at a deeper level, presides among his people. There is a style of presidency that draws people to the leader, and in relation to the eucharist there is even a theology that gives respectability to that. But Christ is found in the liturgy in the assembly, the people who come together and become his body, rather than in one individual. (He is found also in the eucharist in word and sacrament, but that is not our concern at this moment.) The president has to draw together and hold together, but not in order that the congregation may be his or hers, but that it may be Christ's.

One of the things at which worship leaders therefore need to work is the right use of their own personal qualities and characteristics. There are clergy who were trained to exclude everything of themselves in the leadership of worship, especially in the celebration of the eucharist. As far as humanly possible, they left their individual personalities in the vestry as they put on the anonymous vestments of priesthood, and in the celebration played down the gestures of face and eye and hand, and the kind of personal words, that communicated something of themselves. All that for the best of reasons, so that it should be Christ who is proclaimed, not themselves. Yet we can only communicate our faith, our affection and joy in Christ by being ourselves.

For some the problem, if they recognize it, is the opposite one. They have grown so used to communicating the power of Christ through the attractiveness of their own personalities that they cannot see that Christ is obscured, and they are drawing people, not to him, but to themselves. In gesture and in word, the minister must be himself or herself, but very often with a proper restraint, and never more so than when presiding at the eucharist.

Part of the way in which the president in any rite ensures that it is around Christ that the people are being drawn is in the prayerfulness the president brings to the celebration. There is a mentality that can grow up among those who lead worship that they have to sacrifice their own opportunity to worship and to pray in order to manage the business of letting the congregation worship and pray. But this is a wrong sacrifice to make and indeed there is little chance of a congregation experiencing a deepening of its corporate spirituality if its leader adopts this approach. If the minister is to be a person of prayer, he or she must above all else be a person of prayer when presiding at the liturgy. If there is a need to recover for the whole congregation the sense of 'praying the liturgy', there is a need just as much for those who lead worship to believe that they can preside and pray at one and the same time.

The delegating of some parts of the service to others not only affirms something important about the nature of the body of Christ, but also sets the president free to be at prayer during the service. The role of the deacon helps in this respect. By this or other means the president needs to ask, 'How can I set myself free of worry about detail so that I can pray myself and these people through the liturgy?' Part of the answer will be in the preparation that needs to go into every service, but that is not the whole answer. During the service itself the president needs to be sufficiently unencumbered with detail to be free to be at prayer.

The deacon

The tradition of the Church gives us a second, complementary role of leadership in the eucharist, that of the deacon. Always part of the Roman liturgical provisions for the Mass, it was mainly lost in the Church of England, so that even a minister in his year as a deacon before ordination to the priesthood rarely exercised a specifically diaconal liturgical role. The period through the 1980s and into the 1990s, when women had been admitted to the office of deacon, but not to priesthood, was a time when the deacon's liturgical role was re-examined, and the emergence, on however small a scale, of a permanent diaconate of those not seeking ordination to priesthood has also encouraged a fresh look at the deacon's liturgical role.

In relation to the eucharist, the *Common Worship* note on Ministries says:

> In some traditions the ministry of the deacon at Holy Communion has included some of the following elements: the bringing in of the book of the gospels, the invitation to confession, the reading of the gospel, the preaching of the sermon when licensed to do so, a part in the prayers of intercession, the preparation of the table and the gifts, a part in the distribution, the ablutions and the dismissal.
>
> The deacon's liturgical ministry provides an appropriate model for the ministry of an assisting priest, a Reader, or another episcopally authorized minister in a leadership ministry that complements that of the president.

The list of 'duties' might have been expressed a little more broadly. 'The deacon invites the congregation – to confess, to exchange the peace, to make an acclamation, etc. The deacon gives practical instructions – about posture, page numbers, etc.'

Behind this note lie two main assumptions about the deacon's role. The first is that it is a ministry that makes explicit the element of service that lies hidden in all ministries. The deacon serves God in serving both the congregation and the president. The members of the congregation are served by the way the deacon encourages them and helps them through the service. All through the deacon is inviting them to do things, and making it easier for them to do so. But the president is also served by being relieved of some tasks and assisted with other tasks to lighten the burden, and that is important if the president is to be set free to be at prayer. Throughout the liturgy the deacon is holding up to the priest and to the people a model of service, a service that, though it is the deacon's particular ministry, is one shared by the whole Church and by every member of it, priest, deacon or lay person, individually.

The second is that the ministry of the deacon, though it is of service, is not of subservience. That is why it is properly described as complementary. To the deacon is assigned the reading of the gospel, the high point of the Liturgy of the Word. To the deacon is assigned the task of dismissing the assembly at the end. It is a two-person leadership of worship, a kind of team ministry, but one in which roles are clear. The two are not co-presidents, competing for a role, presiding from either end of the table like book ends, or sitting on their side of the chancel knocking the service from one side to the other like a game of tennis. They belong together, often they stand side by side, they support one another, and give way to one another, so that first one, and then the other, may move back into prayer, and then come forward to lead.

The *Common Worship* note speaks of the deacon's liturgical ministry providing a model. This is true in two ways. First of all it does give the shape to the role of a second minister when a church is fortunate to have one. It may be the role in the eucharist for the Reader (see below). It will certainly be the way to use a second priest (the curate as deacon to the incumbent one Sunday, the incumbent as deacon to the curate on the following one, for instance). And, in the absence of a deacon, a Reader or a second priest, some of it may legitimately be delegated to other lay people so that the president does not 'carry' the whole rite.

Secondly what is described as a model indicates something about a second minister in services other than the eucharist. Obviously, where there is a deacon, the role needs developing in relation to other celebrations – baptism, marriage, funeral, etc. Very often the rites speak of 'the president', but also of 'a minister'. In some cases a minister may mean a series of ministers, lay or ordained. But in others it may be right to develop a second diaconal-style ministry. Even an informal all-age Service of the Word might benefit not only from a president, but also a deacon, even if the 'job titles' were not being used. So, similarly, when there is no deacon, it is still worth looking to the deacon model to find the appropriate role for a second priest, a Reader or another authorized minister.

The Reader

Readers play a very significant part in leading worship in the Church of England. Indeed in the rural church they are vital to the maintenance of a pattern of Sunday services in large multi-parish benefices. Where they officiate at Morning or Evening Prayer, at word services and family services, and under some circumstances at a baptism or at a funeral, they exercise presidency, and much that has been written in this chapter about styles of leadership in worship applies to them as much as to the clergy and to other authorized ministers. Where two Readers minister together, they need to take on board, as much as two clergy together, the need to define differing roles, to know who presides and how two complementary roles fit together.

Less straightforward is the role of the Reader in the eucharist. If the Reader is involved because the priest has not arrived (still presiding at a eucharist in the next parish), the rule is clear: 'In the absence of a priest for the first part of the service, a deacon, Reader or other authorized lay person may lead the entire Gathering and Liturgy of the Word.' But it is never ideal that the president of the eucharist should arrive halfway through, and this note simply allows for an extreme pastoral necessity. In the more normal circumstance of priest and Reader being together for the whole service, the note encourages a complementary ministry in which the priest presides and the Reader's role is on the deacon model. The norm set out in the note assumes that, while on occasions delegating much of the Gathering and the Liturgy of the Word to the Reader, the priest will not only give the opening greeting but also the absolution and the collect. But the flexibility of the note does allow that 'when appropriate' only the greeting must be retained by the president, after which a second minister may lead people through the service until before the peace. (The absolution would then be said in the 'us' form.)

The bishop

If we come last to the bishop, it is not because he matters least, but because he is not normally present. His presence is exceptional. Yet his ministry is primary and all those who preside at worship do so as a sharing in the bishop's ministry. To each priest whom he licenses the bishop gives a share in a ministry that is 'mine and yours', and that applies to liturgical ministry as much as to pastoral. The *Common Worship* note on Ministries ends with this sentence: 'When the bishop is present, he normally presides over the whole service.'

By 'the bishop' is meant a bishop within his diocese, the 'diocesan' or his suffragan, not a retired bishop or a bishop from another diocese. When a bishop is present, within his diocese, at a baptism or at the eucharist, he is, almost invariably, the president. Of course, for his own soul's health, he will sometimes be present when another priest presides, but this will be in his own chapel or when he chooses to slip into the back row of a congregation. When he visits a parish, other clergy do not preside, for in doing so normally in the absence of the bishop they do it as his deputy. The old approach (which the Prayer Book allowed and which bishops often encouraged because it was easier for them) of putting the bishop in his chair on the north side of the sanctuary and leaving him there to do nothing except absolve, preach and bless, while the vicar got on with the 'celebrating', as it would have been called, is a theological nonsense. It is the same nonsense when deans claim that cathedrals are somehow different. Of all churches the cathedral is the first where the bishop should be seen to be the normative liturgical president. It does not mean, however, that the other clergy retire from the scene. To see the parish priest standing at the bishop's side or a group of priests gathered around him at the altar affirms something important about the collegiality of the ordained ministers within the larger picture of the priesthood of the whole people of God.

5

Furnishing and Space

~

The place of baptism

The principal furnishings of a church are never simply for practical use, though they do need to be that. There are three principal furnishings: the font or baptistry, which is a permanent sign of entry and of baptism; the lectern or pulpit, which is a permanent sign of the significance of the word of God in scripture; and the altar or holy table, which is a permanent sign of the eucharistic meal. There are other furnishings, but they do not carry the same significance as these three. Thus word and sacrament (through the two dominical sacraments of baptism and eucharist) have equal place and honour, and each should stand out in the church with its own space and dignity, and in proportion to one another.

The font is the place of baptism and of those liturgical moments that put us in mind of our baptism. The font stands for one of the two dominical sacraments. It has a significance parallel with that of the altar table. Yet in many churches, where the altar is fenced off, treated with reverence and seen as a key focus, the font is neglected, used as a repository for books and notices and does not seem to count. Yet every time people come through the door they should see the font as a powerful reminder of their initiation into the Church.

The oldest fonts and baptistries were adequate for the baptism by immersion of adults. Practice varied, but in general it was immersion (kneeling in a pool with more water poured over) rather than submersion (with the candidate disappearing entirely under the water). In such baptistries the amount of water was considerable, signalling both a gracious God best indicated by generously large symbols and also the deadly seriousness of the enterprise, since baptism involves a kind of drowning – dying to the old life. The medieval English font, though intended only for new-born infants (for adult baptism had disappeared), maintained the same principle. It was large and significant, occupied its own space, and a baby could be immersed within; there was enough water that, in theory, the candidate could drown. Since then there has been until recently a decline in font design. The eighteenth-century bird-bath font is all too common. There has even been a line in creating the stone medieval font in wood in miniature to sit on a table, as if it were the shape that mattered. There has been the tendency simply to abandon the great font near the door, because of the bad sight-lines for the congregation, and to baptize instead in a portable bowl at the chancel step. Or there has been the habit, while using the great font near the door, not to fill it with water, but to place a small bowl within it. Finally there has been the trend to move the font entirely into the sanctuary area, where people can see better at a baptism, but with the inevitable consequence that the font loses its own space and becomes confused with the sign of the other great sacrament, the eucharist.

All these are undesirable developments and fortunately they are now being challenged. Indeed, the *Common Worship* initiation rites urge the use of the font not only at baptism, but also at confirmation, with processions to and from it as necessary. Cathedrals at least ought now to consider the provision of a baptistry adequate for the bishop to baptize adults by immersion, for we are returning to an age when adult baptism is likely to be common. Every church ought to consider the adequacy of its font. In some cases this might mean the provision of a new one. In more cases it will mean removing clutter (including possibly some pews) around it, as well as on it, so that it stands out for what it is and what it represents, determining that it and not some substitute be used for the celebration of baptism, ensuring that it is brim full of water when there is a baptism and possibly has water in it at others times (so that people passing it may put their hand into the water to remind themselves of their baptism) and devising the parish's liturgical life so that the congregation gathers around the font at key moments in the Christian Year – Epiphany (with its association with the baptism of Christ), Easter and Pentecost at very least.

The focus of the word

The English parish church, conformed to Victorian fashion, has, as the focus of the word, both lectern and pulpit on either side of the chancel step, standing for two aspects of the place of the scriptures in the liturgy, the lectern for reading, the pulpit for preaching. Some modern churches have just the one furnishing, a lectern, that serves for both reading and preaching. The eighteenth-century 'three-decker pulpit' provided another example of the single focus.

There is of course much to be said for a single focus of the word. All the scriptures might be read from it and the sermon preached from it. Especially when the scriptures are read from the same decent and large copy of the Bible or the lectionary, something about the importance of scripture, and the unity of the Liturgy of the Word, is affirmed, whether in the eucharist or other services.

On the other hand, in an old church, where both lectern and pulpit exist, they ought if possible both to be employed. To leave one in place but unused is unfortunate, and to make a distinction between reading and preaching by using the lectern for one and the pulpit for the other is quite appropriate. Sometimes these furnishings need some modification. The pulpit is too high for effective communication; sometimes it can be lowered without destroying its proportions. The brass eagle lectern may need bringing down a step, or the platform behind it for the reader made higher so that the reader may speak confidently over it, rather than be hidden behind its wings. There needs to be a wariness about replacing these often substantial furnishings with something insubstantial, often 'off the peg' or from the catalogue of an ecclesiastical supplier. The brass eagle was at least a significant piece of furnishing. It suggested that the Bible that lay upon it was central to the Church and its worship. The pulpit, even if it were too high, declared that preaching mattered. Where new furnishings are introduced, they need to be of such substance and quality that they continue to say that reading the scriptures and preaching matter, and they need to be in proportion to the altar table. We hold word and sacrament in equal honour. We need to be wary of creating an imbalance, where the altar is a solid and sizeable furnishing and the lectern flimsy, insignificant or even folded up and carted away halfway through the service. The word must have an adequate focus, and that focus its space around it.

The altar table

If the lectern or the pulpit is the focus of the word, the altar table is the focus for the eucharist, or, to be more precise, for the second part of the eucharist where word gives way to meal. In reality it becomes a focus much more widely. Because, of all the experiences of the presence of Christ among his people in worship, his presence in the bread and wine which they consecrate and share is the most telling, the altar table becomes for many the ultimate sign of Christ's presence in every act of liturgical worship and in the church building itself. It is a kind of extension of that sense of his powerful presence in the eucharistic action.

For this reason the altar table sometimes becomes the place in the church for things other than the sacred meal. Gifts are placed on or around it (whether harvest produce or Sunday School art work or flags of uniformed organizations, or, week by week, the collection). Going beyond that in some places it turns into a kind of lectern for the first, word-focused, part of the eucharist. It is too doctrinaire to say that this is wrong; sometimes the geography of the church, or of a particular chapel, almost dictates it. But we should be wary of using it more like the desk in the vicar's study than as the dining table, lest it begin to lose its real focus as the place of the sacrament of the body and blood of Christ.

The free-standing altar, with space on all sides of it, where the president may stand behind it, at least for the eucharistic prayer, has re-established itself as a liturgical norm. To some extent this is fashion and in some sanctuaries and in relation to some altars the fashion fights both the architecture and the furniture. Nevertheless the celebration with the president facing the people, where this can happen with dignity, enhances the sense of the community gathered in fellowship and thus reflects one of the needs of our own day.

But people have been slow to work through some of the implications of a free-standing altar and a celebration where the president faces the people. First of all the height and shape of the altar needs to be questioned. Altars against the wall are often, in effect, sideboards. But sideboards are not naturally moved to be placed in the middle of the room. In the middle of the room one has a table, lower, deeper, probably nearer a square, depending of course on the shape of the room.

There are also implications for almost every detail of the ritual of the eucharist. What looks right, acted out with backs to the people against a wall, cannot be simply turned around with no further modifications. The first implications are about posture and gesture. When the ministers have their backs to the people, kneeling at the altar is perfectly appropriate, and a genuflexion appears a natural expression of reverence. But ministers kneeling or genuflecting behind the altar as they face the people look comical, and a diminutive eucharistic president with only eyebrows and forehead peeping over the top of the table does not enhance a spirit of worship. The way the ministers use hands and arms in gesture needs to be rethought also (and this is discussed in the next chapter).

There are implications too about what should be on the table. With the sideboard altar and the ministers in front of it obscuring what lay upon it, it was not important how much was crowded on it; and often a great deal was! A cross, two or six candles depending on churchmanship, flower arrangements, often a brass book-stand, were in place all the time, and for the eucharist were added the vessels, covered at first with burse and veil, these later taken off, the one propped up like a cultic object and the other spread out to fill the only available gap. A few churches added framed cards with texts the priest might use and, especially when new services

41

began to appear, clergy often added an increasing number of little books to dip into and pairs of spectacles, with their cases, for every size of print.

But then the celebration was 'turned round', the president facing the people. Some implications were recognized straight away. The cross had to be removed, often relocated on a shelf behind the altar. The flowers moved on to new pedestals where larger and more artistic arrangements could develop. The candles on the table were probably reduced to two. But often that was as far as the rethinking went. The rest stayed and the congregation was exposed to altar clutter.

What needs to stand out on the holy table is bread and wine. They are what the eyes need to be drawn to. Anything that dwarfs them, anything that detracts from them and draws the eye to something else (the propped-up burse, for instance) is not serving the liturgy.

In terms of focus, there is a particular question about cross and candles. The cross is not quite the focus during the eucharistic action that the bread and wine constitute, and yet it is not very far from being so, for they speak of the body broken and the blood shed on the cross. It is therefore appropriate that there should be a cross near the altar, though not necessarily behind it. Sometimes it hangs over the altar. Sometimes it is the cross that has been carried in procession at the beginning of the service, brought in by the ministers and set in a prominent place in the celebration. It follows that it is better to have one cross that becomes a significant part of the celebration than a number of crosses – one behind the altar, one on the altar frontal, one processed in and attached to the choir stalls or, worse, disappearing and only reappearing to lead the ministers out, as if it were a verger's wand.

As for candles, Christians burn them to remind them of Christ the Light. For that reason they appropriately burn on or near the altar table, and especially near the bread and wine over which thanks are being given at the eucharist, because altar and sacrament stand in a special sense for the presence of Christ the Light. It is equally appropriate that they burn near the place of the word, with the sense of illuminating the scriptures, and again reminding us of Christ our Light who speaks to us through their pages. Whether the candles are on or near the altar, whether they are part of the lectern or are brought to be near it, whether there are candles alight in the church before the service, or whether the only lights are those carried in at the beginning and brought in turn to the different foci of worship, will depend on local circumstances, but there needs to be thought about how the use of candles enhances the worship and gives the right emphasis at key moments.

Two detailed points about candles are worth noting. First, if there are candles on the altar, they are better not pushed to the very corners. The altar is a table. If one put candles on the table for supper at home, one would not arrange them on the edge. Aesthetically they look wrong there and do not help the sense of the altar as a table around which the faithful gather for a meal.

Second, when candles are carried in procession, they are not carried to enhance the entry of the ministers. At one level their entry is purely functional; it is so that they are in place to illuminate the celebration and can be carried to the altar or the lectern to highlight a particular liturgical moment. At another level they are part of a procession to illuminate and honour the cross or the book of the gospels or whatever symbol is being brought in. The procession should be formed in such a way as to reveal that.

Mention has been made of the holy table itself as a focus of the presence of Christ. Because it is the place where we focus the presence of Christ in the liturgy, the altar has itself become for many a sacrament of Christ and his presence in the Church, and that is why it is appropriate for people to reverence it, not only in their minds, but with their bodies, bowing to it as they enter and leave the church. It is the altar (and at the eucharist the altar being used) to which this reverence is paid. It is not to the cross. It is not to some distant altar, but to the one in use. Ministers are sometimes seen to come in, turn their backs on the altar at which the eucharist is to be celebrated, and reverence another one in the distance. No sense can be made of that.

The problem arises because there is more than one altar. In theory there ought to be only one altar, just as there ought to be only one font, because both sacraments are about the unity of Christian people in Christ. Nevertheless a determination to remove altars can be philistine if it destroys the essential architectural design and shape of the building. Where everything about the building draws the eye to an altar at the east end, simply to remove it, or to make it the place for the president's chair, is mistaken. If we are to have some sensitivity to tradition, to art and to architecture, we shall sometimes have to compromise on two altars, provided that they are in separate 'rooms' of the building and that care is taken to make the new and central altar sufficient of a focus that the eye is not immediately drawn away from the celebration.

Where a church does opt for a second altar, it must not be of too temporary a nature. We may resist the idea of building it in stone where it is quite immovable, and be thankful for the adaptability of modern church design where everything moves, but if the altar table moves too regularly – to its central place, for instance, only when the eucharist is to be celebrated at it – the sacrament is undervalued, and the witness of the altar to the presence of Christ is undermined. The place that the altar occupies for the celebration of the eucharist should be its normal setting, even if we design it in such a way that it can, on certain occasions, be moved.

In making these decisions, good advice is important and there now exist many examples of bad, as well as of good, practice. A church needs to bring together liturgical principles, pastoral needs and architectural realities, recognizing that all three have to be taken seriously, and the right solution found by taking all three into account. And it is not simply a matter of finding a practical solution. One has to ask: 'What does this ordering say?'

The sanctuary: holy space

The most important thing that needs to be around the altar table is space. This is not only that there may be sufficient room for the ministers and not only that the altar can make its own statement. It is that, beyond these things, part of what people are often seeking in worship is space. Their need is for space in a different sense, a time of rest and recreation in lives that are over-busy, in diaries that are over-cluttered, or in homes where there is no peace. But the need for that sort of space is met also through the provision of physical space. Lack of clutter and lack of fuss in the celebration of the liturgy helps to create it. Space is holy and helpful.

So, in the sanctuary, there need to be minimal furnishings. There is a need, here or close by, for the president's chair, and it may not be only at the eucharist that it is used. If it is true that good presidency requires the worship leader to be visible throughout the liturgy, but not to dominate it, there is a need for the president to sit down in a place where he or she can be seen. The chair needs to have sufficient dignity to stand out from other chairs, stools and benches, but it is not a throne and must not seem too grand. In some churches the solution has been in the use of the chair known before as 'the bishop's chair' (technically only a cathedral has a bishop's chair; that is what makes it a cathedral!) and there is an appropriateness about using this chair, if it is not too grand or uncomfortable, for the president at the eucharist is there as the bishop's deputy and representative.

The chair must be placed so that the president can, when seated, have eye contact with as much of the congregation as possible. That will sometimes mean that it cannot be in the sanctuary, but will be at the chancel step. The fashion for using a clergy stall in the chancel, facing across the church, to preside at the first half of the eucharist, can hardly ever serve the need. Being 'in choir' is quite a different idea from presiding at the liturgy; the angle of the chair is wrong and the desk in front is a barrier between minister and people. And there is truth in that for some other services besides the eucharist. However the question is solved, the chair is more important than it seems. When it is in the right place and used wisely, it can transform the relationship between president and people as the liturgy is being celebrated.

There needs to be a credence table. It is not a mini-altar, with its own cross and candles; it should be inconspicuous, as far as possible out of sight, for nothing happens at it of a symbolic nature; it is purely functional. But if the altar is to be left uncluttered through the service and vessels placed upon it only when they are needed, the credence table needs to be of sufficient size to take all the things that ought to be there and to be a work surface.

There needs to be adequate provision for the distribution of Holy Communion. People need to be able to draw near around the altar. There are occasions when distributing communion from a variety of different points around a building will be right, but something is lost when people do not all come in the same direction to the altar of the celebration to share around the table. People are more willing now to stand to receive, but the Anglican instinct to be kneeling at this point is not to be lightly set aside and that may mean some kind of rails or benches, though in any re-ordering every effort should be made to avoid anything that cuts the altar off from the people and places a fence around it. It should signal openness and invitation, with barriers down.

Church as place of pilgrimage

The crucial thing about the holy spaces is that people should move around them, and the key thing about the font, the lectern and the altar is that people should gather at them. We need to bring to an end the sedentary culture, whereby we enter church, find our seat, leave it only to receive Holy Communion, until we turn round and make for the door when the service ends. Churches, particularly our cathedrals and our great churches, especially when at least partially cleared of pews and chairs, are spaces in which to play at pilgrimage. We should never think of a church as too big for its congregation. The great churches of medieval times were never built to be full, but to provide the people of God with space to move around and to experience the liturgy, and a touch of heaven, from different angles, so to speak. An Epiphany liturgy will take the congregation to the crib and the font, as well as to the altar. The Easter liturgy may well have them outside at the beginning, around a bonfire, and at later points will have them at the lectern, at the paschal candle, at the font and at the altar. A Christmas midnight service may well end up with a procession to the door to tell the good news to the waiting world. And, in a village church on a Sunday morning where thirty people rattle around in a building that could seat five hundred (but probably never has), the prayers of penitence might be at the font (a reminder that baptism into Christ addresses our sinful nature), the people might sit in the nave, at the foot of the lectern and the pulpit, for the Liturgy of the Word, but then move into the chancel for the Liturgy of the Sacrament. They could even go to the porch, if it were not too cold, for the Dismissal. Churches, whenever possible, are for moving about in. There are so many possibilities through the Christian year.

6

Symbols and Gestures

The language of symbolism

One of the areas in which Anglicans grew together in the last years of the twentieth century was in their use of symbolism in worship. The kind of basic questioning that Roman Catholics employed after the Second Vatican Council about their rites and ceremonies gradually gave Anglicans in the catholic tradition the encouragement they needed to do the same, to look at the meaning of what they were doing, to jettison practices that had grown over-involved or else had simply lost their meaning, and to affirm the significance of a limited number of rituals that carried important Christian meaning. This simplification and this desire to use only what has appropriate meaning has enabled Anglicans of a more evangelical tradition, sometimes seeing things through new eyes as a result of charismatic renewal, to re-examine their own suspicion of anything that smacked of ritual. The result is a Church in which the language of symbolism is being recovered.

The difficulty that the Church faces is that, though there is a new openness to the power of the symbol and to the non-verbal in liturgy, it is a language that has been so long lost for many Christians that recovering it is not straightforward and easy. We do things in worship – whether it be the grasping of the hand of another, or lighting a candle, or raising our arms, or allowing our feet to be washed – because in the doing we express truths that defy words. In ordinary life, if we kiss somebody, or put an arm around them, the meaning, depending on the context, is clear. We do not first tell them what we are going to do, and afterwards tell them what it meant. We kissed them or put our arms around them because words simply would not do. The action speaks louder than words. The action has its own non-verbal language. In all sorts of settings in ordinary life we take this for granted.

We need to recover the same sense in the Church, but here the whole language of traditional symbolism has gone somewhat dead on people. In church they do things, they enact rituals. Yet not only do they not know their meaning, but it does not occur to them that there is meaning to be found. They are simply 'what we do', or, more likely, 'what we have always done'. So there is need for good and clear teaching to enable us to recover the sense of meaning, to be able to speak the language, to allow ourselves to be ministered to by sign and symbol.

But the teaching brings its own problem, for, if the symbol and the gesture express what cannot be put into words, the teaching will nearly always narrow down the meaning, always take the power out of the symbol by explaining it away. The moment I try to explain the meaning of things I do in the eucharist, whether kneeling to confess, or bringing bread and wine to the altar, or breaking the consecrated bread, I limit the meaning to my description. Yet the truth is that all these different things are capable of being received at different levels, with a variety of aspects of the truth dawning on me on different occasions. Symbolism allows truth to have no end of strata, and meaning in each, and the resort to words of explanation, even to biblical warrant, can destroy that. We should be wary of explaining away what is beyond words.

Another way in which people have been able to affirm symbolism in worship rather more has been in the recovery of the sense that symbolic and ritual activity in the liturgy is not something that people watch, but something primarily in which they participate. However happy we may be to use words like 'drama' and 'theatre' about worship, it is always on the understanding that we are not spectators, audience, but part of the cast of the drama. Sometimes particular people act out something in which the size of the congregation or the church building dictate that not all can join, but they do it as representative of the whole assembled community, and through them we find ourselves caught up in it. But ideally we all move, we all do, we all act. The principal point of any kind of ritual is not how effective it looks, but what it does to the hearts and souls of those who share in it. We draw close to God in what we do in church as well as in what we say.

Rituals under scrutiny

We need to be ready sometimes to examine the things we do and take for granted in worship, and to ask whether the meaning can still be discerned, whether that meaning is sound, and whether its message strengthens or confuses the offering of worship and the communion of the people with God. We need to be on the lookout for rituals that have lost their meaning, and for those that convey the wrong meaning, just as we need to be looking for new rites and new symbols that communicate grace and truth with freshness.

We need to ask, for instance:

Why in some churches do the members of the choir face east during the gospel reading, turning their back on the reading from the lectern? Is it because they do not want to hear? Or is it because the gospel used to be read from the sanctuary and they turned towards it, but now the reading of the gospel has moved, but they have not changed, because they have forgotten what they are doing and why?

Why in some churches is the high point of the liturgy the collecting and presenting of money, and its elevation at the table with great ceremony? Could it be because, when ritual is suppressed in sensitive doctrinal areas (such as during the eucharistic prayer), it breaks out somewhere harmless, but then overemphasizes the action to which it attaches itself?

Why in some churches does the president say, 'We break this bread to share' and then break only sufficient for those in the sanctuary, and the people respond, 'We are one body, because we all share in one bread', and then proceed to receive their individual unbroken unshared wafers? Is it because they have always used personalized wafers, right back when they used a communion rite that did not make much of the breaking?

In all these cases, and they are only examples, parishes are either using rites and customs that have lost their meaning or acquired a poor meaning, or else are doing things they imagine have no symbolic value, but where meaning, and unfortunate meaning at that, is in reality being conveyed. Occasionally a church needs to be rigorous in examining what it does in the liturgy.

There is a need also to ensure that secondary symbolism does not obscure primary symbolism. In baptism, for instance, anointing with oil and giving of candles contribute to the rite and have helpful meaning, but they become a nuisance if they obscure the primary symbol of water and the meaning its use carries. Similarly in the eucharist, we need to ensure that the primacy of the scriptures and of the bread and wine are not obscured by too many other symbols and rituals, good in themselves, but capable of sowing confusion.

Body and senses

This whole area of ritual and symbol is a taking seriously of the human need to worship God not only with mind and soul, but with body and every sense. It may well be that we express our deepest worship of God when we are still and silent, and even in our pews. But even there we express our worship of God through our bodies, through the different postures we adopt, and through gestures we make with our bodies.

There is a strange suspicion of one another by those who employ different gestures, arising from different traditions of church life. Some Christians, who expect their clergy to raise their arms and use their hands in saying the eucharistic prayer, are quite incapable of coping with lay people who do exactly the same thing as they sing a song of praise. The two are doing the same thing; even the motivation is similar. Other Christians, who do raise their arms to worship, can themselves be suspicious of those who bend the knee to do so. And others, who set great store on the truth that their salvation has been won upon the cross, cannot see the point when some of their fellow Christians make the sign of the cross on their bodies or their foreheads as they share in worship.

All these people are expressing in their different ways the worship of God in the use of their bodies. The movements of the ministers in the liturgy – walking and bowing in patterns as it sometimes seems – are simply an extension of that same instinct to give God glory through the body. The movements and rhythms of those who do liturgical dance are not of another order, but a more vigorous interpretation of that same instinct. The movements of the liturgy are themselves a liturgical dance.

The body has its senses, and there is no reason why opportunity should not be given in worship for all the senses to be used in drawing close to God.

We hear, not just in the words of scripture, but in the fine language of the liturgy, and also through the medium of music which draws many closer to God.

We see. Although the older among us were brought up to put our hands together and close our eyes to pray, we know that all around us in the liturgy is visual stimulus if we will, quite to the contrary, open our eyes wide to worship. Very often the church building itself has its own visual stimulus, whether the sheer beauty of its architecture or what it proclaims in glass or statue, banner or poster. But, more than that, the action of the liturgy before our eyes draws us to God as we allow ourselves to look and see.

We touch. The eucharist invites us to touch. In some settings we may join hands with one another to pray. We touch, whether with hesitant handclasp or affectionate embrace at the greeting of peace. Sometimes we lay on hands or receive that ministry, and there is touch there also, of a sort that puts us 'in touch' with Christ.

We taste. That is one of the great glories of eucharistic worship. Like the psalmist we 'taste and see that the Lord is good', as we receive the bread and wine over which thanks has been given.

If we are to worship God through all the senses, there remains the sense of smell. There is the smell of flowers in the church and for some the smell of incense. The use of incense has never been regular and widespread in the Anglican tradition since the Reformation. What seems to be happening today is that probably even fewer churches are using it at the eucharist week by week, but more and more are using it for some special occasions, as likely at a Taizé-style vigil as for the eucharist, as likely burning in an earthenware pot before the altar or in front of an icon as swung in a thurible.

Both these ways of using incense are open to us. Either it can simply be left to burn, without ceremony, providing its own special smell as a background to worship, the smoke rising up and giving some meaning to the words we use in worship 'that our prayer may be set before you as the incense'. It can burn in a pot; it does not need to be swung in a thurible. Yet it may be used in the traditional way, to highlight moments in the service, censing the gospel book before it is read or the elements before the eucharistic prayer in the eucharist or censing the altar before prayer is offered at Evening Prayer.

It is always a symbol of purification and of prayer, and 'the house filled with smoke', as in Isaiah's vision, is a reminder of the worship of heaven. It needs to be rescued from being thought 'Romish' or 'high church'. The origins of its use are in scripture, and its use need not be restricted to one part of the Church. Where all the senses are to be employed, bring in the incense, but never with that kind of distracting fussiness that has often brought its use into disrepute.

Postures of prayer and praise

The use of the body that no one can avoid is the adopting of a posture through which to worship – prostrate, seated, standing or kneeling. We need to be sensitive to all sorts of physical handicap and never be too prescriptive about 'right' postures. Nevertheless it would be an impoverishment of worship if, in order not to offend, we said nothing about the desirability of standing and kneeling and other postures for different moments in the liturgy. Indeed we need to recover an understanding of how a variety of posture in the liturgy helps to express its different moods.

The *Common Worship* general note on posture states:

Local custom may be established and followed in respect of posture but regard should be had to indications in notes attached to authorized forms of service that a particular posture is appropriate for some parts of that form of service.

And the note relating to posture in relation to the eucharist says:

The people should stand for the reading of the gospel, for the creed, for the peace and for the dismissal. Any changes in posture during the eucharistic prayer should not detract from the essential unity of that prayer. It is appropriate that, on occasions, the congregation should kneel for the prayers of penitence.

In the Church of England we have moved from a Prayer Book norm of kneeling for most prayer to a variety of practice that in many churches has lost the habit of kneeling altogether. Yet the Prayer Book's insistence on the value of kneeling, and its memorable 'meekly kneeling upon your knees' before the confession in the eucharist, is an emphasis that we discard at our peril. It is easy to see why the habit has declined so speedily, for the kind of kneeling we did was often full of discomfort. Sometimes it was half crouch, with back bent double. Often it was with backside trying to reach a pew or a chair just too far away. Occasionally it was on a high and squashy hassock. And very often it was for too long, and so simply had to be endured. The point of kneeling is not that prayer is best offered in discomfort. It is only suitable if it allows us to express humility, penitence and longing. It is the traditional posture to ask favours and to seek forgiveness.

If we did all our praying on our knees, these aspects would gain too much prominence, and our picture of God would be warped. But, if we do no praying on our knees, but always stand as his confident children, or sit as his relaxed children, there will be another imbalance, just as detrimental to our picture of him.

In the Roman Catholic eucharistic rite, the people kneel now only for the eucharistic prayer and only for part of that. The *Common Worship* note allows us the same possibility (providing that the change of posture does not detract from the essential unity of the prayer), but also allows that we may stand or kneel throughout the prayer. If we follow our Anglican tradition we shall continue to see kneeling as the natural posture for penitence, for communion and perhaps for intercession too.

For all that, it is a blessing that we have rediscovered standing as a posture for prayer, as well as for singing, and especially for prayers of praise. We can indeed thank God 'for counting us worthy to stand in [his] presence and serve', as Eucharistic Prayer B affirms. At the eucharist, kneeling to praise God in the *Gloria* seems a pity, or to greet one another at the beginning or at the peace a silliness, and the beginning of the eucharistic prayer, with its 'Lift up your hearts' ought to bring us almost on to tiptoe, even if 'Holy, holy, holy' might bring us to our knees.

As for sitting, we can value this as a posture for meditation, reflection or long periods of prayer, as well as for the attentiveness that ought to mark our hearing of the scriptures and the sermon. We need to leave behind us the extraordinary crouch, that was neither quite kneeling nor sitting, and learn to sit straight-backed but relaxed, and find in that too another posture that opens us in a different way to God.

For those who order the liturgy and plan services there is a responsibility to see that these different postures are widely used, that the variety is there to help express the different moods of approach, and that no one posture is retained for so long that people become anxious or distressed.

The ministers and their gestures

It is difficult to prescribe, or even to describe, the gestures that worship leaders might helpfully employ in the liturgy, for a gesture is such a personal thing that every minister must discover for themselves what use of eye and arm and hand aids their communication. But it is unlikely that they will communicate well with eyes down and arms tight at their sides from beginning to end, so this is something they need to foster. The right gestures, like the right words, do help draw people into fellowship and prayer.

It is the use of the eyes that is most crucial. Communication with eyes averted is difficult. It gives a sense of the self held back, denied to the recipients of the address. Of course there are moments when eye contact intrudes, imposing the personality of the minister when he or she is simply a channel, and some (not all) feel that eye contact at the moment of the distribution of communion is one of those moments. But in general we communicate more with our face, and especially with our eyes, than with our arms and hands.

But arms and hands play their part. In the days when the norm was for the ministers to have their backs to the people at the eucharist, they were taught that when they extended their arms to pray they should do so only from below the elbow, in a fairly tight gesture, and that was right from the back view. When the ministers are facing the people, more expansive gestures, using the whole arm, are more effective.

Three such gestures suggest themselves. One is in normal address to the congregation, in greeting, for instance, or in invitation. It is an extending of the arms out in what is essentially an inclusive gesture towards the people. It is almost like the beginnings of an embrace. It is a relational gesture between minister and people.

53

A second is a gesture over the people, conveying grace, in blessing, for instance, or absolving. The minister extends his or her hands and arms towards and over the people, with the sense of one who is communicating to them something that is coming down from God. It is a variant on the laying on of hands, hands extended over the community, as if hands were being laid on each one.

The third is a gesture of prayer. Here arms and hands are raised, fingers extended upwards, in a gesture that is directed to God, and draws the eyes of the people away from the minister 'heavenwards', so to speak. The convention is for the minister to adopt this gesture when speaking alone in prayer – in the collect or the eucharistic prayer, for instance – but to have hands joined when everyone is praying together, but it cannot be a hard and fast rule. Yet a gesture that raises the eyes, and therefore the hearts, from the minister towards God (even if we know that, at a certain level, God is not 'up there') is particularly important in these days when the worship leader is nearly always facing the people. If the liturgy is to get 'off the ground', if the vertical is to come into play as well as the horizontal, something like this can help.

These are only models. There are no precise rights and wrongs in this area of worship. Ministers must find a style in which they are relaxed and in which they can feel that the people are being drawn into worship. What seems appropriate on one occasion – in a great cathedral, for instance – will suddenly feel quite inappropriate on another – perhaps in a house-group eucharist. Gestures need to take scale, space and occasion seriously. The spontaneous gesture has its place in liturgy just as much as the spontaneous word, even within a fixed form.

7

Cycles and Seasons

∾

The Church's year

One of the joys of liturgy in the Church of England in recent years has been the rediscovery of the variety of the Christian year and an increasingly rich provision for its celebration. Here the Book of Common Prayer, for all its beauty, is at its least helpful. In the eucharist, beyond the collect, epistle and gospel, only the proper preface on eight Sundays or principal holy days of the year introduces a seasonal flavour, though of course generations of church people have supplemented this with hymnody, and choirs with anthems, that give each day and season its distinctive feel.

In the past one of the odd effects of this invariability in the liturgy was that the need for seasonal services was met through non-eucharistic special forms. The high point of Christmas might well have been the Festival of Nine Lessons and Carols, based on Archbishop Benson's model created for Truro Cathedral and popularized by King's College, Cambridge. Good Friday came to be marked more by a three-hour preaching service, that originated with the Jesuits in South America, or by Stainer's *Crucifixion*, than by the liturgy in which by eating and drinking the faithful might proclaim Christ's death until he comes.

We may be glad that the Church of England has developed a skill for fine worship that is not always eucharistic and even not always within its usual liturgical forms. But it is a pity if the eucharist and the other authorized services fail to celebrate as finely the great Christian mysteries of the Church's year. Beginning with the Alternative Service Book of 1980 there has been an increasingly rich permission and provision to mark the seasons. *Lent, Holy Week, Easter* (1986), *The Promise of His Glory* (1991) and, less officially, *Enriching the Christian Year* (1993) have all provided forms, not only for the distinctive and special rites of particular days – the procession with candles at Candlemas, the washing of feet on Maundy Thursday, the Easter Liturgy, for instance – but for seasonal texts

55

at a whole series of points through the ordinary celebration of the liturgy on each festival and in every season of the year. Now, in the *Common Worship* eucharistic material, we are given invitation to confession, gospel acclamation, introduction to the peace, proper prefaces and blessing for each season and principal holy days, and are promised that in a revised and refined form the material in the earlier books will be published within a few years as a 'Book of Times and Seasons', one of the volumes of the *Common Worship* series.

All these are resources to bring alive the Christian year, the Church's calendar. The *Common Worship* calendar has few major surprises and makes no claim to be innovative. Indeed the most innovative proposal – that to create a season 'of the Kingdom' in November – was the only major casualty of the synodical revision process. Instead the *Common Worship* calendar takes as its starting point the calendar of the Book of Common Prayer, so that there may be basically one calendar form in the Church of England, but also looks carefully at the current Roman Catholic calendar and other international and ecumenical provisions, so that there may be unity as far as possible across the denominations in the celebration of the Christian year. It also reflects on some of the experiments, themselves based on ancient practice, in interim proposals such as *The Promise of His Glory* and *Celebrating Common Prayer* (1992). But its fundamental principle, set out in the Liturgical Commission's commentary, is that, 'the calendar celebrates and proclaims the Christian belief in God the Holy Trinity, Father, Son and Spirit, and tells the story of the saving work of Christ in such a way that Christian people today may be helped in their spiritual life and their discipleship'.

Some of the detail of this calendar will emerge in Part 6 of this book. Sufficient here to give the broad outline. It is essentially a simple picture, and rightly so, for the Christian calendar should not be something to confuse, but something the shape of which can be taught and assimilated. The calendar should itself be a good teacher of the faith.

The Christian year is divided into two parts. First there is 'seasonal time', in two sections, one from the First Sunday of Advent until Candlemas and the other from Ash Wednesday to Pentecost. Second there is 'ordinary time', again in two sections, one between Candlemas and Ash Wednesday, the other between Pentecost and the First Sunday of Advent.

Seasonal time is built around the two great celebrations of the incarnation and the resurrection. In each case the shape of the cycle is similar. A season of preparation leads to the great festival itself and a season of joyful celebration then begins, takes in another key festival on the way, one that further develops the theme, and then ends on a final festival that both adds a new dimension of its own, but also brings the cycle to an end.

In the case of the incarnation cycle, the season of preparation is Advent, with its four Sundays, the great festival is Christmas Day, the season of joy is the twelve days of Christmas leading into an Epiphany of four Sundays, the key festival on the way with its own message is the feast of the Epiphany, and the final festival is Candlemas, the Presentation of Christ in the Temple. Then 'ordinary time' returns.

In the case of the resurrection cycle, the season of preparation is Lent, with its six Sundays, culminating in Holy Week and Good Friday, the great festival is Easter Day, the season of joy is the fifty-day period of Eastertide, the key festival on the way with its own message is Ascension Day, and the final festival is Pentecost. Next day 'ordinary time' resumes.

Through these two cycles, one of about nine weeks, the other of thirteen, the Church focuses on the central truths of the Christian faith. They are not over-simplified chronological reconstructions. In Epiphany, for instance, the celebrations move from the visit of the magi to the infant Jesus to the baptism of the thirty-year-old Jesus and later back to a Jesus only forty days old as his parents present him in the temple. But they do both explore the central Christian mysteries through the retelling of the stories that help that mystery to reveal its truths. The rules that surround the calendar are designed to ensure that, during this period, very little can come along to deflect the Church from engaging with these central mysteries. Saints' days may not be celebrated on Sundays, permission to devise a lectionary locally is withheld. There is no encouragement to allow local celebrations that could be located in other parts of the year to displace what the whole Church is celebrating.

It is different with what the calendar calls 'ordinary time', though it could also be called non-seasonal, neutral or ferial time. The first period of it, between Candlemas and Ash Wednesday, could be as little as a few days or as long as five weeks, but more usually will be a period that includes two or three Sundays. The second period is the long stretch from Pentecost to Advent (though the last month of this, from All Saints' Day, may be treated differently – see chapter 33). As the *Common Worship* note puts it, 'during ordinary time there is no seasonal emphasis'. These are essentially neutral periods. The lectionary reads passages of the Bible sequentially, but also gives permission for churches to go their own way for weeks at a time if that makes sense in terms of the church's teaching and preaching programme. Saints' days and other celebrations are allowed to interrupt the cycle of Sundays. There is a freedom that seasonal time does not have. There are few predetermined themes.

'Ordinary time' may be thought a technical term and one that congregations do not need to know. The worship leader needs to know it and, though a new term to Anglicans, it is a straightforward concept. As far as the Sundays are concerned, in order to avoid the prosaic 'ordinary time' in their titles, they have been designated 'Sundays before Lent', 'Sundays after Trinity' and 'Sundays before Advent', but there is a world of difference between Sundays *of* Advent, Epiphany, Lent and Easter, which means that the season sets the tone, and Sundays *before* Lent or Advent or *after* Trinity, which is much more neutral.

The *Common Worship* calendar tries to be pastorally realistic. Although it has to allow for the celebration of the Christian year in places such as cathedrals and religious communities, where every day has potential, the calendar has to be usable too in small communities where weekday worship is rarely sustainable. Thus it gives encouragement to move some weekday feasts to a Sunday – All Saints' Day, The Epiphany (in some years) and The Presentation of Christ in the Temple, for instance – and is more permissive than was the Alternative Service Book in allowing some other festivals that land on a Sunday to stay there. It is also more positive about some of the observances that are important and popular in local communities, even though they are not part of a strict liturgical tradition – Mothering Sunday, for instance, has its own collect, post communion prayer and readings, and the collect, post communion prayer and readings for the Third Sunday before Advent sit comfortably with Remembrance Sunday themes.

Feasts and festivals

Any Church that takes the Christian year seriously needs to have its rules for ordering the year to avoid confusion and imbalance. It is worth noting the simple categorization of holy days that the *Common Worship* calendar employs. First of all there are nine 'principal feasts'. Three belong to the incarnation cycle – Christmas Day, the Epiphany and the Presentation of Christ in the Temple. Three belong to the resurrection cycle – Easter Day, the Ascension and Pentecost. Three stand separately – the Annunciation, Trinity Sunday and All Saints' Day. In addition a church may keep its patronal festival and its dedication festival as principal holy days. These are the days when canon law requires a celebration of Holy Communion, unless the bishop has given permission otherwise. They are days which cannot be displaced by any other celebration (except that the Annunciation is sometimes moved to a different date to avoid Holy Week and Easter Week) and, except for Christmas Day and Easter Day, the feast begins with Evening Prayer the night before. Some of them falling on a weekday can be moved to a Sunday. There are only nine of them; canon law urges every church in the direction of having adequate celebration of them and every churchgoer to celebrate them.

There are three other days of the same status, though they are, for an obvious reason, not called 'feasts'. These other three principal holy days are Ash Wednesday, Maundy Thursday and Good Friday. So, if the Church of England spoke in terms of 'holy days of obligation' (but this is not a very Anglican way of speaking) there would be a round dozen, and it may be worth working away at getting them into the consciousness of Christian people.

The second category is called 'festivals'. These approximate to what in the Book of Common Prayer calendar were often called 'red-letter days', namely the remaining festivals of the Lord and also the festivals of the apostles. To those in the Prayer Book, subsequent revisions including *Common Worship* have gradually added the Baptism of Christ (since 1997), St Joseph (1980), St George (1997), The Visit of Mary to Elizabeth (1997), Mary Magdalene (1928), the Transfiguration (1928), The Blessed Virgin Mary (1980), Holy Cross Day (1997) and Christ the King (1997). There are twenty-eight days in all (or twenty-nine if Corpus Christi is added to them as it may be). Full provision in terms of collect, psalmody and readings is made for them in Holy Communion and Morning and Evening Prayer, with provision also for an optional first Evening Prayer the night before. They are not usually displaced by other celebrations and at some times of the year do not have to be moved when they coincide with a Sunday. But there is no requirement, as there is with a principal feast, for there to be a celebration of Holy Communion.

Thirdly there are 'lesser festivals'. Here is a collection of nearly a hundred saints and heroes of the Church, the large majority of whom are not new to Church of England calendars, though, among others, Aelred of Rievaulx, Janani Luwum of Uganda, Mary Sumner and Elizabeth of Hungary are to be found for the first time. There is no requirement to celebrate any of these lesser festivals, let alone all of them, but they are each supplied with a collect and post communion prayer and with readings for the eucharist. The notes state that the daily readings at Morning and Evening Prayer are not normally displaced for lesser festivals, that they are not celebrated when they fall on a Sunday and that the minister may be selective in the saints that are celebrated. A community with a rich pattern of daily worship may well make quite a lot of these lesser festivals. For some other communities they will be almost entirely irrelevant.

The same will certainly be true of the final category, the 'commemorations'. There are more of these than of the other categories, and most of them are holy men and women new to Church of England calendars. By a conscious decision no person has been entered in this calendar whose death occurred in the last fifty years, except in the case of a martyr, but every other Christian generation and century is represented, and there are more nineteenth and twentieth-century figures and more women than in previous calendars. But commemorations are not intended to displace the ordinary liturgical provision of the day. They have no collect or readings. The note explains that commemorations are 'made by a mention in prayers of intercession and thanksgiving'. In other words the remembrance is intended as a stimulus to prayer rather than as the celebration of a saint's day.

Sundays are not included in these four categories, though their status is much like a 'festival'. Instead a special note helpfully tells us that, 'All Sundays celebrate the paschal mystery of the death and resurrection of the Lord. Nevertheless, they also reflect the character of the seasons in which they are set.' In other words there is a hint of Easter on every Sunday, but that hint must not undermine the sense that we are in Advent or Epiphany or Lent, each of which has a flavour of its own.

Liturgy and the rhythms of life

Why is the Christian year important? It will of course always mean more to some than to others. Even in New Testament times Paul found that some valued holy days, and others thought each day much the same as another. But, if we take the liturgical cycle seriously, we can discover that it is of value to many more than treasure it now.

It is not exactly an historical exercise, a reconstruction of the great events in the life of Jesus and of the early Church in order that we may be taught about them or even that we may be thankful about them, though that does not come amiss. It is by entering into the moods and rhythms of the Christian year, and thus of Jesus in his birth and death and resurrection, that we let him into the moods and rhythms of our life, and find him helping us to live through them in faith, to be tested by them but not destroyed by them, to grow close to God through them. His life and our lives interact in the living of the Christian year. His response to his experiences shape our own as we celebrate the Christian year. If we go deep enough, in its moods and rhythms Christ shows us how to live and also how to die.

This is a difficult truth to express. People can begin to see it as they keep Holy Week, but less obviously it applies to the whole Christian cycle. In a way one can only make sense of it across a lifetime, for the whole point of a cycle is that it has no beginning and no end, but keeps coming round. For this reason it is important to be wary of marking special days by a fresh look each year. Christian worship is refreshed by the innovative. If people were not encouraged to try new things, to modify tradition imaginatively, and to adapt to the circumstances of their day and their community, worship would wither. Yet some of the rites the Church has given us make their mark upon us because they keep coming back. They become part of the rhythm of our lives, and each time we encounter them we go a little deeper. Whether it be ash on our forehead on Ash Wednesday or a candle lit for our departed on All Souls' Day, it needs to become part of us. We must therefore be able to depend upon it. It will happen each year; it will not too often give way to somebody's good new idea.

Contrasting moods

One of the keys to giving to the stages of the Christian year their distinctive character is the ability to create contrast between one season and another. The new richness of seasonal text is part of this, but there is much more besides. There is the opportunity to change the mood by what is omitted and added – no *Gloria* and a fuller penitential rite in Lent, for instance, or cascades of *alleluias* throughout Eastertide. There is the contrast that can be expressed through posture. Easter used to be distinctive because nobody knelt to pray. In churches where people normally stand for penitence and for the eucharistic prayer, in Advent and Lent they might kneel. In places where they normally kneel for intercession they might choose to stand from Easter Day to Pentecost. The use of flowers, plants and foliage, and also the changing liturgical colours, all make their contribution.

Yet much of this is undermined if the choice of music – hymns and songs, anthems and voluntaries – cuts insensitively across it. The mood and the contrast with other times has to be a matter of liaison between clergy and musicians.

All these contribute to the mood of the season. They do not make their impact in one day. But if they become the hallmarks of the season, through four, five or six weeks, they help to create the rhythm of the year.

Contrast of mood can also be a matter of time of day. We have noted already the permission to move some festivals to a Sunday where they can be part of the normal Sunday morning programme, and pastorally there will often be a strong argument for that. There is a loss, however, and it comes in the fact that every festival acquires a kind of sameness when celebrated in the Sunday mid-morning slot. Christmas is appropriately a feast in the middle of the night; people are sensitive to that. But other festivals have their natural time: Easter at dawn, Good Friday in the afternoon, Ascension at midday, and some that are at their best in the darkness, like All Saints and Candlemas, in the evening. Most parishes have lost their tradition of the very early communion. There are times when that, as much as the evening eucharist, might help to give particular days their own distinctive character in the cycle of the Christian year.

61

8

Texts and Traditions

The classical and the contemporary

The *Common Worship* Service Book is comprised of classical and contemporary service forms. The classical or traditional ones are, in the main, services from the Book of Common Prayer of 1662, though in most cases with some of the modifications and variations that have become commonplace, in some cases since early in the last century or before. This is certainly the case with Holy Communion Order Two, which is the Prayer Book communion service as commonly used.

So what is the place of the Book of Common Prayer in the continuing liturgical life of the Church of England? Legally it would take an act of parliament to amend or remove it, and it is difficult to believe that anybody would contemplate that. Beyond that it is both a doctrinal norm and also a liturgical document that has undoubtedly given to Anglican worship since 1662 its own character. Even where new services seem at points to go down a different road, they continue to owe more than is often realized to the Prayer Book. It is, in many ways, the liturgical rock from which we are hewn.

But, however much it stands as symbol and landmark, and whatever its interest to the scholar, what is its liturgical use? Liturgical texts that are not in use cannot form the mind and heart of Christians. In some communities it is the one liturgical book used. They use the Book of Common Prayer and no other. There are not many large and flourishing churches where this is true, but such churches are part of the Anglican picture at the beginning of the twenty-first century and may long continue to be. There are other churches, probably rather more, where alternative services have taken over completely and the use of the Prayer Book has disappeared, sometimes by common consent, sometimes under some pressure from the clergy, though such pressure, where it existed, belonged more to the 1980s than to more recent times. In most of these communities it would be artificial to reintroduce wholesale services from the Book of Common Prayer, though one might hope they might become more open to the treasures of the past. But the majority of churches use both the Book of Common Prayer and the newer services and find value in both. In general they have seemed to find the Prayer Book services suitable on reflective occasions – a quiet Holy Communion service in the early morning and Evening Prayer at the end of the day – and the newer services on occasions when celebration seems even more important than reflection and the sense of community that worships God together needs emphasizing more than the individual's relationship with God.

In publishing within *Common Worship* both Prayer Book services and new forms, the Church has recognized that this approach, 'both ... and', rather than 'either ... or', enriches the Church and should continue. The balance between old and new will vary from community to community, but the ideal that *Common Worship* urges is that churches will find room for both in their programme of services. The hope also is that, quite apart from using complete orders of service, the existence of the two sorts of text alongside one another in the same book will encourage people to draw prayers and canticles from one sort of service into another, so that the rigid dividing line between old and new falls away. For liturgy is an evolving art, where the old and the new can be expected to be found cheek by jowl in a perfectly natural kind of way. If the Alternative Service Book of 1980 was introduced with a message that the Prayer Book was on the way out in a brave new world of liturgical renewal, the *Common Worship* message is rather different. Let there be a level playing field where classical and contemporary forms can both be used to the extent that the local community finds them helpful.

Defending the Prayer Book

So what is it that those who most fiercely defend the Book of Common Prayer believe it has to offer to the Church in the twenty-first century? For some it is its doctrinal stance. They see in all the newer rites, at least in their mainstream form, a shift from the Church of England's Reformation theology. And in relation to the Prayer Book communion service they see also, not a confused rite in which all sorts of liturgical principles seem to have been turned on their head, but a highly creative and ingenious order, with its own rationale, serving its own doctrinal purpose. But that is probably not what attracts the majority of those who continue to value the Prayer Book.

For some it is its lack of variety, seasonal emphasis, permission to insert or expand or omit, its sheer predictability, that allows some people to pray the liturgy at a level other than the text. It is easy to see, in this case, why what makes it attractive to some is the very thing that makes it a burden to others.

For some it is a simple thing about continuity. This is the way our ancestors worshipped. There is something marvellous about entering into their heritage, kneeling where they knelt, and saying the same words. Not everybody would think it necessary to use precisely the same rite as they used to achieve that, and some might think it a rather narrow view of our Christian ancestry to limit it to those whose spirituality was shaped by the Book of Common Prayer. Nevertheless the sense of entering into a heritage is a strong and important one.

Perhaps for the majority of those who hold firmly to the Prayer Book the issue is about language and literature. It is not just a cultural argument that those who grow up unused to the King James Bible and the Prayer Book are missing something as crucial as Shakespeare in terms of English culture and identity. It is that the liturgical language that replaced it has sometimes been terse, lacking poetry and rhythm, and is sometimes banal. And for some it is, more specifically, that only the second person singular form – 'thou', 'thee', 'thy' – provides a proper language form for human beings to address their God. It is with this issue of language that the rest of this chapter engages.

No one will be drawn entirely by one argument, and all these may be present in the attitudes people hold; but it is important to understand what contributes to their sense of unease at the neglect of the Prayer Book in the last thirty years.

Those who have no time for the Prayer Book suspect other motives of its defenders or think them simply out of touch with the reality of life in modern Britain. Perhaps people like the Prayer Book because it does not disturb them. Perhaps it is part of a nostalgia among those who do not want to face life as it really is today. And is not this talk about culture, Shakespeare and poetry coming out of a very narrow educational and social sector of society? It is all worlds away from *Neighbours, Friends* and *EastEnders*.

It had become a stale sort of argument, with very little listening. The Liturgical Commission and the officers of the Prayer Book Society have worked to try to create a different mood in which good can be seen in the classical and the contemporary, like the householder of whom Jesus spoke who could bring 'out of his treasure both the new and the old'. Certainly the *Common Worship* texts represent an attempt to hear what those who most value the Prayer Book have been saying.

The language of contemporary liturgy

The texts of the contemporary services in *Common Worship* are at many points the same texts, or almost the same texts, as those of the Alternative Service Book of 1980. People are not having to begin again, as they did in the 1970s when they moved from Prayer Book texts to the Series Three services, the first attempt to create contemporary liturgical English for the Church of England. But there are a number of changes and some rites, such as the baptismal liturgy or the funeral liturgy, have strikingly different texts. Three motives lie behind the changes.

The first is one to which reference has already been made, the desire to create a culture in which new and old might be used more naturally alongside one another and also Prayer Book resonances restored in some contemporary texts. The 1970s revision proceeded on the assumption that, if you created a contemporary liturgy, everything, absolutely everything, must be conformed to the new style. Thus, in the Alternative Service Book, other than in Holy Communion Rite B that never quite seemed to belong in the book, no classical text survived. Every text was modified and those that had begun life in Latin or Greek were retranslated ecumenically from the original language without any concern for Cranmer's Tudor English texts. That was the conventional wisdom of the day, that all must be new and all 'of a piece', and perhaps that was necessary in order that people might make that quite fundamental jump into a world where God can be addressed in something like the language of the present day.

But, if it were necessary at that moment, there is greater doubt about whether it goes on being necessary. Certainly one can see the foolishness of such a doctrine when it leads to the rewriting of the hymns that accompany the liturgy. If trying to render classical prose into contemporary English is sometimes a testing undertaking, to try to do so with rhyming verse without loss of quality and meaning is impossible. But do we not learn from the use of music in the liturgy that with sensitivity a variety of styles can be used alongside one another in a single service in a way that does not jar, but enriches? I can put into an act of worship a traditional hymn of Watts or Wesley, a modern chorus that probably began life in a charismatic setting but has since been drawn into the repertoire by the wider church, a chant from Taizé, a responsorial psalm by Gregory Murray and, in a cathedral, a motet by Palestrina as well, and, ordered carefully, they can come together in real harmony in an act of worship that draws people to God. If that is true of the music of the liturgy, can it not also be true of the words of the liturgy? *Common Worship* proceeds on the assumption that it can, and notes at various points encourage the importation of texts. For instance, the supplementary material to the eucharistic rites includes both classical and contemporary texts and both can be drawn into the modern language rites and the traditional language rites.

In relation to Prayer Book resonances, the *Common Worship* services at points come closer to the Prayer Book texts on which they are based than were those in the Alternative Service Book. This is true, for instance, in Eucharistic Prayer C, in Intercession 2 of the eucharistic rites (what the Prayer Book calls the prayer 'for all sorts and conditions of men') and in the prayer of humble access. It is also true of that minority of the collects that are based on Prayer Book texts, and here the attempt to resurrect a number of Prayer Book collects and to hold more closely to the language and rhythms of others has already met with considerable criticism, an indication that trying to update traditional texts is often much less satisfactory than letting the old be itself and creating entirely afresh alongside it.

Yet, given that the large majority of the *Common Worship* texts will be contemporary texts, with no Prayer Book antecedents, how does one set about creating texts that satisfy? The cry in the 1960s and 1970s was for intelligibility, immediate accessibility. There were created some prayers of real literary value. Three created for the Series 3 Holy Communion were particularly fine; its confession, 'Father eternal, giver of light and grace . . .', its prayer of humble access, 'Most merciful Lord, your love compels us to come in . . .' and its post communion prayer, 'Father of all, we give you thanks and praise', though the General Synod rejected two, replacing them with something safer, and amended the third (all three now find a place in the eucharistic material of *Common Worship*). But, in general, the style was crisp, terse, functional and intelligible. People got what they wanted and what the spirit of the age dictated.

But it was not long before there was a plea for more poetry, rhythm, resonance and memorability, and a recognition that language that is to be used over and over again needs subtlety such that it does not reveal all at first reading. In some of the transitional books leading to *Common Worship*, there is evidence of the Liturgical Commission seeking a new liturgical rhetoric, where there is a greater richness of language, but without sacrificing intelligibility, even if the accessibility is not so instant. It is, of course, a matter of opinion the extent to which the new texts achieve this aim. But the aim has been clear and the Church has entered the new century with texts intended to last.

The third motive has been the attempt to remain true to the principle with which the Church of England has worked for thirty years that, where there is an internationally and ecumenically agreed text of one of the prayers or canticles we have in common with other churches, we should use it. We strayed slightly from that principle in the Alternative Service

Book by adopting a variant translation of one line of the Lord's Prayer. In the period since then all these international texts have been revised. In most cases the new versions are, by common consent, better. Like Church of England texts they have taken more seriously questions of poetry and memorability, as well, in some cases, as seeking a more accurate translation of the original. We have had no difficulty in adopting most of them. Once again the Lord's Prayer has caused difficulty and this time the Creed also, specifically the line where the agreed international text speaks of the Son being 'incarnate of the Holy Spirit and the Virgin Mary'. The Church of England has opted for '*from* the Holy Spirit and the Virgin Mary'.

But the major difficulty in relation to the international texts, but also more broadly in rendering contemporary translations of our own historic texts and in creating our own new ones, has been the issue of gender-inclusive language. The difficulty for us is that, whereas in the majority of English speaking nations that are party to the agreed texts there has been a significant shift in the use of gender-related language, certainly in relation to human beings and to some extent in relation to God, in England there is no consensus on this, some seeing it as a genuine shift in the use of language that is here to stay, others seeing it as a piece of passing political correctness. While we live at a time when there is no consensus, the task of the liturgist is difficult. *Common Worship* texts do, however, follow an agreed set of principles in this regard. International gender-inclusive texts are followed except where this results in theological imprecision. Historic classical texts are not amended and need to be understood within the context in which they were created. Newly created texts are gender-inclusive. The policy will not please everyone, but at least it is not arbitrary. More time is needed for this matter to settle.

These three motives together mean that the language of liturgy in the Church of England has shifted with the publication of *Common Worship*. It is intended to be richer, more inclusive at a number of levels, and to have the quality to stick in the memory.

The meaning of words

In thinking about the words of worship, we need to take seriously the meaning of the words we use. We need to do this not only at the level of believing the words of faith we proclaim and praying from the heart the prayers we say with our lips. At a much simpler and practical level we want liturgical words to mean what they say. When we say, 'We break this bread', bread needs to be broken, not left unbroken on the plate. When we say 'Draw near with faith' we want to see people, having responded with words, respond also in action and get up to come. When we say 'Go in peace', we want them to go, not settle down for the notices or sing another hymn. So often in the liturgy we use words as if they are pleasing ritual noises that somehow do not carry the literal meaning they would in any other context.

Some might say it does not matter. No great harm is done if people, once invited to go in peace, are nevertheless kept back to sing a hymn. But harm is done if that sort of language fosters in people a sense that what is said in church is somehow not real. How are they to distinguish between the words we apparently do not take seriously, for they are just pleasing sounds, and the ones we do take seriously? Why should baptismal promises or marriage vows not be much the same thing – a pleasing sound but somehow not real? We owe it to people, if we want them to take the words of worship seriously, to mean what we say. We ask no less of them.

9

Scripture and Lection

The word proclaimed

In the Prayer Book communion service, prayer is offered for bishops and curates, 'that they may both by their life and doctrine set forth thy true and lively word, and rightly and duly administer thy holy sacraments'. The proclamation of the word – and not just by bishops and curates – needs to be 'lively', and although the meaning, of course, is primarily that it is to be living in the sense that Christ speaks to us through it, it needs to be proclaimed with the kind of sensitivity and conviction that is lively in the other sense too. The scriptures are good news, and they need to be proclaimed and heard with clarity, with joy and with awe. Never must the scriptures be allowed to sound dull. If they are read as God's word for his people, if Christ is present among his people in the reading of scripture, the atmosphere has to be one of expectation. People should expect to hear a message for their lives.

Mention has already been made of the lectern as the focus of the reading of the word. In some places people need to recover confidence to stand at the lectern and to read the scriptures with conviction. There is much to be said for a well-bound, large lectern-Bible from which people read. Lectern and lectern-Bible (or book of lections) both say something about the centrality of scripture, both indicate that something important is happening. So we need to escape from a culture where people come to stand where they will, sometimes apparently anywhere except the lectern, clutching their own Bible (sometimes not the same translation as the one other people are following) or lectionary or a flimsy piece of paper. Having got them to the lectern standing before the big book as part of their training session, we then need to teach them some other things about the reading of the scriptures:

- to announce the reading simply but correctly, so that we know at least from what book it comes and preferably whether it is from a prophecy or a letter or a gospel that it is drawn;
- to contextualize the opening sentence sufficiently to make the reading intelligible, not to tell everything that has come before and certainly not to say what meaning is to be drawn from the reading (let the listeners discover that for themselves), but sufficient that no reading should begin 'After this he said to them';
- to understand that different kinds of readings need different treatment, that narratives are stories, that poems are poetry, that an epistle is a letter, and that some readings need to be read dramatically and yet others are affective when read in a rather understated way;
- to ensure that the last sentence (often the 'punch line') does not gather speed or fade away, that there is then a pause, before the final acclamation ('This is the word of the Lord' or whatever it be) is said with quiet conviction.

There is of course more to training readers than that, but these are the things that give confidence, and the confident reader soon develops into the reader who knows how to handle the different passages that have to be read.

If the reader is encouraged to read from the large copy of the Bible or the lectionary on the lectern, what of the hearers? How should they follow? There is clearly no one right answer to this. At least four different conventions exist and sense can be made of each one.

The first is that people follow the reading (at least at the principal Sunday service) from a lectionary book. The Prayer Book has the eucharistic lections printed out in full (the ASB did the same). The new lectionary is too large for that, but is published as a separate volume in several editions. This has the advantage that the hearer can follow the exact text, complete with the kind of contextualizations at the beginning of the reading mentioned above. To follow in a lectionary is particularly useful when the passage concerned misses out verses of scripture in an attempt to make a long passage manageable. The disadvantage is that the users end up knowing their way round a lectionary, but not around the Bible.

So a second approach is to equip the church with pew Bibles. This has the advantage that people learn their way around the scriptures, as well as the Bibles being to hand if the preacher wants to expound a passage in the sermon. The difficulty is where the passage being read is not one continuous one; the reader can end up spending longer helping people to find their place than actually reading the passage. It is worth mentioning here the *Common Worship* note: 'When announcing the gospel, if it is desired to give book, chapter and verse or page number, the reader may do this informally before saying "Hear the gospel of our Lord Jesus Christ according to N".' This ensures that the acclamation 'Glory to you, O Lord' is a response to the gospel of the Lord Jesus Christ, rather than to a page number! But the principle can extend beyond the eucharist and beyond gospel readings. Page numbers first and then a strong declamatory announcement of the book from which the reading is drawn.

The third way of putting the text in the hands of the hearers is the printed sheet with the day's readings. This has the advantage of being easy to handle, does not involve the new worshipper in finding their way round a Bible or a lectionary, and makes it all the more likely the hearer will take the readings home and look at them again. The disadvantages are work and paper in producing the sheet and the danger that flimsy paper signals disposable scripture.

There is another tradition, not to be disregarded, that discourages the congregation from following the text, but invites them instead to fix their eyes and ears on the lectern and the reader and to allow that engagement to grip them and convey the scripture to them. Cranmer's collect for the Second Sunday of Advent did not originally say 'hear them, read, mark, learn and inwardly digest', but 'hear them read, mark, learn ...' and, though that may have been because of an illiterate culture, there is something about hearing the scriptures read, all attention through the ears, and the eyes on the reader and the great book. But it does depend on good quality authoritative and sensitive reading.

The Revised Common Lectionary

The Church of England provides lectionary material for Sundays and weekdays throughout the year. For Sundays the heart of the provision is, for Prayer Book users, the epistles and gospels printed in the Book of Common Prayer, and for others what is known as the 'Principal Service Lectionary', intended for the main service of Sunday, whether a eucharist or not. During the months of 'ordinary time' there is provision to depart from this lectionary and this is discussed below. But, as the *Common Worship* note says in relation to the eucharist, 'The readings at Holy Communion are governed by authorized lectionary provision, and are not a matter for local decision except where that provision permits.'

This principal service lectionary is a Church of England version of what is known as *The Revised Common Lectionary* (*RCL*). Its brief history is this. In 1969, as one of the fruits of the Second Vatican Council, the Roman Catholic Church adopted a quite new lectionary for mass. In 1983 that same lectionary was published in a modified ecumenical form (mainly by the addition of canonical alternatives to readings from the apocrypha) under the title of 'The Common Lectionary' and was then adopted by a number of Anglican provinces. By the mid-1980s it was already emerging as a front runner for a genuine ecumenical lectionary across the churches, at much the same time as the limitations of the British Joint Liturgical Group two-year thematic lectionary, which the Church of England had adopted, were emerging. In 1992 the ecumenical Consultation of Common Texts published a revision of the Common Lectionary (a fairly minimal revision, except in one respect) and it is this that is known as *The Revised Common Lectionary*.

There are a number of principles that are at work in the *RCL* and which readers and preachers need to understand:

The *RCL* is a three-year cycle, each year being based on one of the synoptic gospels. That gospel provides the gospel reading whenever possible. This is not followed slavishly. There is not, for instance, a determination to find a gospel reading from Mark for Christmas Day. However, when it comes to the Baptism of Christ, we are given Matthew's account in Year A, Mark's in Year B and Luke's in Year C, and similarly, on the Sunday next before Lent, the three accounts of the transfiguration of Jesus. In general one stays with one evangelist through a year, beginning to understand the distinctiveness of his style, his intention and his theology. This is a sound way to approach the reading of scripture.

The Fourth Gospel is used in all three years, but especially in Year B, the 'year of Mark'. Because Mark is a considerably briefer gospel than Matthew or Luke, there is space to read a good deal of John, though it occurs to some extent in the other two years as well. John is used only a little less than Luke, and much more than Mark, over the three years, so the fact that it does not have its own year does not imply any neglect of it.

The approach to the reading of the synoptic gospels is in two parts. In seasonal time, the readings are chosen from that gospel to suit the feast or season. Thus, in Advent, we have both apocalyptic (on the First Sunday) and John the Baptist (on the Second and Third Sundays), and there is in these parts of the year no attempt to draw passages out of the gospels in the order they occur there. But, in ordinary time, mainly the weeks after Trinity, the remaining passages, the ones not chosen for the seasons, are read semi-continuously in the order they occur in the gospel.

The New Testament reading (i.e. the second reading, what we have tended to call the 'epistle' even when it comes from Acts or Revelation) proceeds independently of the gospel. New Testament letters are set at points in the year that 'marry well' with the liturgical cycle, so there is a seasonal element to them, but there is no predetermined connection between epistle and gospel. New Testament letters are read semi-continuously in much the same way as gospels.

The Old Testament choices are approached rather differently. During the seasons, the Old Testament reading links with the gospel reading, preparing for it, sometimes prefiguring it. The approach is seasonal, with even a hint of a theme. But during ordinary time there are two Old Testament tracks. One continues the approach whereby the Old Testament reading anticipates the gospel and relates fairly directly to it. This track goes back to the approach of the Roman Mass lectionary. The other track allows the Old Testament to speak for itself. Here Old Testament books are read semi-continuously, independently of New Testament reading and gospel reading, with no predetermined link or theme. This alternative track is the one significant change made by the *RCL* to the Roman and Common Lectionaries.

The approach to psalmody is to provide one psalm, or portion of psalm, for each set of readings. In almost every case it relates closely to the Old Testament reading, which at the eucharist would precede it and which at other services might follow it. Where there are two tracks for the Old Testament reading, there are also two tracks for the psalm.

There is provision for readings from the Acts of the Apostles as the first reading in Eastertide. The Old Testament is not provided for on those Sundays, though there is rich Old Testament provision for a series at the Easter Vigil. Acts followed by an epistle is at first a surprise. It works remarkably well and becomes another way of marking out the Easter season as distinct from the rest of the Christian year.

There are principles at work in relation to length of readings in *The Revised Common Lectionary*. They turn out be, on average, just a little shorter than the provision they replace, but not markedly so. Just occasionally the lectionary allows a very long reading, particularly on three Sundays in Lent in Year A where long Johannine narratives – the woman at the well, the man born blind, the raising of Lazarus – are read in full. Were it to happen very often, it would be a problem. Coming rarely as they do, they are three rather special Sundays and the stories are all the more compelling for being told in their entirety.

Common Worship lectionary provision

It is not quite correct to say that the Church of England has adopted *The Revised Common Lectionary*. It has done so with just a few exceptions and these exceptions are to conform it to the *Common Worship* calendar, to restore a few key passages that it was felt were being neglected and to create a series of readings relating to creation to be used on the Second Sunday before Lent (matching the *RCL* provision relating to the transfiguration on the following Sunday), rare examples of a Sunday theme.

So the Principal Service Lectionary is almost the *RCL* and, as has already been said, is intended for use at the chief service of the day, which in most communities will probably be mid-morning. In some churches it will be the only service of the day. The hope is that it will be used week by week, even when the form of service changes on a monthly pattern – eucharist, Morning Prayer, family service, etc. – so that at least those who come every week experience the way the lectionary works, especially as it stays over several weeks with one book of the Bible. (The same set of readings will probably be appropriate for a (second) early morning eucharist where there is such and where the Prayer Book lections are not preferred.)

There are two other Sunday tracks of readings, both of which are specific to the Church of England and not part of the *RCL*, though they are designed to complement it. The Second Service Lectionary is exactly what it says, a series of readings for a second main service of the day. Some churches will not need it. Perhaps the majority who use it will use it for an evening service. Because the cycle of evening services in a parish might include a monthly evening eucharist, a gospel reading is always included in case it is needed.

The use of the Third Service Lectionary is likely to be on a smaller scale. The readings here are (in general) shorter. Not many churches have a service for which a third lectionary is needed. The most likely use is for Morning Prayer, where that is said and is something other than the main service of the morning.

A short schedule of amendments to the Second and Third Service Lectionaries allows them to be used also in conjunction with the eucharistic lectionary of the Book of Common Prayer. In this way, for two services out of three the Church of England has a common lectionary for all its churches.

The Sunday lectionary, especially the Principal Service Lectionary based on the *RCL*, provides a real opportunity and challenge to the preacher. For preachers who have gone with the Alternative Service Book lectionary for the last twenty years or more, with readings that jump all over the Bible but are held together each week by a Sunday theme, the withdrawal of predetermined themes, so that the preacher must come with an open heart and mind to the particular lections appointed and search there for a theme for the sermon, may be seen as threatening or liberating. It is never that there is no theme; themes emerge from every creative engagement with the scriptures. But they do come from that engagement, not from a predetermined list. Sometimes a preacher will find a creative relationship among all three readings and will knit the passages together in preaching, but it is not a relationship that lectionary compilers have spotted and planted for the preacher. It is the work of the Spirit and a different preacher will find a different theme and the same preacher a yet different theme coming to the same passages three years later. Sometimes the preacher will not find a link and will opt to preach about one of the passages set, and let the others speak for themselves, as they so often will.

In any church where there are several people who share the preaching it is important that they meet together sometimes to plan the preaching programme. This is always important if the church's preaching ministry is to be effective and there is to be some cohesion to the teaching. But it becomes all the more important where particular books of the Bible are being read through several weeks. There is a period of ordinary time in Year B when different parts of the sixth chapter of John's gospel are read as the gospel reading for five weeks. Without joint planning it would be possible to have five almost identical sermons on Jesus as the 'bread of life'. With joint planning, not only can this be avoided, but a good course of sermons can be developed on the themes in that chapter.

A preachers' planning meeting would look at where in the lectionary a new biblical book comes 'on line'. If Ephesians, for instance, is being read for four weeks, it may be sensible to let it speak for itself in weeks two, three and four and get on with preaching about the gospel, but in week one it will be important for the preacher to signal that for a few weeks Ephesians will be one of the readings and perhaps to say something of its authorship and its major themes.

For the first time in Church of England provision there is, as has already been noted, an open season in lectionary terms to coincide with ordinary time. What the note says is:

> During the period from the First Sunday of Advent to the Presenta-
> tion of Christ in the Temple, during the period from Ash Wednesday
> to Trinity Sunday, and on All Saints' Day, the readings shall come
> from an authorized lectionary. During ordinary time (i.e. between
> the Presentation and Ash Wednesday and between Trinity Sunday
> and Advent Sunday), authorized lectionary provision remains the
> norm but, after due consultation with the Parochial Church Council,
> the minister may, from time to time, depart from the lectionary
> provision for pastoral reasons or preaching or teaching purposes.

The note may seem to give only faint encouragement and this is partly because the Synod did not want to encourage people strongly to abandon a new lectionary before they had even experienced it thoroughly. In the past many who have sat light to lectionary provision have done so in order to engage with the kind of biblical course on one book of the Bible that the lectionary itself now makes possible. So there may not be huge take-up of this permission. What the note is, in effect, doing is to allow those who never depart from the set provision to be more imaginative and to see whether their church might not benefit from a series of readings and sermons on themes particularly geared to the needs of their church or community and yet, at the same time, to try to draw into use of the lectionary for the key seasons of the Christian year those who in the past have simply followed their own lectionary devices.

Books such as *Patterns for Worship* and *The Promise of His Glory* have already provided a series of modules of readings for this alternative approach, though the freedom is there to devise them locally. A freedom like this would also allow a parish to read in the liturgy some of the great Old Testament sagas that lose half their impact when divided up into lectionary-size extracts. The story of Noah and the flood, for instance, or the Book of Ruth, could simply take over the Liturgy of the Word for the day, with perhaps just a short gospel to provide a Christian comment, though there would be much work to be done in ensuring that the story was presented in such a way that attention was held. The story would need to be well told, probably not by a single voice from the lectern. A dramatized Bible is a fine resource.

For, whether we are talking about alternative and local choices of reading or about official lectionary provision, and whether about a formal eucharist or the least formal of all-age services, there are many ways that the word can be made lively and challenging. A single voice at the lectern proclaiming the scriptures audibly and meaningfully may be the norm, but whether it be by dramatized reading, by the use of lighting, by mime or by the employment of song, there is a variety of means of ensuring the message gets through. And getting the message through is important, for it is the word of life.

10

Sunday and Weekday

∿

Changing Sundays

Common Worship reminds us that 'all Sundays celebrate the paschal mystery of the death and resurrection of the Lord'. Sunday is special for the Christian, special because it commemorates not only the resurrection on the first day of the week, but the first day of creation and the outpouring of the Spirit on another first day of the week, the day of Pentecost. It is special because for most of Christian history it has been the day above other days for collective worship and for the celebration of the eucharist where the risen Lord is known in the breaking of bread. It is special because it is time-honoured; everyone knows that Sunday is about church-going, even those who never do it, but only complain about the church bells ringing too early on Sunday morning.

There has not been one simple pattern of Sunday worship through Christian history and sometimes the Sunday programme of services we imagine to have gone back centuries is a more recent invention. Nevertheless, for a hundred years or so, from the late nineteenth century to the late twentieth century, there was a kind of Church of England norm, with an early communion, almost invariably at 8 o'clock (and frequently with a congregation some of whom came weekly and some just once in every month), a mid-morning principal service, the time of which gradually became earlier through the century, moving from an 11 o'clock norm to a variety of times most of them earlier than that, and an evening service, nearly always Evensong, and usually at half past six. That programme is still in place in many urban churches. In others only the mid-morning service remains, with a variety of service forms within it. In the country it is almost impossible to describe the endless possibilities of service times and forms in a multi-parish benefice where the pattern of worship looks like a rail timetable. In general the trend has been to have less on offer, partly because there are fewer people wanting to come, and one

77

well-attended service is better than three poorly attended, partly because there is a reluctance by most to get up early on Sunday morning and by some to go out at night, partly because services spread across the day can increase the heating bill, and partly because fewer clergy often ministering in several churches are too stretched to provide three services in every church. All this has added up to a considerable reduction in what is available in our parish churches on Sundays.

At the same time, or perhaps more recently, we have seen considerable changes in society that affect how people spend their Sundays. For most churches the main service (for some the only service) is mid-morning. This is the same time as many adults and children have sporting activities, activities that need encouraging if a growing generation that takes less exercise is to be fit and well. It is the same time as the shops open and, like or not, Sunday trading is now well established in towns and cities and is part of the weekend's leisure pattern. It is the point in the day when, with the increased mobility of the population, many people are getting into cars for a day out or to visit relatives and friends. It is certainly not the hour of the day when the young think of gathering socially – eight o'clock at night or later would be more likely to appeal to them. In city centres the churches are often (and not just on Sundays) locking their doors and going home just as people are coming out on the streets as the 'twenty-four-hour day' becomes a reality. It is very difficult to see how exactly the Church should respond to this new pattern. There may be some experiments to be done in service times. There may need to be an acceptance that, even among many of the committed, the pattern of weekly worship has given way to a pattern of monthly worship, and teaching programmes in particular may need to take account of that. With its slightly different approach and its Sunday mass obligation, the Roman Catholic Church has seen the growth of the Saturday evening first Mass of Sunday, with people worshipping on Saturday night and keeping Sunday free. Is this a wise pastoral move or a foolish pandering to the modern age? There are not many signs of Anglican churches developing any equivalent (but for weekday worship see below). If not Saturday evening, can Sunday evening experience more of a revival, with different timings and service forms, in more churches than have so far tried this line? We cannot escape the fact that a huge change in work and leisure patterns ought to be reflected in changes to what the Church is offering and when it is making it available.

In at least two respects we are being pulled at the same time in two directions. First of all there is a tension between flexibility and predictability. On the one hand we want to offer people choice. We want them to be able to choose the form of service they find helpful (and they may not be looking for the same thing every week) and to be able to come at a time they find possible and convenient (which may also vary from week to week). It all points to a varied flexible programme. On the other hand a flexible programme often leaves you wondering where and what the service might be. 'If it is the third Sunday of the month, does this mean that it is Holy Communion at 9 o'clock at Little Addington or is that on the second Sunday? Perhaps it is at 6 o'clock this week and at Great Addington. I'm really not sure.' There is much to be said for a simple predictable and memorable pattern – same time, same place, same service, week by week. It is a genuine dilemma.

So is the tension between the 'menu' approach to worship and the single gathering of the whole community. We all have not only different preferences, but different needs. There is no one service form that leads each of us very naturally to God. However skilled the liturgy is at finding forms that unite us, a broad church needs to have a variety of approaches on offer, and that has long been a strength of Anglicanism. In towns and cities churches are often strong enough to be able to offer several quite different services each week. Alternatively, people will seek out the church where the worship suits them. There is a down side to this, for it destroys somewhat the sense of the church that is set in its own community and serves that community, but it is almost inevitable in a consumer age. In rural communities it is far less natural to seek what you need in another place. You hope to find it in your own parish church or at least in the benefice in which you live. So churches offer as wide a variety of choice as they can over the course of a week or a month. But there is a loss here. For the members of a particular church are the body of Christ in that place. They need to know one another, to pray together, to grow together, not to be divided by preference into smaller interest groups, having little to do with one another and certainly not working together for the establishment of the kingdom of God in their midst. At least sometimes we need to challenge the menu approach and bring whole churches and benefices together. In the end we have to say that the worship of God is about something deeper than individual preference or even need.

Principles of Sunday worship

Even if it were desirable, it would be impossible to set out an ideal pattern of Sunday worship for every benefice and church in the land. Local considerations are paramount. But I think it is possible to lay down a number of principles appropriate to a Church that needs to rethink in changed circumstances and where reversing numerical decline (both by winning back the lapsed and also by making new Christians) is very high on the agenda. These principles do apply with only a little modification to

79

every setting from urban single church benefice to rural multi-parish benefice.

- The pattern of worship should not be shaped by the availability of stipendiary clergy. Through the development of teams of lay people (and where the diocese allows it local non-stipendiary ordained ministers), properly trained, there should be sufficient provision to staff a satisfactory pattern of services that is not over-reliant on the parish priest. The parish priest must work hard on a Sunday, but not so hard that he or she rushes from one service to another, with little time for people and little time for God.
- There should, wherever possible, be a celebration of the eucharist in every benefice on every Sunday. It is 'the Lord's own service on the Lord's own day'. It has been at the heart of the Christian Sunday and its celebration of the risen Lord from apostolic times. Although not everybody wants to share in the eucharist on a weekly basis, it should be available for those who do.
- A service specifically designed to be accessible to newcomers and those on the fringe of the church should be provided in every benefice at least once a month. Ideally of course that should be every week, but not all things are possible everywhere. This is not necessarily an argument for services other than the eucharist and Morning and Evening Prayer; it may be that the form and style of these is tailored to this need. But every benefice should be able to answer the question 'Which is the service where newcomers and those on the fringe are in the forefront of our minds as we plan, prepare and advertise?' And this must not be an 'extra service' for people who do not normally come, while the 'faithful' carry on as usual, going to a quite different service that suits them better, for if newcomers and enquirers are coming in they must find themselves caught up in an existing worshipping community. They cannot easily create a sense of community on their own.
- Almost identically, a service specifically designed to be accessible to children should be provided in every benefice at least once a month. Again ideally that should be every week, but not all things are possible everywhere. And again this is not necessarily an argument for services other than the eucharist and Morning and Evening Prayer; it may be that the form and style of these is tailored to this need. But every benefice should be able to answer the question 'Which is the service where children are in the forefront of our minds as we plan, prepare and advertise?'
- Every church building in the benefice should be prayed in on every Sunday. A church that is not used soon looks and feels neglected.

This is not necessarily a matter of holding a full-blown service. It may mean that two or three people go into the church at a set time, ring the bell if there is one, and spend a short time in corporate prayer. They may read Morning or Evening Prayer or they may use another form. But the church will have been prayed in, the community will know, anyone unable to get to a full service elsewhere will have had a chance to join with other Christians. The signal is that this is a living church and a community being claimed for Christ.

- The pattern of worship in the benefice must not be too complicated. If at all possible something needs to be constant from week to week, whether it be the time of the service or the form of the service or even the place. It must not be difficult to find out what is on offer on any Sunday. Information must always be public, prominent and up to date.

There can be no hard and fast rule about the form of the main service of the day, the mid-morning slot in most churches. In some places it will make sense for the eucharist to occupy that slot every Sunday, though with some variety of style in its celebration from one Sunday to another. In others it will need to be part of a pattern that involves Morning Prayer and other forms. But it is worth looking at the reaction in the last twenty years to the solid advance through the middle decades of the twentieth century of the Parish Communion norm, at least in urban parishes and in some rural ones.

The fundamental principle of the Parish Communion movement was that the eucharist should be the main service of every Sunday. At a whole series of levels, from theology through to the power to fascinate and to maintain interest, the eucharist is the best expression of the Church's nature and the most fulfilling form of worship for the committed Christian. Baptized into Christ, the Christian is nurtured through the weekly meeting with the risen Lord in the eucharist. The chief need is not a retraction of the principle, but a more thorough application of it, so that people become genuinely eucharistic men and women, their whole life and spirituality strengthened by their weekly experience of eucharistic worship of word and sacrament in all its richness.

That stated, recent reaction needs to be taken seriously. Sometimes the protest is because of a fear that there has been real loss in the area of preaching and teaching. The biblical and didactic element tends to be smaller at the eucharist than it was at Morning Prayer. The fault lies not so much with the eucharist, but with the inflexibility with which we celebrate it, allowing word and sacrament to go out of balance.

But there is a more difficult and challenging side to the reaction. It is that, ideal as the eucharist is for the committed, it does not seem to be (as it certainly was not in the early centuries) a suitable vehicle for mission. The Church must meet people where they are, not where it wishes they were. Nevertheless the eucharist can convey a great deal about the Church and about its Lord to the most casual of worshippers simply by the atmosphere of worship and fellowship within the community, and now that non-communicant adults come to the altar rail for a blessing as much as children, there need be no sense of exclusion. Celebrated powerfully, the eucharist brings people to Christ. In John Wesley's much-quoted phrase, it is a 'converting ordinance'.

The answer seems to lie in holding together three aims: first that the eucharist must not be all that the Church offers; second that the eucharist must be celebrated with such flexibility that its mission potential is not lost; third that the programme of worship in a parish must include a policy that will help bridge the gap between the parish eucharist and the non-eucharistic family service. The policy might have two elements to it. First, one month in every four or six the monthly Sunday morning all-age service might include a very simple celebration of the eucharist in the style of the service. Second, in the remaining months material that people will later experience in the eucharist should form part of the service from time to time – a sung *Kyrie eleison* or *Agnus Dei* as a confession, for instance, or the peace as part of the service. It makes sense to have common material that enables people to move from one service into another without too great a culture shock. To ensure adequate eucharistic provision on these Sundays, the eucharist might be held in the evening in places where a second service is sustainable.

In the end we have to hold together two valid principles. The weekly eucharist is the heart of the Church's life, but the proclamation of the good news is the heart of the Church's mission.

As for Sunday afternoon or evening worship, here the possibilities are endless. There are churches where Evening Prayer sung according to the Prayer Book attracts a good congregation with a service that provides a more reflective mood after the celebratory worship in the morning. There are other places where Sunday worship simply cannot be sustained, though it would be a good discipline if the parish priest, perhaps with just a handful of people, would go into the church, ring the bell and say Evening Prayer; one never knows who may feel a need and come.

But for many church communities, where the morning worship has a strong unchanging pattern, the evening may be the time for variety, almost on the basis of a termly or quarterly programme. There might be an evening eucharist once a month, a Prayer Book Evensong, a service with the laying on of hands for healing, a *Common Worship* Evening Prayer, a time of meditation or a Bible study followed by Night Prayer, a

Taizé vigil, a Service of Prayer and Praise. But it needs good planning and, if numbers are likely, at least on some Sundays, to be small, careful thought about what spaces in the church to use.

Weekday worship

There is less weekday worship in churches today than fifty years ago. There is probably just as much church life and more Christians are gathering in homes and groups for Bible study, discussion and worship and the church 'plant' may be in use for some of these gatherings too. But less often than in the past do you find the minister following the Prayer Book injunction to go into the church, ring the bell and say Morning and Evening Prayer, and fewer people are attending weekday celebrations of Holy Communion. The pattern of spirituality of clergy and laity may be as healthy as ever, perhaps more so, but the public impact of it is reduced. There is a certain retreat into a more privatized spirituality.

It would be an immensely powerful witness if groups of Christians (with their priest where possible, but sometimes without their priest, certainly where there is no priest resident in the village) were to ensure that, if not twice a day, then once at least each day they entered their church and prayed a simple office in it. There might be one or two who would be the nucleus of the group and be there most days. Or there might be a rota of people, just two a day even. And there would certainly be others who might come sometimes and many more who would be glad to know it was happening. If they could manage to ring the bell, the community would know and that would be a bonus. It might be very cold in winter, but wrapped up well and only there for fifteen or twenty minutes, they would survive! Too easily have we accepted locked churches and deserted churches and this needs reversing. Communities need to be prayed for every day. Churches need to be prayed in every day. Clergy need to recover a sense of obligation about the 'daily office' which is where their public role and their personal spirituality ought to meet, and we now have sufficient flexibility of service form that no priest need feel 'this is not my sort of spirituality'.

There is also a case for reviving the weekday eucharist in places where it has fallen away. Patterns change and early mornings suit fewer people. More are at work, though mid-morning still appeals to some. In city centre and maybe other places midday and lunchtime may be better. For some the weekday evening eucharist might have a place. Obviously there are places – cathedrals, religious communities, minster churches at the heart of groups and teams, churches with a clear catholic emphasis in worship – where the daily eucharist is well established and which, in a sense, undertake this offering of the world to God on behalf of the whole Church. But there is a need in other communities to at least look again at the weekday eucharistic provision for two reasons. First for the reason already discussed that some people are not able to come to church and to the eucharist on a Sunday; Sunday is special, but we need to develop worship patterns that give people other opportunities. Second, if our only experience of the eucharist is in its full, sung, whole-community form, which is a very proper norm, we nevertheless cut ourselves off from its power to strengthen us when it is celebrated quietly, simply, briefly even, with just a few gathered together. It ministers to us in a different way then. Our forebears experienced it when they got up and went to the early communion and we would be foolish to lose out on the intimate eucharist, however much we value it in its full-blown Sunday form. It does not need to have lots of words. There needs to be real willingness to strip the rite down to essentials with good times of silence. The weekday communion is not just the Sunday eucharist without music. But it is a treasure worth keeping and sharing.

In terms of lectionary for a weekday eucharist, *Common Worship* continues the provision made by ASB 1980 of providing daily readings based very closely on the Roman Catholic daily Mass lectionary. This accords well with the Sunday provision. However, it is at its best in a community where there is a constant congregation through the week, for its approach at some points in the year uses biblical books semi-continuously. There is, for those where the congregation is different every day, or where there are only one or two weekday eucharists rather than a daily tradition, the use of the third weekday lectionary track. It is primarily for an office, but it is also 'an alternative eucharistic lectionary' that does not rely nearly so much on a semi-continuous approach. Because of its possible use at the eucharist, it is provided with psalmody to follow the first reading and always has a gospel provided.

Except in very small churches, there is a need to reassess where in the church small services happen. If clergy or laity, or both together, are to gather in small groups for worship, they do not want to be rattling about in a large space. They need to create a more intimate room. It may be a side chapel. It may be the chancel. But it is a space that needs to feel lived in and prayed in. When the service is the eucharist, it may mean being gathered around the holy table itself.

A word may be said finally about Saturday evening. Simply to reproduce the Roman Catholic Saturday night eucharist provision, counting as part of Sunday, probably would not meet the same need in the Church of England, at least not in many churches. But is there a case for a short service in the late afternoon or the early evening at which at least a few might gather? It might be a simple form of Evening Prayer and at one and the same time it could be a coming together of those who are going to lead in some way in the services next day, completing their preparation by worshipping together, a time to gather at the font on the day that stands each week for the Lord buried in the tomb and perhaps to renew the water of the font and to say the baptismal (apostles') creed as a renewal of baptismal life, a looking forward to the worship of the next day by reading and reflecting on its gospel reading, and an opportunity for those who cannot come next day to have a small part nevertheless in the worship of that Sunday. That is simply one example of the kind of fresh thinking that is needed if churches are to be filled with worship 'seven whole days not one in seven' and if the needs of people in a fast-changing culture are to be met.

11

Young People and Children

Some basic affirmations

The Church has a lot of guilt about its children, and indeed its lack of them. Commissions sit, reports are written, helpful courses are devised. There are model parishes that seem to get their children's work right, but most places struggle. It is not always that church people have a negative view that children are, in the common sense of the phrase, 'in the way'. They are affirmative of the place of children in church life and worship. But somehow they have failed to find a formula that integrates all ages. There are, I believe, some helpful principles with which to begin, though there is a real struggle in putting them successfully into practice.

The first principle is that children belong in the liturgy. They are not in church on sufferance. They do not come in from where they really belong, in a Sunday School or Children's Church, to share a part of the liturgy, or go out, after a token gesture, to where they really ought to be. They are not in training as the Church of tomorrow. They belong, simply by virtue of their baptism, to the Church of today. That has to be the starting point.

The second is that they belong at the altar, sharing the sacrament. And here our half-hearted attempts to reform our Anglican practice in relation to admission to communion has us in trouble. We should perhaps have moved into a timed transitional stage, but with a clear objective that a new policy across the land would be in place within so many years. Instead we have a different overall policy from diocese to diocese and a different procedure in every parish. The truth is that, if we are not ready to admit children to Holy Communion at an early age, we ought not to have gone down the path of making the eucharist the Sunday morning norm. While that is the norm, even on some Sundays in the month, the case for the admission of all the baptized to Holy Communion is overwhelming. This ought not to mean permission for a deviation from confirmation before communion in some self-selected places, creating pastoral confusion as people move from church to church, but a national shift that recognizes that sound theology and pastoral needs have come together to make a new practice imperative.

The third affirmation arises from this, but it applies equally when children are not communicants and indeed when the service is not eucharistic. It is that children need not be absent from the liturgy because of its demands in terms of wonder, awe and mystery. For they have these in greater measure than adults. They do not come with age; if anything they are lost with age. For a child everything has fascination, everything is worth exploring, everything is full of life. As part of that, children are easily caught up into mood and atmosphere. If they walk into church and find adults totally gripped and caught up in something full of wonder, something that has taken them over at a deep level, they will not be immune to that atmosphere. They will be quiet. They may even be still if they are entranced. Our problem is not that children have no sense of mystery, but that they do not find it when they come into church. If they are bored and restless, it is often because the adults are not far off boredom and restlessness themselves. It is not so much worship for children that needs to be more full of life and of wonder, but worship for the adults as well.

The fourth principle, which follows naturally from the last, is that we shall never make worship intelligible and attractive to children just by simplifying the words we use. This is partly because children often have a fascination with language that is more to do with pleasure at a sound than a worry about its meaning. Of course words in worship that simply do not engage ought to be avoided. Certainly the language of worship needs to be strong, concrete and pictorial if children are to respond to it. But children understand that the power of language is not all in the immediate accessibility of its meaning.

More fundamentally, we shall never make worship intelligible and attractive for children if we imagine that text is the key issue. It is the total experience that will grip them or fail to grip them. Much time has been spent in the search for eucharistic prayers suitable when children are present. But just as important as the words of the prayer or even the length of the prayer are the music of the prayer, the gestures of the prayer and where the children are placed, so that they can both see the action and be part of it.

From principles to practice

There are two models of children's participation in the liturgy. The ideal is not that a church opts for one, but that both models have their place within the pattern of church life. They are both models of 'all-age worship', though that term is used more often to describe the first of them.

The first is the kind of worship where the whole community remains together throughout the service. Children are present in the church alongside adults from beginning to end, and the style of the service is intended to take their needs seriously, but also not to disregard the needs of adults.

The second model is where the community divides for part of the liturgy. Adults and children worship, learn and pray at their own levels, but come together, probably at the beginning, almost certainly at the end, to affirm their unity. For the parts where they are together there is a special sensitivity to the needs of children as well as adults. This may sound simply like a description of the old model of sending the children out, and it might just be that. But what is intended is the sense of one body, where all have equal value, but which chooses to go into different groups, appropriate to age and Christian experience, for part of the time together. And that would feel very different from the old model of sending the children out. Sometimes it might be the adults who might move to another space. Sometimes the priest might be with the children.

If there is to be a sense of one community working at a series of different levels, care needs to be taken to see that, at whatever the level, the community is engaging with the same truth or theme or scripture. In some ways this is less easy now that clear overall predetermined themes have disappeared from the lectionary. But there is a wealth of material for use with children and young people that follows the provisions of the *Revised Common Lectionary*, and the very large overlap between the *RCL* and the Roman mass lectionary means that we can now make use of a good deal of the children's material devised to go with that sequence of readings. It is important to achieve this sense of worshipping in parallel, partly as a symbol of the one worshipping community, partly so that the parts of the service that all share together should be relevant to each, and partly so that there is the kind of overlap that enables adults and children to talk afterwards, over the lunch table for instance, about each other's insights. It makes no sense for the adults to be engaging with Daniel and the lions while the children are working away on the Parable of the Sower.

The music of the eucharistic prayer has already been mentioned and music is an important consideration in relation to young people in the liturgy. First of all, both in parishes that have strong choirs of young people and also in parishes that have music groups with young singers and instrumentalists, we need to be conscious of younger people whose liturgical ministry (for that is what it is) places them throughout the service in what may be a very adult environment. Being conscious of it does not mean needing to change it. Children can be very professional about operating in an adult world and often learn more from it than we realize. Nevertheless to be conscious of it is to ensure that their presence is always taken into consideration, not least in the preaching.

In Tune with Heaven, the report of the Archbishops' Commission on Church Music (1992), gave strong encouragement to churches to make better use of the instrumental resources on offer from children. We have seen something of a decline in the number of child choristers in parish churches and, though the reasons for this are complex, one contributory factor has been the decline of singing in schools. But despite the requirements of the National Curriculum, music is very much alive in schools. The emphasis, however, is on composition and on playing instruments, rather than on singing. More young people are playing musical instruments than ever before. Churches do well both to make sure they are using the musical potential of the young people they have got, but also to be on the lookout for other musicians who could bring their talents to the service of the church and perhaps be drawn to faith through it. Even in a village church, where there may be no choir and not always an organist, there may be a flautist, a violinist and a keyboard player among the young members of the community. This is talent to be tapped. Or, to put it differently, these are ministries to be used.

There is a problem relating to musical repertoire. Today there is almost no overlap between the music of the average parish church and the average primary school. The problem is not restricted to churches that use only traditional hymnody. There is not much more overlap between the school repertoire and the kind of song emerging from charismatic and evangelical sources. There is no one solution to this problem, certainly not that the Church should cave in, abandon its heritage and sing only what children know. It may mean a better dialogue between the local church and those responsible for religious education and for music in the local schools. It may mean some time in church devoted to teaching adults and children each other's songs. It will almost certainly mean a sensitivity about the choice of music at points when children are sharing in worship with adults. If children come in to a difficult tune and unfamiliar words, it is a dreadful start to their experience of that day's liturgy. Yet they are only part of the community, and cannot expect to sing only their own songs. Sometimes the younger of them would do better to bring in simple home-made musical instruments to accompany the singing than struggle with words and tunes they do not know. Best of all, everyone, irrespective of age, needs to learn more songs.

If children have more to contribute to the liturgy than we sometimes realize through their musical gifts, we should also remember that, as members of the community of the baptized, they should be exercising a ministry more broadly within the liturgy. It should not be a bit of tokenism that children sometimes read the lections, offer the prayers or bring the gifts to the altar. There should not be a special Sunday when it is the children's turn. Week in week out, they should be found on all the worship rotas. Something has been said already of children as servers, and here is a ministry that some will exercise faithfully through many years. But there is scope for less formal involvement. Servers do not need to be 'dressed up'. The gospel does not necessarily need two robed acolytes on either side of the book of the gospels; it might have a whole circle of children around it holding candles. And, although some children would not do well if asked to speak in front of a large congregation, they can be encouraged to make their contribution among the children as they meet separately from the adults. There may be scriptures to be read or mimed there and prayers to be said. This too is all part of young people exercising liturgical ministry.

But we must be conscious of age changes. Young people go through phases. We need to allow them to let things go, when what had been a natural pleasure becomes an embarrassment to them, and help them find a new way to express their membership.

Indeed in general we need to be wary of assuming that what is true of one age group among the young is true of another. The needs of young people change and develop as they grow. In the life of the church we often need to lump together young people of different ages. If our Sunday School or our Youth Club are small, that is inevitable and young people cope with this age spread just as older and younger siblings cope in families. But whenever we can we need to try to identify and meet the needs of particular age groups.

This is never more true than when trying to engage teenagers in the life of the Church. They belong much more naturally in an adult world than a children's world, for that is the kind of culture our society has created for them. They are playing at adulthood while still half children. Sometimes we need to allow them to live in that halfway world unchallenged. But, as well as making them adults young, society has also encouraged them to see themselves as a separate group in society, with their own lifestyle and values and culture. Whatever else the Church does it needs both to respect that and also to value them as part of the whole Church. Gently we should try to hold them within the mainstream of the parish's liturgical life, letting them play their part in shaping it and leading it, but we should also be open to them, additionally, doing their own thing.

There is a whole new world of alternative worship that the churches are only beginning to understand. It is by no means unliturgical. Of course there are dangers of which to be wary, but in general we should welcome the fact that there are those who are doing liturgy on the boundaries, and pushing those barriers back, engaging with the world of new-age concerns, and the desire to see youth culture christianized. Like any new movement it will have its failures and its excesses, but it will also bring new life to the mainstream worship of the Church. Not every church will be placed to provide a home for young people's alternative worship, but the message that needs to be heard is one of encouragement. We need more people who understand and value the liturgical tradition, but who are willing to sit sufficiently light to it that good and creative new things can emerge. Many of those, if we have taught them well, will be the Church's own young people helping to bring their generation to faith in Jesus Christ.

12

Clothing and Colours

❧

Why robes and vestments?

Canon law does not at present permit the clergy at public worship to dispense with the customary robes and vestments. There is of course a good case for changing the rules, which are over-restrictive and, in anticipation of such a change, some clergy have abandoned them in favour of the every-day, or in some cases the Sunday, clothes of modern life. There is a need for more flexibility, but there are arguments for distinctive liturgical clothing and they are worth restating. Some of them apply only to the historic vestments of the eucharist, but some have broader application.

The first argument is about origins, history and continuity. I suspect one cannot defend the view that vestments are a natural development from the everyday clothes of Jesus and his disciples, though that is sometimes said. There is more of a case for seeing their origin in the ordinary dress of the Roman gentleman at the time when the Christian Church emerged from persecution. But their significance lies more in their historical continuity in Western Christendom than in their precise origins. Priest and deacons at the altar for the eucharist have worn these vestments through fifteen hundred years. They have modified them; they have been preserved from fashion only a little more than any other clothes. But the continuity has been there, and their use today is one way of rooting what we do in the liturgy with what the Church has always done.

That argument is, of course, the precise reason why some have wanted to abandon the use of the traditional eucharistic vestments of Western Christianity. They would want to say that what the Church did at the Reformation was to make a break with medieval doctrine, and the vestments were part of the way that doctrine was expressed. They have feared that a return to these vestments in the Church of England marks a return to unacceptable doctrine. To reassure them, canon law affirms that they have no doctrinal significance.

A second reason for their use is that those in the sanctuary are engaged in a great drama, and for this they need, not the practical clothes of daily life, but the long-flowing garments of the liturgy, garments that are pleasing to the eye and are suited to the spaciousness of the liturgy and its movements. The argument has its weak point in the fact that everybody, the whole congregation, is a participant in the drama, and logic might suggest that everyone, on entering the church, should put on a white robe. Nevertheless, if we accept that certain people have a representative function in worship, and also that in the use of our senses in worship the visual is important, the case is well made. Where a group of people share in liturgical dance, there is nearly always a degree of uniform to what they wear; it may be black leotard, rather than the white alb, but there is a recognition that the clothing needs to suit the task.

There is also a recognition that excessive individualism destroys the unity or distracts from what is important. Though ministers must be themselves as they lead worship, there is a proper restraint in the use of their own personalities, and personality is very often expressed through clothes. There is nothing false or wrongly theatrical about dressing for a role.

The vestments of the ministers also prevent them from being classified in a way that makes them belong to only part of the congregation. If a minister leads worship in a suit, one set of signals is sent out about where the minister belongs socially. If the minister wears jeans and sweat-shirt different signals are sent out. In a strange way there is something neutral about vestments that do not make the minister the property of any particular group.

The final argument is about focus and justifies the colourful and often striking vestments of the ministers. In the liturgy the eye needs to be drawn to where the action is, whether at lectern, font, pulpit or chair. If all the colour in the church is static, whether in the windows or on the walls or on the holy table, the eye is not drawn to the liturgy itself as it moves around the building. What the ministers wear should make sufficient impact to focus the eyes on the celebration, but not so much as to detract from it.

The vesture of the ministers

Although some regret the gradual disappearance (except at Morning and Evening Prayer) of the long and full English surplice as part of the vesture of the minister at the liturgy, the alb has established itself, right across the traditions of the Church, as a seemly, unfussy and convenient basic garment for the leadership of worship. To it the clergy add the stole.

At the eucharist in some places they add the chasuble and on other festal occasions the cope. Changes in styles of stoles and chasubles are partly a response to the circumstances of the new liturgy, where, at the eucharist, the president faces the people over the altar, and where more expansive gestures seem appropriate. But vestments must suit a building, as much as a liturgy, and the style of the building, the quality of the light, the basic stone colours, as much as any other colour within the building in glass or carpet, for instance, needs to influence the choice. Some of the modern styles, with strong primary colours, are designed to draw the eye to the celebration in new buildings where walls are often plain and glass uncoloured. Something very different and much more subtle is needed in an ancient building already full of colour. A parish often needs the help of someone with an expert eye for this. Buying by catalogue will hardly ever do.

Whether the president wears a chasuble (at the eucharist) or a cope (at another service) will be partly a matter of theological tradition, both the minister's and the church's. But it can also be influenced by the style of the celebration and the number of robed ministers involved. When the priest stands alone, or almost so, at the altar, it does not need an expansive and colourful garment to indicate presidency of the rite. In a sanctuary with many ministers, lay and ordained, in their white albs, it does need this. Setting and style of celebration ought to influence policy and practice in these things.

Not that in this area the minister is free to decide without consultation. Because this has been a sensitive doctrinal issue in the past, the question of dress for the priest at the eucharist is protected by canon law. Any change in a church's custom in relation to the eucharist needs to be by resolution of the Parochial Church Council. The minister, including any visiting minister (even the bishop), has no right to substitute his or her own preference for the locally established custom.

The distinctive sign of the deacon in the liturgy has been the stole worn over the left shoulder and sometimes the long tunic called the dalmatic. In the current Roman Catholic practice, a priest never wears his stole deacon-style, even if fulfilling some of the deacon's traditional ministry. But this is because, in the Roman Catholic way of seeing things, he will nearly always be a 'concelebrant', exercising his priestly ministry. In Anglican terms, the logic is that, when a priest is exercising a ministry as a deacon in the liturgy, then the stole should be worn as a deacon wears it.

There has been a change in the use of the stole. It follows partly from the popularity of the alb as an all-purpose liturgical garment, often replacing both cassock and surplice. In the past people have seen the wearing of the stole as the sign of sacramental activity; the priest (or deacon) only wore it when administering the sacraments. Today it is more usual to see it as part of the general liturgical vesture of ordained ministers, with the liturgical colour often indicating the season, appropriate to any liturgy, and not specifically sacramental. Similarly the previous practice in the catholic tradition of carrying the stole in (or having it in one's place) and putting it on to do a particular thing, such as preaching the sermon or taking part in the distribution of communion, has all but disappeared. In the latter case it is particularly inappropriate, for distributing the sacrament is not a specifically priestly or diaconal function.

Should servers and those who assist with the distribution at the eucharist be specially robed? It can be argued both ways. These are essentially ministries 'out of the congregation' by people who otherwise sit in among the people. That is made the clearer if, when they take their turn at the altar, it is in ordinary clothes. And yet, if their role involves a visual part in an unfolding drama, they may need, just as much as the ordained ministers, to wear garments appropriate to that drama. That may argue for a different answer on Sundays and weekdays, and a different answer between those in the sanctuary throughout the celebration and those who come up to do something and then return. So much depends on the building, the style of the worship, and local custom. It is not an area where great principles are at stake.

The liturgical colours

Liturgical colours, both for the vestments of the ministers and the hangings of the altar and sanctuary, need not be as uniform as they seem to have become. In England there have been the alternative sequences of Rome and Sarum, though these only emerged in their present and precise form in the nineteenth century. Most churches have opted for the Roman and these form the basis of the (non-mandatory) provision in *Common Worship*. In the end, there are few rights and wrongs, and the provision of different colours for different days is about variety and even more about contrast. You come into church on the First Sunday of Advent or on Easter Day, and the colour has changed, signalling a change of mood.

A church might simply have three colours, festal (best), ordinary, and plain (penitential). The festal might not be white and the plain might not be purple, but providing there is a local customary use, those who worship regularly will soon learn to read the signals and enjoy the contrasts. Where a church has not three colours, but six or seven, the sequence will be more complicated, but the principle the same.

That said, it may be useful to give the rationale of the Roman four-colour sequence in general use in the Church of England and set out in *Common Worship*.

White is for the festival seasons, Christmas to Candlemas, and Easter to Pentecost Eve, on the feast days of Christ and of the Blessed Virgin Mary, and on the days of the saints who were not martyrs, or on the days that commemorate something other than their martyrdom. It is the 'festal' ('best') colour, and so is used for any sort of festival, except when red has a special claim, for the Dedication Festival, for All Saints' Day, at the eucharist on Maundy Thursday, at weddings and at the funeral of a child.

Red has two sorts of use. Red for blood and red for a king both make it the colour of Holy Week (except the Maundy Thursday eucharist). It also makes it suitable for the weeks between All Saints' Day and Advent, when there is a celebration of the 'reign of Christ' (but see chapter 33 for a discussion of this period). Red for blood also makes it the colour for the martyrs, and, since all the apostles and evangelists except John are venerated as martyrs, for their festivals also.

But red is also for tongues of flame at Pentecost, and so for the Holy Spirit. Red is therefore the colour for the last day of Easter, the Day of Pentecost, and for any other occasions that celebrate the gift of the Spirit. As such it is used increasingly (in preference to white) for baptism, confirmation and ordination.

Purple (meaning anything from a very pink purple to a dark blue) is for penitence, prayer and preparation, and so is used for Advent and for Lent until Palm Sunday, though some churches have a 'Lent array' of unbleached linen for Lent. It is the normal colour for funerals, expressing the penitence and prayer proper to the occasion. Some, of course, would prefer white to express resurrection hope (though this is expressed in other ways in the funeral liturgy). Where white is used for adults, it needs to be used consistently; white for some and purple for others suggests a judgement we cannot make.

Green is the colour of growth. It is for use through the weeks of 'ordinary time'.

As for those other days that every community has, with their special themes and emphases, local decisions need to be made, consistent with the sequence of colours normally used and designed to achieve contrast and signal change, when that is the aim.

Precise rules in this area do not matter much. But one thing does. Beautiful vestments, fine fabrics and a variety of colours all witness to the truth that we do not leave in the natural world outside the church the glories of creation, but delight ourselves and honour the Creator by employing them in his worship. They are all his gift and they give him glory.

13

Fellowship and Wonder

Part Two of this book has been concerned with some of the principles, worked out in practice, that apply right across the liturgical life of a church community. It began with the people of God and the prayerfulness that they need to bring to the liturgy. If some subsequent chapters have been less about them, and more about liturgical rules and conventions, let it end, in a kind of postscript, with a return to the people of God and what needs to be in their hearts and minds as they share in the celebration of the liturgy. There needs to be a constant interaction between the sense of fellowship, that has such contemporary appeal, and the sense of wonder, that timeless element without which worship will never take off.

It has proved difficult in the contemporary Church to find quite the right expression of fellowship. In some churches, there has been much talk of it, but it has been seen principally as an activity after worship. For all its real value, the parish 'breakfast', or getting together over coffee, have obscured the truth if they have allowed people to think of fellowship as what happens when the service is over. The fellowship proper is in the service – at the eucharist it is around the table – and what happens afterwards is simply an extension of it. This is nothing new in the Church of England. Thomas Cranmer envisaged it in the sixteenth century when he intended communicants to 'draw near' quite literally, not in some spiritual sense, and kneel together around the holy table for a considerable part of the eucharist.

Other churches have received the message, but at a superficial level. They are characterized by too great an emphasis on the greeting of peace and by an inappropriate *bonhomie* at that point in the service. The restoration of both the words and the gesture of the peace is one of the gains of liturgical renewal and, although its introduction in some parishes was painful and divisive (for there is a risk and a vulnerability about it from which people sometimes shrink), it is now rightly established as an integral part of the liturgy in a very large number of churches. But in a minority of parishes there has been an exaggeration of its significance and it has become the expression *par excellence* of the community's fellowship. It is the sharing of the bread and the cup that is properly at the heart of such fellowship. That is the point of communion one with another, just as it is the point of communion with God. Brothers and sisters are drawn into fellowship with one another by their fellowship with the Father. It is sad when the greeting of peace so dominates a service that this truth is lost. The peace becomes the high-point when it lasts too long, so that the flow of the service is destroyed, or where there is a sort of uninhibited enthusiasm that marks it out as the principal moment of emotional release in the service. For most congregations that has not become a problem. For many the difficulty remains the opposite one, that there is too much inhibition and too formal and stifled a greeting. Nevertheless the peace has degenerated when it becomes the time of a cheerful five-minute walk around, chatting to friends about a great variety of matters.

For the assertion, 'We are the body of Christ', perhaps the most often used of the biblical verses that introduces the peace, is, rightly understood, as breathtaking and stupendous a truth as the 'This is my body' of the eucharistic prayer. That God is really present in the assembly, the congregation, that the body of worshippers constitutes the body of Christ, is as great a wonder as the presence of Christ in the shared bread and wine. It follows that the hand that is stretched out to receive into it the hand of another should reach out with the same joyful reverence as the hand that is stretched out to receive the consecrated bread. The idea of the Church, including its local expression, as 'a wonderful and sacred mystery', bringing reverence and awe to the exchange of the peace, needs to be understood if this attractive and powerful symbol, which need not be restricted to eucharistic liturgy, is to retain its effectiveness.

There is a series of reasons why the element of fellowship has received such emphasis in contemporary worship. In part it has been simply that the liturgists have said that it is good (congregations often resist very firmly what the experts tell them is good, although this emphasis has met with a significant answering groundswell of support among ordinary churchgoers). In part it has been a laudable desire to make people feel welcome. In part, at least in some churches, it has been a conscious desire to give liturgical expression to the 'body of Christ' theology. But there are other reasons too – one is to do with the sorts of communities in which we now live. In a small settled rural community in the past, overt expression of fellowship during worship would have seemed unnatural and unnecessary. For in a community in which everybody knew one another, and met one another all through the week in various situations that formed part of village life, suddenly to greet one another in church in a solemn affirmation of what was self-evidently true was peculiar. But in our strange new world, the Church is very often not reflecting natural community life, but creating among rootless people and in places without tradition or common history a sense of community. The creation of community calls for a more overt expression of it than the mere maintenance of it would do.

Additionally, the expression of a warm and reassuring fellowship within the community is a real need for a Church that feels threatened by an increasingly alien world. Strength is derived from the clinging together of those who feel isolated or a little afraid. As such the language and ritual of fellowship is both a reassurance and a danger – leading to insularity and exclusiveness – in the life of the Church.

None of this is intended to imply that an emphasis on the Church's fellowship is mistaken. It is simply that alongside friendliness and welcome, fellowship in the deep Christian sense also means joyful wonder. Where that has been understood, there is less likely to be the tension between those who emphasize the transcendence and those who emphasize the immanence of God. The contrast has become something of a cliché, but in a more subtle form it goes on worrying many churchgoers. Those who make much of active participation and of fellowship sacrifice something of the majesty and dignity of worship which we need if we are to draw close to God, or so the argument runs. The other side rejoins that God is to be found not in the distance – at a high altar, way up there, so to speak – but in the fellowship and mutual concern, sometimes the hubbub, down in the nave. But the tension need not be there. Where the fellowship expresses itself in joyful wonder, then, far from detracting from the sense of the numinous, it helps to create it. Indeed a healthier understanding of the nature of the Church emerges where that sense of 'the sacred' is attached to the community more than to the building or the furnishings within it. 'Wonderful and sacred mystery' properly describes the Church universal, the liturgy itself, and the community that in every place celebrates it with fellowship and joy.

PART THREE

The Eucharist

14

Rites and Orders

Bread for the world

Part Three of this book is entirely concerned with what *Common Worship* calls 'The Order for the Celebration of Holy Communion, also called The Eucharist and The Lord's Supper'. All three titles for the sacrament of Christ's body and blood have something to teach: 'Holy Communion' that what we seek together in the sacrament is a real experience of God in Christ; 'eucharist' that in offering thanksgiving and praise we do both what Jesus himself did and what has become the heart of Christian prayer; 'the Lord's Supper' that what we do has its origins in the upper room on the night before Jesus went to the cross for the sins of the world.

In this sacrament we also have a constant reinforcement of the divine initiative in our lives. We may try to grasp the heel of heaven, but the truth is that we have a God who stretches down to us. Indeed one of the marvels of the eucharist, one of the reasons why it is so satisfying a form of worship, is that we have no sooner lifted hearts and hands to symbolize our desire to be in heaven than we are celebrating a God who in a very special sense has come among us. Although Christians will never entirely agree about how they understand that presence in the eucharist, the truth that Christ is present, as the assembly hears the scriptures read and gives thanks over the bread and wine they are to share, is one in which all can rejoice. So it is one of the paradoxes of our faith that at the very point that we reach up to heaven we are reminded that ours is a God who in Christ is very much on the earth. This is not contradiction, only paradox, and in paradox one needs to hold on to both truths.

We need to guard against a churchiness that excludes the world from our worship, and especially from the eucharist. We sometimes make it a hopelessly churchy affair; we can almost believe that is the way it has got to be. But the eucharist is full of the world. There is penitence, and when we have penitence as part of public liturgy it is a recognition of the corporate nature of human sin. There is intercession, and at their best the prayers of the eucharist are broad in their concerns and sympathies, and become a lifting up to the Father of the whole of his creation. There is bread and wine and, for all their specific Christian symbolism, these are universal symbols of life and work and leisure. There is the cross, there is the blood shed for all for the forgiveness of sins, there is the Lamb of God who takes away the sins of the world and grants peace. We should be suspicious of being 'sent out into the world', for the eucharist is set in the world and proclaims God's salvation.

All this leads us to take the eucharist with the utmost seriousness, never to celebrate it without a yearning to be joined to heaven, never to celebrate it without a vision of a world redeemed, and never to celebrate it without offering ourselves as what the Prayer Book calls 'a reasonable, holy and lively sacrifice'. That will mean care for the detail, as well as openness to the Spirit.

Two orders, four rites

Common Worship prints four complete eucharistic rites and yet claims to have only two orders. This is not a piece of nonsense, but a recognition that shape is all important. For there are only two orders in the sense that there are only two differing shapes and structures.

The first of these orders is the classical shape of the eucharist that we find in the earliest evidence we have of eucharistic rites, a shape that the catholic Mass just about held on to through the centuries, a shape that is common to almost every twentieth-century revision of the eucharist among the churches of the West, and the shape adopted in the Church of England's Holy Communion Rite A in the Alternative Service Book of 1980. You can call this both 'classical' and 'ecumenical'. In terms of contemporary church life, you can also call it 'normative'.

Holy Communion Order One is a gentle revision of the ASB's Rite A. There have been few changes of great substance, except in the provision of a greater number of eucharistic prayers and a greater range of style within them. The language of Order One is little changed from that of Rite A.

But there is a second rite within this order. It is called 'Order One in Traditional Language' and that is exactly what it is. The order is the same, the points where there are choices and options are nearly all the same, the opportunity to insert seasonal material is identical. There are only two forms of the eucharistic prayer, but they are traditional-language versions of Prayers A and C. Indeed it is only in the language that this rite is different from the main Order One. Like Rite B of the Alternative Service Book, it uses where appropriate the texts of the Book of Common Prayer and supplements these with texts that address God as 'thou' that are compatible with the Prayer Book language.

However, Order One in Traditional Language is different in a number of respects from Rite B. First of all it follows much more closely the shape and structure of the contemporary-language rite of which it is a variant. The prayers of penitence, for instance, are at the beginning. Second, when dealing with texts other than those in the Prayer Book, it provides – as in the confession or the communal prayer after communion, for instance – texts precisely parallel to those in the contemporary-language form of the service, rather than the slightly different texts with minor variants that found their way into Rite B in 1980. Third, the permission to insert seasonal and other variable material into the text at points such as the invitation to confession and the introduction to the peace is extended. What is achieved is what is intended by the title – the contemporary eucharistic order adapted for those who wish to retain the classical texts of the sixteenth century. Two rites, but one order.

Order Two is different, therefore, because of the shape and structure of the material. Here is the distinctive order that Archbishop Thomas Cranmer adopted in his second Prayer Book of 1552 and which has been in constant use through more than three hundred years in the Book of Common Prayer of 1662. Cranmer's order is distinctive in a number of ways, but principally in the way that the communicants receive the sacrament almost, as it were, within the eucharistic prayer. For the traditional elements of that prayer have in fact been divided into three: the first part, the preface, is followed by the 'prayer of humble access'; the second part, the prayer of consecration, leads immediately to communion; and the third part, leading into the doxology, comes after the distribution, as does the Lord's Prayer. The dominical actions – taking, giving thanks, breaking and giving – are also treated differently. Whereas in the classical/ecumenical order each of these marks a stage in the rite, in Cranmer's rite the actions are all brought, as far as possible, into a single moment, when the words of the Lord at the supper are recalled and the people eat and drink. This 'Reformation' Order is not a jumble; it has its own logic and integrity. But it has been left behind by most churches in their recovery of the classical order that has both a longer and more universal usage and also a greater clarity of structure.

Order Two is the Reformation or Prayer Book order. Again it exists in two forms and to meet two quite different constituencies. The mainstream Order Two is in traditional language, because at root Order Two is the Prayer Book rite. The form in which it is printed in *Common Worship* is in fact the Prayer Book 'as commonly used', in other words with the small deviations from the strict order that pre-date any of the liturgical revisions of the last fifty years. The summary of the law or the *Kyrie eleison* may replace the commandments, the priest may greet the people before the collect, an Old Testament lesson and psalm may be inserted, the customary responses may be used at the gospel, there may be biddings before the prayer for the Church, the long exhortations may be omitted, the *Benedictus* ('Blessed is he that cometh...') and the *Agnus Dei* ('O Lamb of God...') may be added. Perhaps more significantly, a note allows the rearrangement of the material around the consecration to move the prayer of humble access to a place before the preface and the prayer of oblation before the distribution to create the eucharistic shape often referred to as the 'interim rite' and briefly authorized as Holy Communion Series One.

But the majority of the users of this rite are not looking for that rearrangement. They are looking for the Prayer Book service, loosened up a little by minor additions and omissions, available in the same book as the contemporary services, and printed in such a way that it looks like a rite for today rather than belonging to yesterday. People will not often advertise it as Rite Two. They will be speak of the 'Prayer Book Service' and only the very legalistic will say they are wrong.

The fourth rite is a modern-language version of that Prayer Book rite – 'Order Two in Contemporary Language'. The need here is different. In ASB Rite A it was met by a provision in the appendix for 'The Order following the pattern of the Book of Common Prayer'. *Common Worship* makes it a separate rite, but the principle is the same. It is to provide for those (mainly conservative evangelical Anglicans) who want to use contemporary texts, but who believe that the Prayer Book's order and shape best preserves the doctrinal insights of the Reformation, in other words it is a genuinely 'reformed rite'. Order Two in Contemporary Language therefore follows the Prayer Book shape in modern English. It does not always provide only an updated Prayer Book text, not least because the Prayer Book texts sometimes defy updating. But it does try to be faithful to what the Prayer Book is trying to do. Thus, for instance, there is a new (but shorter) exhortation before the invitation to confession, the form of confession alternative to the one in the Prayer Book is the fullest of the contemporary texts ('Father eternal, give of light and grace...') and the prayer after communion is not the short 'Almighty God, we thank you...' which is inadequate when there has been a prayer of consecration ending at the words on institution without moving on into the final part of the eucharistic prayer ending in the doxology. There is also freedom in this rite to introduce as much of the seasonal variation as makes sense within it.

It has to be said that there was no great enthusiasm for this rite during the revision process and, in order to achieve a Prayer Book order in contemporary English, some unhappy literary compromises had to be made. The rite is unlikely to have widespread use, but it is provided, for it meets an important need for some.

Clean text: supplementary material

The intention of the Liturgical Commission in producing the *Common Worship* eucharist was to produce a main text that was as 'clean' as possible, with a minimum of notes and instructions, as few texts as possible that were likely simply to be passed over in favour of some seasonal or other variant and altogether a service where people need not be confused. That intention has meant that quite a lot of material has found its way into supplementary material printed before and after the rites. Most, though not all, of this material need not concern the majority of the congregation – they do not need to be asked repeatedly to turn to another page – but those who lead the worship, and especially the presiding minister, need to be aware of what is to be found in the supplementary material. It would be a great impoverishment if much of it were not used and indeed, at some points in the service, some of it is necessary.

The material is basically of three kinds: notes, a form of preparation and supplementary texts.

The notes are themselves divided. Three quite crucial notes, which all worshippers ought to know about, are printed prominently at the beginning of the eucharistic material. They relate to preparation for the sacrament, ministries within the service (already discussed) and the invitation to communicant members of other churches to receive Holy Communion. The other notes are printed at the back of the section. Some of them have already been discussed in this book (posture, traditional texts, for instance), others will feature as Order One is examined in detail, but there are others of a more general nature that deserve attention. There is advice on the use of sentences of scripture, acclamations and greetings through the service, on the place for silence and for songs, and to some extent a loosening up of rubrics that in the service itself may not seem to allow so obviously for spontaneity and variation. Thus, 'Acclamations, which may include congregational response (such as "The Lord is here: His Spirit is with us" and "Christ is risen: he is risen indeed") may be used at appropriate points in the service' in note 5 encourages a spontaneous, even charismatic, approach to the liturgy. Although there are some notes specific to Order Two and some of the Order One notes that cannot apply to Order Two, the intention is that the notes apply as far as possible to both orders. Some are clear rules, others are more in the style of 'coaching hints' aiming at good liturgical practice. Worship leaders do not need to be constantly checking things out against the notes, but they do contain much wisdom, succinctly expressed, and merit occasional revisiting.

The 'Form of Preparation' is a different kind of text. It is printed before the main rites in order that it may have prominence, not least because it includes the printing of the text of the ten commandments (which Order One does not do). It consists of:

- *Veni Creator* ('Come, Holy Ghost, our souls inspire...');
- a short exhortation;
- the commandments or the summary of the law or the comfortable words or the beatitudes;
- silence for reflection;
- confession ('Father eternal, giver of light and grace...');
- absolution ('Almighty God, who of his great mercy...').

Three uses of this preparation are suggested. Individuals may use it as part of their personal preparation in advance of the eucharist. It might, on some occasions (the first Sunday of Advent or Lent are both obvious days or a vigil eucharist before a festival), be drawn into the eucharist itself, so that it follows the opening greeting and replaces everything until the collect, giving the eucharist a more distinctly penitential flavour than might be right on most occasions. Or it might, with the addition of a greeting at the beginning and the peace and the Lord's Prayer at the end, together with hymns and other suitable liturgical material, become a separate service. Again, the evening before a festival is a possible time, or a weekday evening in Lent. It may be added that, in addition to the three uses specified, what *Common Worship* has given us is, in a prominent place, some of the classic texts of Christian worship, a fine resource to use as we will as part of the core of common prayer.

At the other end of the material the supplementary texts are a rich liturgical resource: penitential material, gospel acclamations, creeds, forms of intercession, introductions to the peace, prayers at the preparation of the table, words at the giving of communion, forms of supplementary consecration, prayers after communion, blessings and seasonal provisions. Again the intention is that, as far as they are applicable, they should be available for use across the four rites, allowing old and new to stand alongside one another.

The seasonal provisions are particularly useful. Brought together on one double page for each of fifteen seasons or principal holy days is an invitation to confession, a gospel acclamation, an introduction to the peace, prefaces for the eucharistic prayer and a blessing. One marker in this page will allow the minister to have easy access to all the seasonal material that can enrich the liturgy on that particular day. Of course it does not preclude the use of other seasonal material (and indeed the *Book of Times and Seasons* will provide more), but it gives a certain priority to these texts which, if used consistently throughout a season, will begin to get into the liturgical memory of worshippers in a way that must be good.

Holy Communion without a priest

Common Worship does not make provision for the distribution of Holy Communion outside a full celebration of the eucharist, but the General Synod has engaged with both the principle and with orders of service. There are, of course, grave theological reservations about the practice, and not only from evangelicals, but, because there is a clear unwillingness in the Church of England to consider lay presidency and while there is a shortage of priests, pastoral solutions need to be found to enable communities to have weekly communion if that is what people clearly want.

There is more than one possible way of providing for communion 'by extension'. What has been proposed in the Church of England is an extension of place, whereby the sacrament is taken immediately from the eucharist in one church of a benefice to a service of the word with the distribution of communion in another. Except for those who cannot countenance the idea of the consecrated elements being 'reserved' in an aumbry for a while, an alternative, and perhaps better way forward, would be extension in time, by which a community, having celebrated the eucharist on one occasion would then communicate a second or a third time from the elements consecrated at that eucharist. There is good precedent in the West – both in the traditional reception on Good Friday of the elements from the Maundy Thursday eucharist and in the early Church practice of the faithful taking some of the consecrated elements home to receive communion through the week – and parallel practice in the Eastern churches. Such a way forward avoids the difficulty of people receiving the elements from a eucharist at which they have not been present.

However this is not the path that, in the main, the Church of England has followed. This is not the place to explore any further the theological issues involved. Sufficient it is to say that, as far as the liturgy is concerned, what the services brought to the General Synod and revised there try to do is to ensure that, where there is Holy Communion in the absence of the priest, the service is seen to be distinctive from the eucharist and has nothing within it that might be mistaken for a consecration, but which nevertheless has sufficient resonances with the Last Supper and with the eucharist that people are put in mind of the death and resurrection of the Lord before they eat and drink. It is a subtle business, for people must be given a satisfying liturgical experience that enables them to worship and to be fed, but which still holds out to them as the norm the participation of the priest and people together in the whole eucharistic action of taking, giving thanks, breaking and giving. There needs to be thanksgiving, but not the great thanksgiving prayer. There needs to be familiarity and yet difference. Part of the familiarity will come from using the 'order' (whether One or Two) that the community is the more familiar with, but with the adaptations that clearly signal the difference. It has to be hoped that, authorized nationally or only by the local bishop, it represents only a temporary pastoral expedient while better solutions are found.

15

The Gathering

Coming in

In the following four chapters we take a trip through the eucharistic rite. The particular rite on which the comments focus is Order One. But nearly everything that is said will apply to Order One in Traditional Language and a fair amount to the two forms of Order Two, and the reader is asked to make the necessary adjustments and to disregard when common sense dictates. Similarly the rite is explored in relation to a principal and sung eucharist, but much of it can be applied usefully to smaller, quieter celebrations. It assumes a variety of ministers, ordained and lay, and a fair amount of movement and ceremonial, but again, with adjustments, it applies in a setting where these are not possible or make little sense.

Few people arrive at church for the eucharist on Sunday morning ready and prepared. Among families, for instance, there has been the squabbling over the bathroom, the disagreement over what clothes should be worn, and the argument about who sits where in the car. Or it may be that the phone has rung just as you were on your way. People do not always walk through the church door on the tiptoe of expectation, bursting with praise, and wholly open for the Spirit to pour in. Nor do they arrive feeling like a congregation, as an assembly. They arrive as individuals, their own needs to the fore, and very often find themselves being asked to share with people they have not seen in the intervening six days since last Sunday morning or perhaps for a longer period still. Only on the very special days of the Christian year do any but the most liturgically aware come with a clear view of what today's celebration will bring. What will be its flavour and its mood? How will it be different from other Sundays?

Common Worship calls the first part of the service 'The Gathering'. It is a recognition that we need binding together with our neighbours if we are genuinely to be a congregation and the body of Christ. We need gathering time to prepare. We need to be got ready for communication with God. We need to begin to understand what it is that we are specially to celebrate or reflect on in this day's eucharist. This gathering and preparing is the function of this first part of the rite.

In some churches today people prepare for worship by the singing of songs and choruses for a time before 'the service proper' begins. It is a recognition of the same thing that liturgy has nearly always seen, that we need time to warm up – to God, to each other and to what we are to celebrate. Everything between the greeting and the collect is warming-up material, serving the same need as the chorus or song.

In some communities the moments before the liturgy begins seems the best time to give out any notices, especially if they are to relate to the service itself (and there may be a new tune or chant to learn). What makes little sense is for the president to do so, in advance of a more formal entry and liturgical greeting to the people. Notices, if they are given now, need delegating to another minister; it may be to a lay officer.

The entry of the ministers through the congregation and their approach to the altar, probably during the opening singing, has a liturgical significance. It should be designed so that the procession moves among the people, and is not simply an entry from right or left somewhere in front of them. In moving through the congregation the ministers in a sense gather its members up together and symbolically take them on towards the sanctuary. The symbolism is also present that the ministers, clergy and laity alike, are drawn out of the congregation. And there is also the idea of pilgrimage only just below the surface.

The singers, even if a robed choir, do not necessarily need to be part of such a processional entry. They will often be better in place before ever any singing begins, and in any case progress to their seats does not carry the same meaning as the procession and other ministers to the sanctuary.

The cross may be part of the procession but, as has been said already, the emphasis is on the cross being brought in by the ministers so that it may make a bold statement about the nature of the celebration, rather than on the cross leading the ministers in.

Common Worship notes that 'at the entry of the ministers, a Bible or book of the gospels may be carried into the assembly'. If it is a Bible (and indeed if it is the lectionary) it will be carried to the lectern. If it is the book of the gospels, by tradition it will be the deacon (or whoever is to read the gospel) who will carry it in and will place it upon the altar until it is needed. This bringing in of the book, held high, is common to both Roman Catholic and Presbyterian worship, parallels the bringing in of the bread and wine as the service moves from word to sacrament, and indicates something about the equal value we accord to them. When the book is the gospels, one ancient and strong strand of tradition understands it to be an icon of Christ symbolizing his presence among his people in the reading of the scriptures.

'At the entry of the ministers, a hymn may be sung' and the use of the word 'hymn' is not intended to signal a particular musical style. The opening music of the liturgy is sometimes called the 'gathering song' and that indicates at least part of its function. In most communities on most Sundays this will mean something that everyone can sing, for singing together is part of the process of gathering and binding. This is the point to sing the hymns that invite people to join in worship. 'Enter now his courts with praise' is a good line as a congregation begins to worship and the ministers move towards the sanctuary. It makes little sense at the end of the service.

The other function of this opening music is to set the mood. At some times of the year, it will be seasonal, but mood is more important. Is this to be a service with a particular air of joy and celebration? Or is it a day with a more sober and reflective character? The choice of this first hymn will send out the signal.

Greeting

Before the greeting, the president may say

> In the name of the Father,
> and of the Son,
> and of the Holy Spirit.

This is new in Anglican provision for the beginning of the eucharist, though it has been a frequent way of beginning prayer. It an optional beginning, but it does place the worship firmly at the start within a trinitarian context and takes us to the heart of what we are about: meeting with God.

The president greets the people. Two texts are given – the classic and brief 'The Lord be with you' and the more extended 'Grace, mercy and peace from God our Father and the Lord Jesus Christ be with you', both of which invite the same response. Other forms are of course appropriate, not least, when the 'In the name of the Father...' ascription has not already been used, the trinitarian

> The grace of our Lord Jesus Christ,
> and the love of God,
> and the fellowship of the Holy Spirit
> be with you.

The greeting, especially 'The Lord be with you', looks insignificant, but it performs an important function. The president greets the people and so, as the Roman instructions rather grandly express it, 'constitutes the assembly'. It is in this exchange that individuals are brought into relationship with the president and, through the president, with each other. Men, women and children become 'the congregation'. It is clear therefore why it is a presidential text, not delegated to others, and also why these need to be the first words the president addresses to the congregation. One does not greet someone halfway through a conversation, but before the conversation begins. When the president enters, greets the people with a 'Good morning, everyone', gives out notices, announces a hymn, and only five minutes later says, 'The Lord be with you', that greeting has been robbed of its meaning and function. If there are less formal words of welcome or a theme to be introduced, they arise naturally out of that more formal liturgical start. Thus the rubric adds, after, not before, the greeting: 'Words of welcome or introduction may be said.'

Care needs to be taken to see that any alternative is genuinely a greeting. *Patterns for Worship* has a series of 'introductions', but they do not have the same sense of exchange and relationship that the true greeting needs. This was the reason for the removal at this point in the service of the ASB's 'The Lord is here'. It was more acclamation than relational greeting. Similarly the special Easter form – 'Alleluia. Christ is risen' – because it is more acclamation than greeting is made additional, rather than alternative, to the greeting for the fifty days from Easter Day to Pentecost.

There may then follow the 'prayer of preparation', as *Common Worship* calls it. Traditionally we have called it the 'collect for purity'. It is an eighth-century prayer that calls down the Spirit right at the beginning of the liturgy. It can be a useful tool of gathering and preparing. But its use is optional and there will be occasions when the president's words of introduction after the greeting lead very naturally straight into the prayers of penitence.

Being penitent

A prominent place for penitence in liturgy has always been a part of Anglicanism. The classic expression of it is in Morning and Evening Prayer in the Book of Common Prayer, where the minister says, 'Although we ought at all times humbly to acknowledge our sins before God; yet ought we most chiefly so to do, when we assemble and meet together.' The purists may tell us that corporate penitence at the eucharist comes late in the tradition, but the Anglican instinct has been to recognize its importance. First, in so doing we acknowledge that our sinfulness is part of a fallen world; all sin is, in one sense, corporate, and that needs expression in a general confession we make together. Second, we know that the burden of sin, even when we do not realise it, impairs our relationship with God, and that no act of worship is complete without a recognition of that and a desire to put it right.

Prayers of penitence, therefore, form a significant part of the eucharist, but the tendency in recent years has been to play down this element. It has been both a reaction to the very full emphasis on it in the Prayer Book and also a concession to the spirit of the age. It has not been restricted to the Church of England. In some other Churches an emphasis on penitence in worship has been played down in favour of joyful praise. The truth is, of course, that our praise is, above all else, because we know ourselves penitent sinners who have been forgiven and restored. What is needed is a recovery of balance. Penitence ought nearly always to be part of our approach to communion, but on occasions it should be brief and to the point, while on other occasions we should be prepared to give more time and space to this element in our worship.

Order One has ended the ASB Rite A provision of printing the prayers of penitence at two alternative points in the service. Instead it opts firmly for penitence at the beginning of the service, recognizing that we cannot come to worship, we cannot relate to our Father in heaven, unless we first put right the relationship that sin has marred. It is as in any human relationship, where a rift needs to be healed before ordinary conversation can be restored. We cannot sing God's praises when we have not yet said sorry.

But of course a case can be made for penitence, not as part of preparation, but as a response to the word of God read and preached. This is where Order Two puts it and a note allows those using Order One to transpose the prayers of penitence to that later point. But they are not printed there in the text. There are certain days in the year, Ash Wednesday in particular, when a major liturgy of penitence may well come later in the rite. There are also days – and a note permits this – when the penitence might be in a very low-key brief form, perhaps led by an assisting minister, before the opening hymn and greeting. There might be some great feast days when this might be appropriate. But the norm is penitence after the greeting and (optionally) the prayer of preparation.

Although it can be extended by the use of the commandments, the beatitudes, the comfortable words or the summary of the law (the last of these four being printed in the rite), there are four basic elements to the prayers of penitence: an invitation, a time of silence, the confession and the absolution.

First a minister (not necessarily the president) invites the congregation to confess their sins. There are fifteen seasonal forms for use at the appropriate times and the rubric gives these some priority. There is a 'default text' in the main rite ('God so loved the world...'). There are four other texts in the supplementary material, two of them versions of the Prayer Book's 'Ye that do truly and earnestly repent . . .' And beyond that the minister has the freedom to look to other sources or to use his or her own words to introduce the penitence. Whatever the text, the immediate response, however briefly, ought to be silence; time for all present to call to mind their sins.

Then comes the confession. Order One provides two texts in the main body of the rite and some alternatives. Of the two texts, one is almost that of ASB Rite A, the other is from Series Two Morning and Evening Prayer, a fine text, well worth recovering. The supplementary texts provide three more (including the Prayer Book's 'Almighty God, Father of our Lord Jesus Christ . . .') and elsewhere in *Common Worship* can be found a wider selection of authorized confessions and absolutions. Care should be taken to choose confessions that are broad in their embrace. This is a general confession, where people bring a whole variety of sins for forgiveness. They are not served by a confession that narrows their sin down to pride or environmental pollution or lack of faith. Most communities will want to opt for a normative text (or perhaps a normative text for each season) with variations when appropriate.

There is a further approach to the confession in the main text. It is the use of the *Kyrie eleison* with penitential sentences. A note states, 'When the *Kyrie eleison* is used as a confession, short penitential sentences are inserted between the petitions, suitable for seasons and themes. This form of confession should not be the norm on Sundays.' The final sentence of the note is a way of recognizing that this is a fairly lightweight confession, more suitable to weekday celebrations, brief penitence on great festivals, confession at a eucharist with many children present, than as the normative form Sunday by Sunday. There is also the need to see that the sentences inserted, however seasonally chosen, or however much they reflect the readings of the day, are nevertheless genuinely penitential. A note also allows the *Kyrie eleison*, without such interpolation, to be used instead after the confession or after the absolution, in a way to which we have been accustomed.

The prayers of penitence end with the absolution. Only one text is given in the main rite, but there are two others in the supplementary texts and, again, wider provision elsewhere in the book. The italicizing of *you* and *your* in absolutions is not entirely because of their use by deacons and lay people. There is the option for bishops and priests also to use the more inclusive 'us' form, though the declaratory 'pardon and deliver you' is a powerful calling down of God's mercy.

Although no rubric indicates it, it is an appropriate mark of the absolution for the president, when using the declaratory form, to make the sign of the cross over the people as the words 'pardon and deliver you' are said. It is a reminder that our forgiveness is because of the sacrifice of Christ upon the cross. When this sign is used, it needs to be a bold and strong gesture if it is to witness to the power of the cross.

From penitence to collect

After the absolution may come *Kyrie eleison* if it has not been used already or *Gloria in excelsis*, though neither need be used every day, and both could be. Both are texts in liturgical use since the fourth century, both have a repetitive quality, both can help set the mood of the service (*Kyrie eleison* giving it a more penitential character, *Gloria* a more festal), especially when sung. No note controls when the *Kyrie eleison* is to be used, but a note indicates the use of the *Gloria* except in Advent and Lent and on weekdays that are not principal feasts or festivals. Its omission normally marks out a penitential or neutral day; its use means it is a Sunday or festival. But local conventions can be established.

Then comes the collect, and a rubric in the text indicates a change of practice for many churches:

> *The president introduces a period of silent prayer with the words 'Let us pray' or a more specific bidding.*
> *The collect is said, and all respond:* **Amen**

Everything in the rite between the greeting and the collect, except for the bare bones of the penitential section, is optional. The classic start to the eucharistic liturgy is that the president greets the people and invites them to pray. Silence follows as they pray. When they have prayed long enough, and so been drawn deeper into their relationship with God and one another, the liturgy can proceed, its undercurrent of prayerfulness established. And so the president then says the prayer that collects up their praying, logically therefore called the 'collect'.

That has not always been the way. Very often the collect has emerged straight from the *Gloria* with no bidding and no silence. The rubric urges a new style. The president is to say 'Let us pray', the people having been taught not to regard this as an instruction to change posture, but to remain standing praying silently (or in some more charismatic settings, out loud) for a while. Or the president may want to give the bidding a little more shape and direction – 'Let us pray for . . .', but not too much direction for this is a broad open prayer at the beginning of the liturgy.

The collect is the last element of the Gathering; it is not the first element of the Liturgy of the Word. It will at some times of the year be highly seasonal, but it will not enunciate a theme to be developed in the readings. That is not its function (and is in any case all but impossible when the readings are not united by a common predetermined theme). The collect is a presidential text, or at very least a text for a single minister. It is not designed with corporate recitation in mind and the congregation does not need to have the text. Their part is the praying in response to the bidding; the president simply rounds it off in the collect.

It is intended that there should be only one collect. A string of them makes no sense in this understanding of the collect's function in the rite. One collecting prayer is all that is needed. Where there are secondary themes to be developed, this is better done in the prayers of intercession than by an additional collect here. Those who wish to are free to use only the shorter 'through Jesus Christ our Lord' ending wherever such an ending makes sense of the collect, but, if there is only one collect, the long trinitarian ending does provide an appropriate high point on which to end this first section of the eucharist.

16

The Liturgy of the Word

❧

Reading and singing the scriptures

The people have gathered, prepared and prayed. Now they sit down to hear the reading of the scriptures. The notes plead that, wherever possible, all three readings are used at the eucharist. If only two are read, 'the minister should ensure that, in any year, a balance is maintained between readings from the Old and New Testament in the choice of the first reading'. The principles underlying the Church of England lectionary have already been discussed in chapter 9 in relation to their use at the eucharist and at other services, as have the qualities needed in the reader, the training that needs to be given and the high standards of reading that are needed if people are to be gripped and challenged by the scripture readings.

The rubric indicates that 'the psalm or canticle follows the first reading'. It goes on to allow other hymns and songs between the readings, but there is a priority given to the psalm. But first it should be said that there does need to be something between the readings; one straight after the other does not allow the first to be assimilated. At very least silence; better a song; best of all the psalm appointed.

The near disappearance of the psalter from the worship experience of many Christians is worrying. A Christianity that is not fed on the psalms will be an impoverished thing. This need not mean Anglican chant week by week, any more than it need mean the now more fashionable responsorial psalms. Perhaps the answer lies in variety – Anglican chant, plainsong, responsorial psalm, song from *Psalm Praise*, metrical psalm, sometimes sung, sometimes said.

Because the psalm is chosen so specifically to echo the first reading, this place immediately after the reading is very clearly the right point for it. If it is to be said in a responsorial way, it may be right for the reader of the first reading to stay at the lectern to lead the psalm. The congregation does not need the entire text, providing they have on the service sheet, or hear clearly articulated by the reader, the text of the response. The psalm between the readings at the eucharist does not traditionally have 'Glory to the Father . . .' at the end; the christianizing of it, if that is needed, comes in the New Testament reading that follows, but in any case a Hebrew song is an appropriate response to the Hebrew scriptures. Unless the psalm is one of particular praise and joy, people do well to remain seated through it. We are now in a reflective part of the service as the scriptures are opened up through readings and psalmody.

A different rubric follows the second reading. Again hymns and songs are allowed, but additionally 'an acclamation may herald the gospel reading'. If a hymn is to be sung at this point, it needs to be chosen for its suitability to this point in the liturgy, which may mean some relationship to either the reading that precedes or the gospel that follows, but more importantly it needs to be quite brief. It needs to maintain the impetus towards the gospel, rather than be a stage of the service in its own right.

'An acclamation may herald the gospel reading' is a novel rubric and 'herald' an unexpected word to find in such a setting. But it is a long-established custom in some traditions to prepare for the gospel with a burst of *alleluias* around a sentence of scripture. *Common Worship* provides fifteen seasonal texts and seven for ordinary time. There is much to be said, especially where the provision is new, for staying with this limited selection so that they become thoroughly assimilated, but, that said, there is nothing to prevent people from choosing other sentences of scripture, enveloped by *alleluias,* and music is readily available for singing these in a variety of styles. Traditionally the *alleluia* is omitted during Lent and a different text envelopes the sentence of scripture. *Common Worship* opts for 'Praise to you, O Christ, king of eternal glory'.

There is a case for reading the gospel from the lectern, so that the unity of the scripture readings is accentuated by the reading of them all from there. Equally the custom of a procession into the midst of the people of the book of the gospels and the reading of the gospel there has a thoroughly incarnational slant to it. Or it may be read, not so much in the midst, but further 'west' towards the door – the gospel that is to be taken out and proclaimed in all the world.

The tradition assigns the reading of the gospel to the deacon, and where someone is fulfilling that role in the eucharist, they will probably read the gospel. Where there is no deacon, Anglican provision does not specify who reads it. In some churches only a priest reads the gospel, but the only logic of this tradition is that the priest does because he or she is also a deacon. It is perfectly proper for a lay person to proclaim the gospel.

In some places the desire to reserve it to an ordained minister is simply to enhance its significance as the high point of this part of the liturgy, but this can also be achieved in other ways.

The significance of the gospel is sometimes signalled by the deacon receiving a blessing from the president before reading it. Usually under cover of the pre-gospel song, the deacon bows to receive a blessing such as:

The Lord be in your heart and on your lips
that you may worthily proclaim his holy gospel;
in the name of the Father, and of the Son, and of the Holy Spirit.

The formula for announcing the gospel discourages details of chapter and verse and gives instead the strong declaratory announcement, 'Hear the gospel of our Lord Jesus Christ according to N.' The response here and at the end differs from that in ASB Rite A. Because the versions used since Series Three were not addressed specifically to the Lord, present in the reading of the word, a presence focused above all in the gospel reading, there has been a return to the more traditional forms that address Christ himself:

Glory to you, O Lord.
Praise to you, O Christ.

What follows from that change is another small one. The gospel reader says at the end 'This is the gospel of the Lord' and it is this that elicits the response 'Praise to you, O Christ'.

There are places where, in order to cover the return of a gospel procession, at this point there is a fanfare, usually from the organ. An alternative is to repeat the *alleluia*. But if there is to be instrumental music, although there are days of the year when a fanfare is appropriate, on most Sundays what is needed is an extemporization on the gospel that has just been read, and that will probably have involved the musician playing it to have studied the gospel reading in advance. It will often need to be reflective, without even a hint of fanfare.

Preaching the word

The sermon follows the gospel because it ought to be grounded in the scriptures that have preceded it. Styles of sermon may vary, but where there is no sense in which the preaching arises from what has gone before, something important is lost.

All Church of England rites indicate that the sermon is normative. It is not, in the Prayer Book, a case of a sermon 'may be preached' and in this rite the main text assumes a sermon. One of the notes does however soften the obligation somewhat:

> The sermon is an integral part of the Liturgy of the Word. A sermon should normally be preached at all celebrations on Sundays and principal holy days. The sermon may on occasion include less formal exposition of scripture, the use of drama, interviews, discussion and audio-visual aids.

The need to preach on weekdays is therefore removed, but the obligation (as in the Book of Common Prayer) remains to preach at all celebrations on Sunday. One of the arts that those who lead worship need to acquire is the ability to pick up on a phrase in the readings and draw out a single point in just a few sentences. It is more of a thought for the day, than a sermon in the way we normally understand that word. That will often meet the need at the Sunday early-morning eucharist.

At the main service of the week, and especially if there are children in the congregation, preachers sometimes want to give the message a less intimidating tone, or to justify a very different sort of style from usual, and so at this point comes 'The Talk' rather than 'The Sermon'. There is a lot to be said for staying with the traditional terms – 'preaching' and 'sermon' – if they help to remind us that this is a serious moment of encounter with scripture and therefore with the God who speaks to us through it. But that does not mean that there is only one form to the sermon, and the note helpfully indicates the possibility of drama, interview, discussion (perhaps in groups) or teaching with audio-visual aids. But it is still the 'sermon', because, whatever its form, its purpose is to preach the good news of Christ and to do so partly by expounding the scriptures. Under a variety of guises there is nearly always the need to have a sermon preached.

Affirming faith

The creed follows the sermon as the people's response to the reading and preaching. There are a number of reasons why people found the requirement in ASB Rite A to use the Nicene Creed on every Sunday constricting. One was its sheer length and complexity, a solid and tight theological block of material in the middle of the rite. A second was the fashion for insisting that the creed be said, rather than sung, turning what for generations had seemed like a doxological song into a doctrinal statement. A third was the recognition that much of what it said duplicated all that was going to be said with greater clarity in the preface of the eucharistic prayer.

Common Worship responds to this by loosening up the provisions. The Nicene Creed remains normative and is printed in the main text. The note states that it is used on 'Sundays and principal holy days'. That is already a reduction in the number of days, for the whole category of 'festivals' has been removed. But the note immediately goes on to say that 'on occasion the Apostles' Creed or an authorized Affirmation of Faith may be used'. The effect of the rubric is to give the Nicene Creed a priority – it would be sad indeed if a Christian community never used it and people were unaware of it as a core text – but not to require it absolutely on any particular day, instead allowing local decision on what the occasions might be when either the Apostles' Creed (printed in the supplementary texts) or an affirmation of faith (found elsewhere in the book) might be used.

There are some points that need to be noted in relation to the affirmations of faith. The first is that this is not an open-ended invitation to create one's own statement of faith, whether based on scripture or any other form. It adds to the traditional creeds eight specific texts. Two are versions of the Apostles' Creed (one of them interrogative, the other metrical), one a version of part of the Athanasian Creed, one a version of the baptismal promises. The other four are passages of scripture – verses from 1 Corinthians, Philippians, Ephesians and Revelation. These, together with a responsorial version of the Nicene Creed and the international text of that creed without the *filioque* clause for use 'on suitable ecumenical occasions', are the only texts permitted, except that the rubric would also cover the use in Order One of the Prayer Book text of the Nicene Creed.

The second is that the word 'creed' is not used except of texts derived from the three catholic creeds. Other texts are specifically called 'affirmations of faith' to keep a distinction clear.

Third, the seasonal emphasis of the affirmations is worth exploring. The Revelation text is particularly suitable at All Saintstide and in Advent, the Philippians text both at Christmas and in Lent, the 1 Corinthians text in Eastertide, the Ephesians text at Pentecost and Trinity, though all of them have wider application.

But the Nicene Creed, even if its use becomes one for special occasions rather than for use week in week out, ought not to be sidelined. It would also be good if once again it were sung. To say that it is a statement of faith, rather than a song of praise, is a false distinction, and doctrine in worship always needs to be turned into doxology. When the creed is sung, it does not lose its doctrinal content, but it does become a great song of praise. Composers should set to work.

A note provides a text for the president to use in introducing the creed, useful if everybody is to make the affirmation with which it begins, 'We believe in one God'. The introduction is 'Let us declare our faith in God,

Father, Son and Holy Spirit', though other cue lines could easily become established.

Praying for the Church and the world

A note suggests that the notices may precede the prayers of intercession. If they are placed here, they need to strike a note that makes them lead naturally into the prayers of intercession. This is logical, for, if a matter is important enough to announce, it is important enough to pray about. But the relationship needs to have been worked out. There is no better place in the service for notices, especially if they are to be given by the president, though some may prefer the option before the dismissal.

Intercession is a natural response to the reading and preaching of God's word. This is one of the points in the service where the undercurrent of prayer comes to the surface, and this time the prayers have an intercessory flavour. A note makes the point that 'intercession frequently arises out of thanksgiving; nevertheless these prayers are primarily prayers of intercession'. That point is well made – the prayers of penitence have happened, thanksgiving is focused in the eucharistic prayer still to come, but this is the point of prayer for the Church and the world.

These prayers have traditionally been called 'the prayers of the faithful' or 'of the people', and that sense needs preserving. It is not necessarily about who leads them, but about who prays them, and everything that has been said about praying when all is silent and still applies very strongly here. The growing custom that these prayers are led by a lay person is a good one, though there is a case for the opening invitation ('In the power of the Spirit and in union with Christ, let us pray to the Father') and the final collect or ending to be said by the president as one of those moments when the representative figure draws the community together. There is also a tradition of assigning the intercession prayers to the deacon. It is certainly better for the deacon to lead these than the president, but lay leadership at this time will normally express more strongly that these are the prayers of the people.

The main order of service provides no text for intercession. Instead it sets out something about shape and structure:

> *The prayers usually include these concerns and may follow this sequence:*
> *The Church of Christ*
> *Creation, human society, the sovereign and those in authority*
> *The local community*
> *Those who suffer*
> *The communion of saints.*

Possible versicles and responses are also provided here in the main text. If the prayers of intercession are to provide the setting for the people's prayers they need to retain a broad sweep. There are services where intercession rightly focuses on a few precise and defined areas. But the eucharist is not like that. It has to encompass everything that people bring to prayer. There will always be someone present who is feeling deeply about some atrocity or sadness in the world, somebody with an urgent prayer for a sick neighbour or a friend in trouble, somebody for whom it is the anniversary of the death of a member of their family. If the intercessions are too narrowly focused, these needs will not find their place. The sequence of five categories that the service gives as the norm ensures that the prayer remains broad, and the eucharist the setting for offering to God the whole of his creation.

So the shape is clearly established, but the text is left open. Turning to the supplementary material, the leader of intercession can find five forms.

1. The first is almost identical to the mainstream text in ASB Rite A, a series of set paragraphs, into which can be inserted both the leader's own material and also silence and set versicle and response, or which can be used as a continuous text after biddings.
2. The second is a version of the Prayer Book's prayer 'for all sorts and conditions of men' (though the 'men' have disappeared) with an additional paragraph relating to the departed.
3. The third is the prayer for the church from the Prayer Book of 1928 which was also found in ASB Rite B. It is a full, rich and continuous text that needs only brief biddings to focus it. A note allows the omission of some paragraphs.
4. The fourth is a litany, based on the full form of the litany elsewhere in the book. Any biddings need to come at the beginning, for the rhythm of the text would be destroyed by interpolation.
5. The final form is another looser form of litany, in which insertions can be made.

Several of these forms indicate places for silence, either through the text or just before the end, and the need for a concluding form of prayer (collect or ending); a set of eight of these are provided for use either by the leader of the intercessions or by the president.

In addition to all these forms there are a number of seasonal intercessions, most of them in *Patterns for Worship*. Sometimes they are of the kind where local insertions make sense, but sometimes the prayers are sufficiently tightly constructed that it is better to give brief biddings that focus on immediate and local needs and then to use the set text without interpolation.

Seasonal texts (and sometimes other forms of intercession) introduce variant congregational responses. The key here is preferably to have the printed response in the hands of the congregation, but certainly to enunciate it clearly at the beginning of the intercession and to use it immediately. There is also a growing understanding of the place of music in intercession, both through the sung response and the use of song as a background to silent prayer.

But the freedom is there for the leader to devise entirely their own form of intercession, though usually within the guidelines printed in the text. The leader needs to be very clear from the beginning what shape and style they are adopting, what congregational response (including silence) they are seeking and whether their basic approach is by bidding or by prayer. This last distinction is not always understood.

A bidding is addressed to the congregation ('Let us pray for peace in God's world', for instance). The intention is clear. The leader invites the congregation to pray. The leader is talking to them. They then in the silence of their hearts do the praying they have been invited to do. They are talking to God.

But a prayer is when the leader does not address the congregation, but talks directly to God, carrying the people along through the dynamic of the prayer. Thus 'We pray to you, Father, for the peace of your world' is prayer, not bidding. Once a leader has begun intercession with address to God, they have committed themselves to an approach through prayer, rather than bidding, and any more sentences beginning 'Let us pray for . . .' are out of place.

Both styles have long precedent. Both are legitimate and helpful approaches to prayer. But it is better not to mix the two in such a way that neither leader nor congregation knows to whom the words are addressed. The confusion is all too common.

There is of course an opportunity here to be much less structured, to have, in effect, a time of 'open' or 'free' prayer. Those who are at home in this style know its difficulties in a large assembly, especially in terms of audibility, and also that, for all its openness and its freedom, it needs organizing and holding together. Whether it be the spoken extempore prayer of a single voice, or an occasion when many will contribute out loud, it fulfils the brief of 'other suitable words' providing there is the breadth of content and sufficient space between the words for everybody to feel that their prayer has a place within it.

In the end, whatever forms are used, and whether they follow the conventions or break the rules, the fundamental truth to hold on to is that these are the people's prayers, and the praying often begins when the leader stops talking.

17

The Liturgy of the Sacrament

Making peace

In the place that Order One assigns to it, in the same place that it has in Justin Martyr's second-century description of the eucharist, the greeting of peace has a pivotal role in the liturgy, and marks the transition from word to sacrament. It follows naturally from the Liturgy of the Word in the sense that it is the seal of the prayers of the people and it looks forward to the Liturgy of the Sacrament, both by being a ritualizing of the command of Jesus to be reconciled to our neighbour before bringing our gift to the altar and also in being, in effect, the opening greeting of this second, table-based, service. The Prayer Book rite includes the invitation, 'Ye that do truly and earnestly repent you of your sins, and are in love and charity with your neighbours . . . draw near . . .' and the peace attempts to express something of the same sense in which the communicants must be reconciled to their neighbours before they bring their gifts and share around the altar table. It is this emphasis that has made the text 'We are the body of Christ . . .' so popular an introduction to the peace (though it is now one of seven texts in the supplementary material). Yet there is a danger in seeing the peace too narrowly. It is a sign of a much broader reconciliation in Christ. In the sign of peace, those sharing in the eucharist express not only their love and charity for those present with them in the celebration (though that is sometimes a painful and demanding thing), but symbolically the reconciliation of the whole of humankind in Christ. When the peace follows the prayers, with their emphasis on the world and its sorrows, that becomes very clear.

So how is this greeting to be given? People need to be standing. Even in a community where the peace is not 'passed' there must be, as the words are said, a consciousness of the community and a sense that we are addressing one another. The president may use a sentence of scripture to introduce the peace. Besides the seven texts listed in the supplementary material for ordinary time, there are fifteen texts in the seasonal section. But the words of the greeting itself will sometimes be sufficient.

Where there is a deacon, it is sometimes the deacon's, rather than the president's, task to say 'Let us offer one another a sign of peace.' The service does not make this sentence presidential.

How the peace is exchanged has already been discussed (in chapter 13). Restraint is not out of place because what is being affirmed is an awesome thing. Being the body of Christ, being in love and charity with your neighbour, being reconciled through Christ, are none of them light and cheery things. There is a proper reticence to the way we express them, though how reticent will depend on the kind of people we are. The exchange ought to include the worship leaders moving among the people, rather than sharing the peace only with other robed ministers.

Restraint is also important because the momentum of the service must not be lost at this point. We are embarking on something. The peace begins the Liturgy of the Sacrament and must propel us into that. It is a lovely and significant moment in the liturgy; but at another level it is only a preliminary to what is to come.

A note emphasizes the suitability of the peace at this point in the liturgy, but also allows it to be transposed to be the opening greeting or to form part of the text of the breaking of bread or the dismissal. At the beginning it changes its character to become a welcoming rite; at the end it becomes part of the taking leave. Both can be appropriate, but both lose some of the undercurrent of reconciliation. A better case can be made for the position, adopted in the Roman rite, that associates the peace with the breaking of bread. Here it draws the sense of reconciliation close to the words of the Lord's Prayer ('Forgive us our sins, as we forgive those who sin against us') and of the *Agnus Dei* ('grant us peace') and also retains the body imagery ('We break this bread to share in the body of Christ'). But any movement about the church at this moment can seem an intrusion at the point where the communicant is preparing to receive.

Laying the table

Order One now brings together a number of rubrics, but no text, under a double heading:

THE PREPARATION OF THE TABLE
THE TAKING OF THE BREAD AND WINE

The double heading may alert us straight away to the fact that this apparently simple moment in the rite has hidden complexity. To unravel this we need to take each of the rubrics in turn.

The first is that a hymn may be sung. It has several functions. It may cover all the other actions that the rubrics suggest at this point. It may move the service on from word to sacrament. It may prepare the people for the eucharistic prayer. If it does its task well, everyone will be ready to 'take off' into the dialogue with which the eucharistic prayer begins. But if it has been too short, or very much too long, or has failed to encapsulate the mood, the eucharistic prayer has to struggle from a poor launching pad.

The second rubric is that 'the gifts of the people may be gathered and presented'. Here is an intentional ambiguity. The 'gifts' may mean the collection of money. But the 'gifts' may also mean bread and wine (and sometimes water) brought in procession to the holy table. 'Offertory processions' predate the 1960s liturgical reforms. They began as an attempt to relate liturgy and life through affirming that in the eucharist we bring to God symbols of human work, and it is these that he takes and uses in the eucharist, transforming them and giving them back to us. This emphasis continues to have popular appeal, because people recognize in it something important that they need to express. Their daily lives and their Sunday worship are related. The eucharist is not a narrow churchy thing, but a bringing to God of the whole of creation.

But there have always been those who were alarmed at this sort of emphasis. We come to the eucharist with nothing. We come to God empty, hungry, needing to be fed. He gives us richly, and his giving is not in response to ours. Everything is his initiative and his grace.

This is another paradox of the eucharist. At one level we can and do bring nothing. God does not need our gift. He is not dependent on us. And, at one level, all that matters is the offering of Christ upon the cross and the way that the eucharist renews his death and life within us. And yet our love for God is what makes us approach him wanting to offer, to give. It is the knowledge of the sacrifice of Christ that creates in us the yearning to consecrate our lives and the life of the world, and so, in a sense, to lay them on the altar. To keep these truths in the right proportion we need to ensure that the 'offertory', if we call it such, is not a high point of the liturgy. We may have a procession, but it needs to be restrained. It must not claim too much. Something important is being said, but something infinitely more important is still to come.

The third rubric says that 'the table is prepared and bread and wine are placed upon it'. This is thoroughly practical. It is better that bread and wine are not placed on the altar until now, whether brought in procession or simply carried from the credence table. The minister of this table-laying is by tradition the deacon, setting the president free to sit quietly and to prepare for the eucharistic prayer. Whoever the minister, sufficient bread and wine are now placed upon the altar table. If it possible to have just one paten and just one chalice (perhaps with a flagon of additional wine), the sense of unity of the sacrament is enhanced. At the fraction the bread can be broken on to several plates and the wine poured into several chalices, but the visual impact of 'one bread and one cup' through the eucharistic prayer is strong. Where there are several vessels on the altar, they should be arranged so that one cup and one paten stand out as a focus.

The long tradition of mixing a little water with the wine is almost certainly utilitarian in origin, but people identify it now with John's account of the blood and water flowing from the side of the body of the lifeless Christ, and it also provides a link with the water of baptism that brought us into the community that shares the bread and wine.

The fourth rubric allows for the saying of one of the 'prayers at the preparation of the table'. Unlike ASB Rite A there is no text in the main order, but the supplementary material provides twelve texts, one of them Rite A's familiar 'Yours, Lord, is the greatness...', another the Roman provision ('Blessed are you, Lord God of all creation...') with some small amendments that render them theologically more widely acceptable ('to set before you', rather than 'to offer') and provide a stronger ending ('the cup of salvation', rather than 'our spiritual drink'), a third based on the old prayer in the *Didache* ('As the grain once scattered in the fields...'). The others are newly composed. Seven require only an 'Amen' from the congregation and three only 'Blessed be God for ever'. Only two involve congregational words that would need them to have the text in front of them. They offer a number of different emphases – some focus clearly on bread and wine, others on the money collected, others are much broader. Their style is intentionally understated. Some of them are almost give-away lines. This is in order that they contrast with the eucharistic prayer and do not begin to anticipate it. To some extent they seek to serve for what in the Roman Mass are two quite separate stages of the preparation – the unchanging offertory prayers and the variable prayer over the gifts. None of them are mandatory and there is a strong argument, at a sung celebration, for allowing the momentum of the hymn to lead straight into the eucharistic prayer without any intervening text.

The final rubric says that the president 'takes the bread and wine' and a note fills this instruction out:

> In Holy Communion, the Church, following the example of the Lord, takes, gives thanks, breaks and gives. The bread and wine must be taken into the president's hands and replaced upon the table either after the table has been prepared or during the eucharistic prayer.

The scholars identify the four actions of Jesus, of which the first is taking, as very fundamental to the eucharist and the repeating of them part of how we recognize the Lord among us. For some time the 'taking' was identified with all the practical business of getting sufficient bread and wine ready upon the altar. But we now know that 'taking' was a simple symbolic gesture emerging from Jewish practice, whereby the president, when the table-laying was over, lifted the bread and wine a few inches above the table in silence and then replaced them, thus indicating, before the prayer began, the bread and wine over which thanks were to be given.

The rubric encourages exactly that, the first of the four dominical actions, immediately before the prayer begins. But the note allows that some will think this a gesture that has lost its meaning and will prefer instead to take the elements into their hands at the words of institution, which is a more dramatic moment, and which is in line with a long tradition reflected in the Book of Common Prayer.

Giving thanks

Gathered around the altar table, with bread and wine as their focus, the president and people now pray the eucharistic prayer, a sustained out-pouring of praise, that identifies with Jesus in the second of the four actions at the supper, but develops beyond this into thanksgiving for the mighty acts of God in Christ himself, recalls the supper and the words during it, calls down the Holy Spirit in relation to the gifts and the people, and offers the duty and service of Christian hearts. It is a single prayer from opening dialogue to concluding doxology. It needs different shades and moods if it is indeed to be a sustained outpouring of praise, but it remains a unity.

It is the whole prayer that is consecratory. There is a human need to identify a moment. The whole eucharistic rite is in one sense about focusing the presence of Christ. He is present in the entire celebration. There are those who do not want to say more than that. But Christians have usually wanted to say more. It is in the eucharistic prayer that bread and wine are sanctified to be the body and blood of Christ. Thus we may see Christ's coming in that prayer and his presence in that bread and wine. People may express it, and indeed believe it, in a variety of ways, but to focus to that degree seems right. It is there that the rite tries to hold the line, and it is probably a psychological and devotional need, more than a theological one, that wants to focus still further on particular words or actions. Where there is that need it focuses around the words of institution and around the prayer for the Spirit in relation to the gifts (*epiclesis*). In traditional eucharistic prayers in the West the prayer for the Spirit has preceded the words of institution, even if there is a later prayer for the Spirit in relation to the congregation. In the East, the prayer for the Spirit has never been divided in this way. Those who use the Order One eucharistic prayers will find that they variously reflect both Western and Eastern practice, and this means that some of the old manual actions and gestures of catholic liturgy fit ill with some of the texts.

Gesture nevertheless has its place. The variety of mood and the dynamic sense of the prayer will nearly always mean the generous use of gesture – perhaps taking the elements into the hands of the president at the words of institution, the hands outstretched over elements and then over the people in the different phases of the prayer for the Spirit, the elements raised (perhaps with the president holding the bread and the deacon the cup) at the doxology. It may mean eyes raised to heaven and arms uplifted (and not only necessarily by the president) for much of the prayer. In different ways the offering of prayer to heaven and the sense of the Spirit hovering over the celebration needs to be signalled. There may also, despite recent emphasis to the contrary, sometimes be an argument for a change of posture during the prayer to express a change of mood.

There will also be the need to recover, on some occasions at least, a good deal more music than has sometimes been the case in the eucharistic prayer in recent years. This must not mean the delegation of presidential texts to a cantor. From the opening words this prayer is essentially a dialogue between president and people. If necessary the president's words must be said, not sung, but clergy should be encouraged to recover their singing voices and musicians to provide them with texts that they can sing confidently. But at least the people will be able to sing – in *Sanctus*, acclamations and the great 'Amen'.

There is a good case for the voice of a second minister on some occasions, especially in the prayers (A and F for instance) with oft-repeated congregational acclamations. A deacon may acclaim or sing these, the congregation repeating the deacon's words. A second voice can be part of the prayer's variety. It can also mean dispensing with congregational texts so that eyes may be on the eucharistic action.

Music is one of the ways in which the whole congregation participates. Their vocal participation varies from prayer to prayer. In some their words are simply responses of praise to the words the president speaks for the community. In others, notably in Prayer H, the text the people say more obviously moves forward the logical progression of the prayer. What ought never to vary is their participation through praying this prayer with real faith and commitment. It is the Church that gives thanks and the entire community that consecrates, even if one person articulates what is in the hearts of all.

There is a choice of eight eucharistic prayers. It would be possible to allocate their use seasonally, but this would in some ways be artificial, for they all celebrate the same Christian mysteries and several receive their seasonal emphasis more from special prefaces than from their basic text. But equally the text does not need to be arbitrary. There are criteria for choice. A longer or shorter prayer? A prayer with more rather than less in the way of responses and acclamations? A prayer into which a long seasonal preface can be inserted? A prayer with a strong credal element to it? A prayer where the prayer for the Spirit comes earlier or later? A prayer with creation imagery? A prayer with a place for intercession? Unlike the four eucharistic prayers of ASB Rite A, each of these eight has a character of its own.

Prayer A has its roots in Series Three and ASB Rite A Prayer 1. It is a traditional 'Western' prayer, with an invocation over the gifts before the words on institution and a prayer that the people may be renewed by the Spirit later in the prayer. Its full preface is thoroughly credal, but this can give way to either an extended or a shorter seasonal preface. It has an optional repeated congregational acclamation and a final congregational doxology. It is one of the two longest prayers. Printed as the first and with its particular history, it has something of the sense of a norm.

Prayer B owes something to the eucharistic prayer of Hippolytus and to one of the prayers in the contemporary Roman Mass and is, little altered, Prayer 3 of ASB Rite A. Again it follows the classic Western shape and can be used with both an extended and a shorter preface. It does not have congregational text beyond the four basic elements of opening dialogue, *Sanctus*, post-narrative acclamation and 'Amen'. It is of average length.

Prayer C has roots in the Prayer Book preface, consecration prayer and prayer of oblation and, in almost its present form, is Prayer 4 of ASB Rite A. More than the other prayers it is focused on redemption through the cross and many, while finding it too austere for most of the year, will use it in Lent. It follows the classic Western shape, though the prayer for the Spirit is entirely before the words of institution and prays only that 'by the power of your Holy Spirit we receiving these gifts of your creation . . . may be partakers'. Its preface does not rehearse the mighty acts, a short seasonal preface may be inserted into the prayer, but it cannot be used with an extended preface. It is of a little more than average length.

Prayer D is newly written, has the presence of children very much in mind, involves a high level of vocal congregational participation in a repeated response, has a set text without the possibility of seasonal prefaces, rehearses the whole salvation story succinctly, and has the prayer for the Spirit in relation to both gifts and people after the words of institution. It is among the shorter prayers.

Prayer E is also new. There is no congregational text beyond the four basic elements. There is provision for shorter prefaces, but an extended preface is encouraged. The prayer for the Spirit is located entirely before the words of institution. This is one of the shorter prayers.

Prayer F has its origins in the Liturgy of St Basil. Unsurprisingly therefore it has an Eastern shape, with the invocation of the Spirit after the words of institution. Its acclamations, which vary through the prayer, make it highly participatory. It is strongly credal, but has no provision for proper prefaces. It has a significant section on creation. It has space for intercession. It is one of the longest of the prayers.

Prayer G is a modified modern ecumenical text that, in a slightly different form, was among a group of eucharistic prayers that was brought unsuccessfully before the General Synod in the mid 1990s. This too has the Eastern shape, an emphasis on creation, opportunity for intercession and an unchanging preface. The congregational text is restricted to the four basic elements and a final doxology. It is a prayer of average length.

Prayer H differs from the others in that the congregational text is more than acclamatory. It carries some of the essential logic of the prayer. Newly written, it has no opportunity for special prefaces, has the prayer for the Spirit in the later position, has the presence of children in mind, and is the shortest of the eight prayers.

Not every church community will use every prayer. Indeed that would probably create too much variety. But each needs a coherent policy on which prayers it will use and when it will use them, and it would be an impoverishment if a parish restricted its repertoire to only one or two.

Breaking bread

It is natural that the Lord's Prayer finds a place in the eucharist and natural also that that place should be close to the breaking of the bread. As we press on towards communion, the words 'give us today our daily bread' take on a special meaning, and the petitions relating to forgiveness make links with the words that will follow soon that speak of the one 'who takes away the sin of the world'.

The prayer is printed in two forms, as in later editions of the Alternative Service Book, but now there are two distinct introductions, so that people may be clear which text they are to be asked to say.

'Breaking' is the third of the four actions of Jesus. Originally utilitarian, ensuring that the bread is broken for all to share, it ought now to recover both that utilitarian function, and also to develop more clearly the symbolic meaning that has long been attached to it. It is not only about sharing, important as that is, but about brokenness. The bread that Christ gives in the eucharist is always his broken body. Something about the scandal of the brokenness of the Church is present, linked with the sense of the body of Christ broken upon the cross. For that reason alone it is better that people receive into their hands bread that is broken, ragged and torn, simply because it is the broken body that redeems, and because the vocation to follow Christ is in part about accepting brokenness. The neat rounded host says nothing of that. Nor indeed of the bread that is shared.

Churches will differ in their solution. Some will go for a genuine loaf, broken apart at this point in the service. Others will opt for one of the many new sorts of unleavened wafer or biscuit bread, in a variety of sizes, that can be broken for sharing. At very least, people may opt for the use of nothing but the larger hosts that can be broken into four, six or eight. Here, even if there is not quite one bread, at least there is breaking.

The main service order lays down that the president breaks, provides two texts that are used at this point and then two versions of *Agnus Dei* ('Lamb of God...') for use 'as the bread is broken'. The note amplifies this:

> Sufficient bread for the whole congregation to share may be broken by the president, if necessary assisted by other ministers, at this point in the service. *Agnus Dei* may accompany this action. The words provided at the Breaking of the Bread must be used on Sundays and principal holy days. On other days the bread may be broken in silence or during *Agnus Dei*.

What is being encouraged here is that the entire breaking, the third dominical action, should happen at this point. What needs to be avoided is 'fraction by stealth', a few breaks now, a few more after the invitation to communion, a few more during the distribution itself. In this way a significant action is lost. Here is the chance for the *Agnus Dei* to fulfil its original and proper function, to be the song that is sung while the bread is broken. Its text makes all the connections between the broken bread and the body on the cross.

Feeding on Christ

The fourth of the actions of Jesus is the giving of the bread and wine. In the accounts of the last supper he gives to those at table with him. In other stories of eucharistic character, the feeding of the multitudes, he gives to the disciples that they may distribute.

What is going on in this fourth action? People entitle the whole service 'Holy Communion', but they also refer to this point as 'taking communion', 'making communion' and 'receiving communion'. Order One calls this section of the service 'the giving of communion'. Yet today one of the most popular phrases is 'sharing communion'. There is truth in all these terms, and the appeal of 'sharing' is obvious in an age that has wanted to regain the sense of the corporate in the eucharist. For people do some times still speak of 'making *my* communion', which is excessively indivi- dualistic. Our communion is always with one another as well as with the Lord.

Yet we must guard against the opposite danger that we shall see the distribution of the bread and wine almost entirely in terms of a fellowship meal in which we share, a meal blessed by God certainly, but where the giving is very much of ourselves to one another. The giving of the bread and the cup is a solemn moment of encounter with Christ. However we understand it precisely, we are sharing principally with him, renewing our participation in his death and resurrection, and receiving his life into our life. Somehow, without losing all the welcome contemporary insights that restore the sense of fellowship around the table, we need to recover the truth that we come to have communion with our Saviour, and to feed on Christ in our hearts.

The president invites the people to come to communion. This is intended to precede any reception of the elements, even by the ministers. Their communion is not of a different order from other people's. Four forms of the invitation are given, all printed for ease in the main body of the text. The fourth is for the period from Easter Day to Pentecost, but the others have more general use, though a church might choose to use them seasonally. Or it may choose to follow the ASB convention of always using the first, with its classic statement of Anglican eucharistic theology – 'Draw near with faith. Receive the body ... Eat and drink...' – adding one of the three others according to season.

But that might be too much if the next option is to be exercised. Order One has relocated the 'prayer of humble access' where it began in the rite of 1549, immediately before the distribution. Here it becomes an oral response to the invitation to draw near, immediately before the con- gregation approaches the altar. They indicate something about the spirit in which they are to come, not 'trusting in our own righteousness, but in your manifold and great mercies'. This is likely to prove a better resting place for this classic devotional prayer than its place in some earlier rites. Its use is not, of course, mandatory and some will prefer the invitation to lead into the distribution straight away. Those who do use the prayer need to note that there are two versions. Alongside the traditional one (with the lines 'that our sinful bodies may be made clean by his body and our souls washed through his most precious blood' restored) is the contemporary alternative, 'Most merciful Lord, your love compels us to come in...', first written for Holy Communion Series Three.

The rite does not specify who shall receive first. This is in contrast to the Prayer Book where the priest is to receive before anybody else. Some have been anxious to commend a new practice of the ministers receiving last. It would make for a swifter move into the general distribution. It might also seem to be good manners; serving oneself last. But there is another view, that because the president and other ministers are not the hosts of the rite – only Christ is the host – that is a false argument, and they need to receive the sacrament first to be made worthy to share it with others.

When the ministers do receive first, there is no need for all in the sanctuary to receive in some sort of hierarchical order. All in the sanctuary gather around the table, the circle open so as to admit symbolically the rest of the congregation to it, and share first the bread and then the cup, perhaps with the words being spoken once only and the elements passed in silence. So often the eucharist seems to come to a grinding halt at what should be a moment of expectation, simply because the distribution is so laborious.

The supplementary texts include five sets of words for use with each communicant, from the long Prayer Book form, through three variations, to the short 'The body of Christ' and 'The blood of Christ'. A text such as 'The body of Christ broken for you' is particularly appropriate in Lent.

Some of those who come forward are not communicants. We owe it to people to make clear in our churches, whether on notice boards or service sheets, sometimes by a word from the president or deacon in the service itself, who is welcome to receive communion, and how others, whatever their age, are invited to come forward to receive a blessing. A text for this blessing is given in a note. It is important that no one feels second class or unwelcome or just uncertain about where they stand.

During the distribution, the rubric permits hymns and anthems. They need to be suitable to this moment in the rite. People are drawing near to feed on Christ. The music must enhance that spirit of approach. Silence is also a blessing.

A text is provided in the supplementary material if the bread or wine prove insufficient. The president returns to the table, adds more and says the authorized words. There is no provision for adding silently.

A rubric follows relating to consuming what remains. Other than any needed for communion (i.e. to be taken now to the housebound or to service in another church or else to be placed in an aumbry for later distribution), what remains is to be consumed now or after the service. It does not have to be done by the president. It certainly should not be done at the altar. Quietly, away from the main action, perhaps at the credence table, perhaps at a side altar, perhaps in the vestry, those appointed consume what remains reverently. It is unseemly to consume the left-overs and do the washing up in full view of the guests.

Meanwhile the distribution of communion and perhaps the music that has accompanied it has given way to silence (which at this point is a mandatory part of the rite). That silence is broken, when it has gone on long enough, by the president, who invites the people to pray (whether standing or kneeling according to local convention), and says the *Common Worship* post communion prayer set for the day (or some other prayer). No second prayer is required by the rubric, but in nearly all cases the Liturgy of the Sacrament will be brought to an appropriate end with a congregational prayer. The rite provides two in the text, both familiar ('Almighty God, we thank you . . .' and 'Father of all, we give you thanks . . .'), but the supplementary texts provide three more. When one of these prayers has been said together, all that is needed is to be sent out 'to live and work to his praise and glory'.

18

The Dismissal

The fourth section of the eucharist, The Dismissal, consists only of two optional elements and one mandatory one, together with an instruction to the ministers and people to depart.

The community has said its final prayers and now, at a sung celebration, people will be standing to sing a final hymn. The rite allows other points for this final hymn, but this is the preferred moment for it. The hymn may, like a seasonal prayer, bring back at the end the particular theme or emphasis of the day's celebration. Or it may strike a note of thanksgiving, especially at the end of a season or at the conclusion of a project, though it will not want to detract from the primary thanksgiving in the eucharistic prayer. Very often it is the hymn that can move the mood of the service into the final phase of 'sending out'. The kind of hymn that reminds people of their vocation, of the Church's mission, of Christianity lived out in daily life, that helps turn their minds towards the task before them, is what may be needed here.

Then may follow the blessing, optional but almost always included. Some believe that communion constitutes the ultimate blessing, after which presidential words are superfluous. Others think that a blessing needs to be a mark of a special occasion, rather than form part of the liturgy week in week out. But the blessing survives in most communities. There is in many an ingrained sense of its appropriateness at the end of the service. There is also the likelihood that there will be present some who have not come forward for communion or individual blessing. They need to be included.

The main order gives priority to the seasonal blessing (one of the set of fifteen), but also provides the treasured Anglican text that Cranmer put into his first rite of 1549 ('The peace of God, which passes all understanding . . .') and seven other texts for ordinary time in the supplementary material. *Patterns for Worship* and the other books that will provide material for *The Book of Times and Seasons* also offer a series of 'solemn blessings' for principal holy days, each with three clauses prior to the usual trinitarian formula of the final clause. These solemn blessings should be used sparingly if they are to mark out days of special significance.

The people are often sent out with the sign of the cross, made over them by the president in giving the blessing. They have celebrated Christ's death upon the cross, and now they are going out, marked with the cross, to tell the good news of his salvation from day to day. So it is right and proper that they should be dismissed with this sign, made over them strongly and boldly.

All that remains is for them to be told to go. The text of the dismissal, which is mandatory and which needs to be the last word if it is to make any sense at all, is not necessarily presidential. Traditionally it is part of the deacon's role. There are two versions of the text, and a third form with *alleluias* specifically for the fifty days from Easter to Pentecost.

There remains only the question of how 'the ministers and people depart'. Whereas there is important symbolism in the movement of the ministers through the congregation at the beginning of the liturgy, there is no equivalent significance in their departure. A procession to the altar is a symbolic pilgrimage; a 'recession' to the vestry complete with a 'recessional hymn' is a strange invention.

What, if anything, is symbolized at the end of the rite is that the assembly is dismissed and begins to disperse (even if only to coffee!). The ministers are part of that dispersal, and the choir has also been dismissed. The going out should therefore be orderly, but with minimal fuss and ceremony. When the ministers reach the vestry there is nothing more liturgically to be said. The assembly has been dismissed already. It does not need another dismissal. Music that is played at this stage also needs to give the same message: 'The eucharist is ended. Go in peace. Go to love and serve the Lord.'

PART FOUR

Word Services

19

A Service of the Word

Flexible structure

'A Service of the Word' has been authorized in the Church of England since 1994, though its origins are in the first edition of *Patterns for Worship*. It is not a service in the sense of a full provision of texts, but an outline order, a list of minimum content and a guide to good practice. Its presence in *Common Worship* brings what it envisages into the main stream of Anglican worship and is in some ways the most radical provision in the book. Indeed some of those who most value the commonality of Anglican worship may see it as something of a Trojan horse, at least in relation to its provisions for a service of the word with the eucharist.

Published originally in the same book as authorized confessions, absolutions and affirmations of faith, its original intention was to provide a broad and permissive outline for non-eucharistic Sunday worship, for the family service and for all-age worship, but with some frontiers set and some landmarks that need to be kept in place. That intention remains. But, in addition, it has proved to be the legal framework within which to develop new forms of Morning and Evening Prayer and, beyond that, to provide the model for almost any special service for which the minister wants some guidance about core content and about order. 'A Service of the Word' helps, whether one is devising a carol service, a memorial service or a service for One World Week. As its notes say, 'it provides a structure for daily prayer, for Sunday services and for services of an occasional nature'. It can be read at three levels – first the core table of order and contents, second, the notes that spell out this order and clarify some points and, third, what it calls the 'introduction', but which is more in the nature of a commentary, a guide to good practice.

In terms of structure, it identifies four stages to a non-eucharistic service – Preparation, Liturgy of the Word, Prayers and Conclusion. Although some of the titles of sections are different, this can immediately be seen to be the same structure as the eucharist with the Liturgy of the Sacrament omitted. Equally one can see here the classic shape of the daily office. So what 'A Service of the Word' does is to bring to the surface, for those who have not seen it, a basic structure that experience teaches makes good liturgy.

'Preparation' at its fullest would move from opening greeting, through prayers of penitence, and then a song 'or a set of responses' to the collect. In this fullest form, especially if the song were the *Gloria*, it has the look of the conventional Gathering section of the eucharist. But there are variants. The only absolutely mandatory text at this point in the service is the greeting. Prayers of penitence must be included, and must be in an authorized form, but need not be part of the preparation. Instead they can come in the 'Prayers' section of the service later where they become a response to the Liturgy of the Word. The song, though it might be the *Gloria* or indeed the *Kyrie eleison*, might have something of the flavour of Morning Prayer about it by the use of the *Venite* ('O come, let us sing unto the Lord . . .') or it might be any other hymn or song that established a sense of worship and belonging at the beginning of the service. In its place, or more likely in addition, might be a set of responses, whether the 'O Lord, open our lips . . .' of Morning Prayer or a less familiar set from *Patterns for Worship*. The collect also, though it is placed here in the Preparation as the same kind of opening prayer that it is at the eucharist, may be transposed to the Prayer section, where it serves to collect up and conclude the prayers, in much the same way as it is intended to do in the daily office.

The Liturgy of the Word moves through four stages – readings from scripture, a psalm or 'if occasion demands, a scriptural song', a sermon, and an authorized creed or 'if occasion demands, an authorized affirmation of faith'. If the psalm precedes the readings and if there are scriptural songs as well, there is the classic shape of the daily office Liturgy of the Word. But there could be a quite different feel. The notes spell out that the readings might be dramatized, the psalm might be metrical or the song simply a chorus text with strongly scriptural words, the sermon, as discussed in relation to the eucharist, might include less formal exposition, interviews, discussions etc. Indeed the note relating to this now included in the notes for the eucharist began life in this Service of the Word context. The sermon may come after either of the readings or, as in traditional Morning Prayer, later in the service after the prayers.

'A Service of the Word' is more permissive than the eucharist in relation to readings and to lectionary. First of all it assumes two readings, rather than three, and allows that there may be only one. Second, it widens the period during which official lectionary provision may give way to local choice. Whereas in the eucharist, official provision is ordered from the first Sunday of Advent until Candlemas and from Ash Wednesday until Trinity Sunday, leaving only 'ordinary time' as an 'open season', 'A Service of the Word' orders the official provision only from the Third Sunday of Advent until the Baptism of Christ (four or five Sundays) and from Palm Sunday to Trinity Sunday (nine Sundays), the heart of the liturgical year, leaving three quarters of the year open, including a long enough period in the autumn for a locally devised course of themes or sermons and the freedom to devise these also for the first five Sundays of Lent.

'The Prayers' section specifies intercessions and thanksgivings and the Lord's Prayer. As we have already noted, the prayers of penitence may also be transposed to this section, as may the collect to conclude the prayer section. The inclusion of thanksgiving, alongside intercession, is of course important. Whereas in the eucharist, thanksgiving focuses in the eucharistic prayer and the earlier prayers rightly major on intercession, here, where there will be no eucharistic prayer, it is important that praise and thanksgiving feature in the prayers, and also in the choice of hymns and songs.

The final section, 'Conclusion', is, like the equivalent 'Dismissal' of the eucharist, brief. Often there will be a hymn or song. All that is specified is a 'liturgical ending', which a note tells us might be the peace, the grace, 'a suitable ascription or blessing' or a responsive conclusion such as one of the dismissal texts from the eucharist.

Planning the service

Although the main purpose of the table of structure and contents of a Service of the Word is to identify shape and order, from it we may also deduce the irreducible core that we may expect to find in any service that lays claim to being good liturgy in the Anglican tradition. At least we can almost do so, but we need to know that some of this irreducible core applies only to Sundays and principal holy days and some applies only to the principal service of the day. Here nevertheless are the ten constituent parts of the core if the service is on a Sunday or principal holy day and is the principal service of the day:

- greeting (in a recognizable liturgical form);
- authorized prayers of penitence;
- a collect (not necessarily that of the day);
- a reading from scripture;
- a psalm (or any text of scripture sung);
- a sermon (though not necessarily formal preaching);

145

- an authorized creed or authorized affirmation of faith;
- prayers of intercession and thanksgiving;
- the Lord's Prayer;
- a liturgical ending.

To this would, of course, be added hymns and songs at various points, and perhaps other elements too. On a weekday the list is shorter and is intended to enable a Service of the Word to provide the structure for a daily office (see chapter 20):

- greeting (in a recognizable liturgical form);
- a collect;
- a reading from scripture;
- a psalm (or any text of scripture sung);
- prayers of intercession and thanksgiving;
- the Lord's Prayer;
- a liturgical ending.

These are useful checklists for any who are preparing worship.

But in a sense there are prior questions that need to be asked before ever the list of the irreducible core can be helpful. The cluster of questions with which any discussion of the service should begin include:

- For whom is this service principally intended?
- In what season is it set?
- What is its particular purpose or theme?
- What length should it be?
- What style of service would be appropriate?

The question of style is an important preliminary. There are no right or wrong styles, though there is an appropriate style to a particular occasion. Styles may range from a formal, choral service, highly rehearsed, with solemn words and dignified ritual, to an informal and more spontaneous service, with lighter music, words close to everyday speech and a minimum of ceremonial (though possibly some congregational movement and perhaps near the heart of the service some act of giving or receiving). Both styles have their place. Both ought to have their place if possible in the same church. And there is a whole range of styles between. It is important to have some picture of the style that is needed before ever the detailed task begins. It is not that a style needs to be followed slavishly; a service can, to its enrichment, include variety, but no style at all will make for a hotchpotch of irreconcilables that will please no one.

It is then that those who are planning the service begin to look at questions of structure, sense of development and content, and here 'A

Service of the Word' with its flexibility, but its clear guidelines, is of real help. Both *Common Worship* itself and also *Patterns for Worship* and the seasonal books supply rich resources.

But it is worth pausing for a moment to reflect further on what is written above about 'some act of giving and receiving'. Although the guidelines mention drama, they do not say much about the fact that worship often engages us when we do something. The getting up out of one's seat, the moving forward, whether it is to gather in another part of the building, or to be given a gift or to make an offering, acquires an almost sacramental character, even outside the context of the celebration of the sacraments themselves. Receiving flowers on Mothering Sunday, carrying christingles in procession at Christmas, or bringing apples, marrows or tins at Harvest – the sorts of things that happen in family services – are the equivalent of some of the more formal liturgical experiences such as receiving ash on the forehead at the beginning of Lent or carrying branches on Palm Sunday. Very often moving, giving and receiving deepens our experience of worship. We need to be imaginative and creative in how we build these things into a Service of the Word.

There are more questions to ask when structure and content has been provisionally decided in order to check the balance of the service. Special services sometimes exaggerate out of proportion some aspect of worship at the expense of others. So at this stage we need to ask:

- Does this service feel like a joyful celebration of the people of God?
- What is the nature and level of congregational participation?
- Will the service have a sense of wonder and reverence?
- Are the elements of penitence, intercession, thanksgiving and praise all present?
- Is the gospel of Christ being proclaimed?
- What is the teaching element of the service?
- What expression is there of the Church's fellowship?
- Are there too many words? Is there too little silence?
- What will be the balance between the role of the presiding minister and other leaders?

Finally there are 'stage directions' for those taking a leading part, and decisions about standing, kneeling, turning and moving. There are decisions of personnel and the rehearsing of them. There are sometimes questions about furnishing, staging, lighting and sound. There is also the need to provide an attractive service sheet, so that not too many instructions will need to destroy the continuity and momentum of the service, but the congregation will be able to participate fully.

147

Making the eucharist more flexible

Holy Communion Order One is a flexible eucharistic rite, and for Sunday use provides as much choice and variation as most parishes will need. But 'A Service of the Word' increases the flexibility by providing a form in which the two combine. What is then given as the order is surprisingly conservative. It is in fact the same order as is found in the main eucharistic rite. Where it is radical is in the way that, while keeping the order, it removes the requirement to use the customary texts at points such as the greeting, the gospel responses, the peace, the breaking of bread, the invitation to communion and the dismissal (while retaining them for the prayers of penitence and the eucharistic prayer). But the note at the head of the table spells out that this freedom is intended for very specific, limited and well-prepared occasions: 'This rite requires careful preparation by the president and other participants, and is not normally to be used as the regular Sunday or weekday service.'

A much more likely use of the provisions is by using the permissions of 'A Service of the Word' to free up the Gathering and Liturgy of the Word parts of the eucharist, to make them even more flexible in an all-age context, while keeping the Liturgy of the Sacrament within the usual eucharistic framework (probably with one of the briefer eucharistic prayers), and using throughout the service the customary greetings and acclamations. So the content will be much the same as any other eucharist (though perhaps with less text than on many occasions), but in the first part of the service the shape may have been altered or stretched.

There is a lot of freedom here, but it will not go wrong and undermine the common worship of the Church if the lessons about structure and core content are understood.

20

Daily Prayer

∾

A lawful variety

This is a transitional time in the daily prayer life of the Church of England, and the *Common Worship* service book, published in 2000, makes no new provision, allowing instead for new forms to emerge, within the legal framework of 'A Service of the Word', and to be published in a later supplementary volume in the *Common Worship* series.

The forms of Morning and Evening Prayer in the Book of Common Prayer remain part of the total legal picture, and indeed *Common Worship* reproduces them in the 2000 book, though more in the recognition that they have a continuing place in the Sunday pattern of some churches, than in order to bolster their weekday use. They are forms of great beauty and have led to the unique English tradition of the daily choral evensong in cathedrals and collegiate churches, which is an art form of its own, with a unique musical repertoire, and the tradition shows no sign of decline; indeed, like other parts of cathedral worship, it is a growth point in the life of the Church. Quite apart from this particular manifestation of it, the strength of the Prayer Book offices is exactly what for others is their drawback. Though the psalmody and the lessons change, the prayers and canticles of the office do not change from one day to the next or one season to another. The strength is that, armed only with a Bible for the psalm and readings, one can say the daily office by heart.

But the effect of the provisions of 'A Service of the Word' is to make a whole series of other forms of service proper and legitimate forms of daily office in the Church of England. Among these forms of service are Morning and Evening Prayer in the Alternative Service Book of 1980. Although the legal life of that book may have come to an end, these forms – the full Morning and Evening Prayer and the shorter versions – fall within the provisions and may continue in use. That use may not be considerable, for as forms of daily office they have no great appeal. Essentially the Prayer Book forms in contemporary language, with a few alternative canticles, they have little of the beauty of the originals without asking some of the more fundamental questions about what we might need in daily prayer today that might have given them fresh appeal.

'A Service of the Word' provisions also cover such forms as the daily prayer of the Roman Catholic breviary and the office book of the Taizé Community, and people were turning to forms like these (the Roman office particularly seemed to more helpful when praying alone than some of those more clearly geared to a community gathered for prayer) until the publication in 1992 of *Celebrating Common Prayer*. The work of Anglican religious community members, led by the Franciscans (the revision of whose office book it technically was), and a number of other liturgists, including members of the Liturgical Commission, this was intended to put on the market a very different sort of office book, in order to test out ideas in preparation for a new official office book in or soon after 2000. In the preparatory work much emphasis was laid on the need for a form of daily prayer that would, at one end of the scale, provide for the rich liturgical needs of a religious community, meeting corporately at least four times on every single day, and, at the other, draw more obviously within the daily praying life of the Church those who once a day sit down at home with a Bible and maybe a book of prayer for a time of quiet Bible-reading and prayer. In the event, *Celebrating Common Prayer* came out looking rather complex (actually looking more complex than it really was), but a shorter 'pocket' edition, shorn of the complexities, followed. The take-up was enormous. Unofficial as it may be, *Celebrating Common Prayer* has become widely used, both by individuals and in places where people say daily prayer together, and certainly does give some strong indications of what more long-term official provision might mean.

But 'A Service of the Word' does not simply recognize and legitimize published attempts to provide a daily office for the Church. Where an individual or a group share in a form of prayer which includes the seven elements in the irreducible core of 'A Service of the Word' – greeting, a reading from scripture, a psalm (or another scriptural song), prayers of intercession and thanksgiving, the Lord's Prayer, a collect and a liturgical ending – then not only are they clearly part of the daily praying of the Church, they are also formally part of a company that celebrates a daily office and, if they are clergy, they are fulfilling the obligations that their calling lays upon them.

A praying Church

What does the Church need today in terms of its daily prayer? More important than anything in particular about forms of service, it needs to recover this sense of a great company of Christians who give glory and praise to God and hold up to him his creation every day, each individual and community doing this in the way appropriate to them, but each encouraging one another, part of a conscious company of people praying in solidarity. As part of that great company at least four categories need to be sustained and encouraged.

The first is the large number of places across the land, which includes cathedrals, collegiate churches and religious communities, but is not restricted to them, where it is possible to maintain, publicly at set times, a rich liturgical offering of prayer, often with musical resources, often drawing in casual worshippers to join the regular praying community. The existence of that solid dependable public prayer becomes a witness for the life of a Church that gives God praise and glory 'seven whole days, not one in seven' and a source of encouragement for those whose resources are smaller, opportunities to meet together fewer and who sometimes find it a struggle to pray alone.

The second category is the clergy. It may be true that the daily office belongs to the whole Church and should not be clericalized, but it is also true that a praying ordained ministry is necessary for the renewal of the Church. Because the only forms of authorized daily office until recently were constricting, and did not seem to match the praying needs of so many clergy, too many of them abandoned the daily office. Some of them put something with more freedom and flexibility in its place – and they need now to be shown that what they are doing is within the overall picture of the Church's daily prayer, part of something corporate, not just something personal and individualistic. Some of them, to be honest, put very little in the place of the daily office they abandoned or never knew. Fresh forms and freedoms need to challenge them to climb on board the 'company of voices' that make up the Church's daily offering of prayer.

The third category, already discussed in chapter 10, is the group of (mainly) lay people who need to be encouraged to come together to see that in every church of the land there is public prayer offered every day or as near to that ideal as they can manage. It does not need to be more than once in the day, there is not one hour that is more sacred than another (it might be a form of Midday Prayer), the form of prayer does not need to go beyond the seven core elements, and fifteen minutes might well be long enough from beginning to end. They would not need to sing (though breaking into song does not require an organ; a tuning fork will do). They would not need to have great professional skills. They would simply need to overcome their reticence to pray out loud together. It would be good if they could ring the bell. They would derive encouragement from the fact that they were part of something bigger. Groups like that across the land would be an immense spiritual resource.

The final category (which will have some overlap with the second) is those who pray alone and who need to know that what they do, perhaps what they have always done, is part of that something bigger, part of the Church's daily offering. They may be sitting at home, or on a train, or grabbing ten minutes in their lunch hour at the office. They may be getting out their Bible, or their pocket *Celebrating Common Prayer* or their Scripture Union notes. But they would be helped to know that they are part of a great enterprise and, if there can be some overlap between the material they use and that being used in churches and in cathedrals and communities, the sense of being engaged in something that has the power to change things will be all the stronger.

The content of the daily office

'A Service of the Word' has already given us a series of core elements for daily prayer. We need to look at some of these in turn. But first it is useful to look at the ways that Anglicans have been conditioned to think of the office by the provisions of the Book of Common Prayer, for in some ways, for all their ingenuity and beauty, Cranmer's forms of Morning and Evening Prayer may blind us to more universally recognized insights.

The first relates to the use of scripture. Scripture is obviously the major source of text for the Church's daily prayer, but in the broad tradition it has been seen as the source of prayer and praise, rather than as lection. The Church prays through the psalter, which is very much at the heart of the office, and through the canticles. It may also use small passages of scripture as lection, but that is not the principal use. Cranmer's office put the emphasis more clearly on lection and gave it a more didactic feel. The clergy were to use the office to learn the Bible, two chapters a morning, two chapters an evening. It was a perfectly legitimate aim. But it has given Anglican offices an unusual emphasis. To some extent the revisions leading to the Alternative Service Book strengthened this. While keeping long lessons, they reduced the psalmody, sometimes to only about ten verses, instead of the twenty-five to thirty that the Prayer Book's monthly cycle gave, thus reducing the scripture used as prayer and praise.

The second relates to what has become known as the 'gospel canticle'. Through a long tradition, whatever else changed from day to day the climax of praise was a canticle from Luke's gospel. At Morning Prayer it was *Benedictus*, the Song of Zechariah, at Evening Prayer *Magnificat*, the Song of Mary, at Compline (Night Prayer) *Nunc Dimittis*, the Song of Simeon. After the canticle came a time of prayer. Because Cranmer combined Evening and Night Prayer into one office, he moved the Song of Mary from its key position at Evening Prayer, placing it between two lessons, and importing the Song of Simeon after the second lesson. From this there emerged in Anglican thinking (though whether it was in Cranmer's mind was uncertain) the sense of a logical sequence through Evening Prayer from psalmody into Old Testament lesson, into a bridge canticle (the Song of Mary) that made the transition from Old to New. So there then followed the New Testament lesson and a second canticle that seemed to express faith in Christ (the Song of Simeon). This sequence then affected revision of Morning Prayer also, with the Song of Zechariah as the bridge canticle and *Te Deum Laudamus* as the Christian response at the end of the sequence. The result of this is to create a different expectation of the shape of the office from the one that is offered in most contemporary forms, and also a failure to see the pivotal place that tradition assigns to the gospel canticle.

The third relates to prayer and in particular to the role of the collect. Contemporary forms of the office see the gospel canticle leading into a time of prayer, probably 'open' and 'free', probably involving silence, but concluded with a single collect and with the Lord's Prayer. At the time at which Cranmer was at work the principle of the single 'collecting-up' prayer had given way to the series of collects (at Morning and Evening Prayer he uses three). A series of collects clearly has a different liturgical function than a single summing-up prayer. But Cranmer's offices still retain something of the collect's concluding role, for the collect of the day comes at the end of a litany of intercession. We have come to call that intercession the 'versicles and responses', but they have the character of a litany of intercession, which the collect concludes. In course of time, however, because of their strict form and unchanging character, they have ceased to be thought of as prayers of intercession. So more prayers have been added to the office, after the collect, which can no longer fulfil its function of concluding the prayer time, a function that passes instead to the 'grace'. It needs to be understood that contemporary forms of the office return to a sequence of (mainly intercessory) prayer leading into a single collect and the Lord's Prayer.

Contemporary forms vary, but not much, and a typical present-day sequence (excluding some of the responsories and antiphons found in some richer forms) would run:

- greeting or responsory, sometimes with an opening prayer;
- invitatory canticle;

153

- psalmody;
- variable canticle (here or between the scripture readings);
- reading(s);
- gospel canticle;
- time of prayer;
- collect, Our Father and conclusion.

A word needs to be said about the psalmody and lectionary provided for weekdays in *Common Worship*, for although new office forms have not been provided immediately, psalms and lections have in order to integrate with the shape of the Christian year and the Sunday provision.

In terms of psalmody, there is a departure from traditional Anglican practice for part of the year. For the weeks of ordinary time, the psalms continue to be set for use sequentially, from 1 to 150, through Morning and Evening Prayer six days a week. This principle, of saying the psalms 'in course' follows the same principle as the Prayer Book's monthly cycle. But during seasonal time the psalms are selected for their suitability to that season and the particular Christian mystery being celebrated. So the choice moves around the psalter (and in some seasons always ends at Morning Prayer with one of the 'praise psalms') and repeats itself each week of the season. This is another traditional way of using the psalter and one that may enrich our experience of the cycle of seasons.

The lectionary provision continues to make two sets of readings (apart form the daily eucharistic lectionary) available, both with a lesson from the Old and the New Testament. They are not specifically allocated to Morning and Evening Prayer, though the assumption is that most people will use the First Office Lectionary for Morning Prayer and the Second Office Lectionary for Evening Prayer. The first has the longer readings and more opportunities for semi-continuous reading of scripture in both lessons. The Second Office Lectionary has shorter lessons than has been our custom, is more prepared to omit passages that would need a good deal of explanation and sometimes abandons semi-continuous reading of a Bible book for one of the two lessons in order to draw from all over the scriptures a passage complementary to the other lesson.

There will, as we have noted, always be those who are seeking a single office each day, whether Morning or Evening Prayer or a form that draws on both and might even be at midday. They are free to choose their lectionary and indeed how many readings to have. They are also provided with an alternative psalm sequence that takes into account the fact that there is only one office a day.

A word may be said about combining Morning and Evening Prayer with Holy Communion. The Alternative Service Book made provision for doing it (so that the office becomes the Liturgy of the Word for the eucharist). There will be times and places where this is right, and without it a community of people sharing both office and eucharist one after the other can end up with biblical indigestion. But the reality is that office and eucharist are distinctive and each is sufficiently rich better to stand alone. Ideally office and eucharist should not follow one another, but be at different times, or at least have a significant silence between them. The worst of all worlds is an office cut off after the gospel canticle with another service following immediately. For the praise has been leading into prayer and yet, the moment the prayer time is reached, the office has been brought to a premature and unsatisfactory end. At very least there must be a moment of silent prayer and the collect, but preferably rather more.

The truth about the Church's daily prayer is that very large numbers of people are doing it, though in a rather privatized way. If they can be made more aware of the company to which they belong and if the world can see it happening in churches in cities, towns and villages each day, the sense of a praying Church will be much stronger than it is.

21

Celebrating the Sunday Office

∾

From office to celebration

Because the *Common Worship* Service Book of 2000 is intended to be a Sunday book, it does not provide daily forms of Morning and Evening Prayer. But it does provide these for Sundays. It does so in two forms, first by reproducing the texts from the Book of Common Prayer, with some simplified rubrics and a number of small deviations from the strict order that have long been in common use. It also provides contemporary forms of Sunday Morning and Evening Prayer, along the lines of the principles discussed in the last chapter, and as outworkings, in some ways no more than examples, of how services can be created by using the provisions of 'A Service of the Word'. It envisages their use as a simple office, not unlike Morning and Evening Prayer on any day of the week, or as the Liturgy of the Word for another service which is to follow immediately, or as the principal service of the day. Whichever need they meet, the introduction states that 'the central core consists of the Ministry of the Word interwoven with canticles to supply the response of praise, followed by intercessory prayer in one form or another'. It is the third use, as the principal service of the day, that this chapter examines.

What is involved when an office becomes the principal service of the day is, first of all, that from the point of view of legal provision, it must include material not always present in the office, namely prayers of penitence, a sermon and a creed or authorized affirmation of faith, and these are all included in these orders. But second, and perhaps more fundamentally, the service changes something of its character, for though at one level it remains an 'office', at another it becomes a 'celebration'. Perhaps we ought always to think of the office in terms of celebration, though that will take a lot of adjustment, but certainly in this Sunday context as the main service of the day it will mean, among other things, a style of presidency and leadership more high profile than we usually associate with an office, more movement, ritual and use of symbols than we usually associate with an office, and some rethinking of the traditional choreography of the office with minister and choir facing across the chancel at a right angle to the people.

The structure of the Morning and Evening offices is all but identical, so it is easier to consider the two services together. The structure is, as one would expect in a form derived from 'A Service of the Word', one that divides into four sections: The Preparation; The Word of God; The Prayers; The Conclusion.

The Preparation will begin with the entry of the ministers. The pressure will be strong to enter during the singing of a hymn. This cannot be entirely wrong (though it has always been odd to say or sing 'O Lord, open our lips and our mouth shall proclaim your praise' when we have already done just that in a strong entrance hymn). If people can be persuaded to begin this particular celebration in a different way, the place allocated for the first hymn, after the penitence and towards the end of the Preparation, is more appropriate.

The first words are either of greeting (and this is text perhaps more obviously suited to a celebration) or an opening responsory (more in the style of a more reflective office). An optional scene-setting introduction by the minister follows. Then come the prayers of penitence, with an authorized text provided for the invitation, the confession and the absolution, but of course any of the variants could be used. There are then several different ways of concluding the Preparation:

- a prayer of thanksgiving – in the morning for creation and the light of the new day, in the evening for the light of Christ in the darkness;
- an opening hymn;
- a canticle in the morning and verses from Psalm 141 or Psalm 104 in the evening;
- a bidding, silence and an opening prayer.

The canticles recommended in the notes for use at this point in Morning Prayer are *Venite* ('A Song of Triumph') in Advent and Lent, *Jubilate* ('A Song of Joy') in Christmas and Epiphany, The Easter Anthems in Eastertide and *Benedicite* ('A Song of Creation') in ordinary time. In many places a canticle at this point will be unnecessary, when a hymn has just been sung. In general, fine as the texts of the thanksgiving prayer and the opening prayer are, after opening greeting and penitence, there is a need to avoid the danger of too much material in the Preparation, though the kindling and blessing of light at Evening Prayer at dusk has strong appeal.

157

The section entitled 'The Word of God' covers psalmody, scripture readings, responsory, gospel canticle, sermon and creed. The psalms and scripture readings are appointed. If this is the principal service of the day, they will be those from the principal service lectionary and the note in that lectionary commending the use of all three readings will apply. If only two are used, there is no requirement that they be one from the Old Testament and one from the New, nor is there a requirement that one of them be a gospel reading. Because this is not the eucharist, the 'open season' in lectionary terms only excludes the period from the Third Sunday of Advent to the Baptism of Christ and Palm Sunday to Trinity Sunday, but if this service is part of a monthly pattern that does include the eucharist, there will often be sense in staying within the tighter lectionary rules as they apply to the eucharist.

Two responsories are provided for the readings. One the familiar 'This is the word of the Lord. Thanks be to God' formula, the other a more extended spoken responsory (different in morning and evening), best said still seated, with a change of mood and posture immediately after when all stand for the gospel canticle.

There is also provision for canticles before or between the readings (with Old Testament canticles in the morning and New Testament in the evening, though that cannot be an absolute rule). There are places in which musical resources will allow for several sung canticles during the service, but in most parish settings what will probably be appropriate is a single spoken canticle, either said between minister and people, or recited together, or led by a single voice with a congregational response. The canticle is another opportunity for seasonal input, and a table in the notes makes specific suggestions. Where music is needed between the readings a scriptural song or a scriptural chant from Taizé would meet the need.

But the gospel canticle (the Song of Zechariah in the morning and the Song of Mary in the evening) is a different matter. Because of their pivotal place as a climax of the 'Word of God' section of the service, it would be a pity if either were omitted or said rather than sung. To be the high point in a musical service the text needs to be sung. Composers will go on making musical versions in a variety of styles available, and there are also metrical versions of both canticles. To replace the gospel canticle with another hymn or song would severely damage the integrity of the celebration.

Several different positions are given for the sermon, each with its own logic. It may be immediately after the readings, to which it will presumably be related. It may follow the gospel canticle and precede the creed which becomes a response to it, as at the eucharist. Or it may follow The Prayers and precede The Conclusion, probably enveloped by hymns or songs, and occupying the traditional place of the sermon at the Anglican Sunday office.

The section entitled 'The Prayers' indicates that intercession is to be their principal emphasis, but no text is given. A note indicates the same subjects and sequence as in the eucharist, and worship leaders may go to the intercessions in the eucharistic supplementary material for texts. But here is an opportunity to develop a variety of styles of prayer different from the eucharist, and so people are free to turn to different books and resources, as well as to develop their own approach and to ensure that silence is not squeezed out. The prayers are to be drawn together in the collect and in the Lord's Prayer and, if the time of prayer has been led by someone other than the presiding minister, it would be appropriate for the president to say or sing the collect and to introduce the Lord's Prayer.

The Conclusion, which almost certainly will begin with the kind of hymn that is either a hymn of praise or of sending out, may include a final prayer suitable to the time of day and then a blessing, or the grace or the peace. If a blessing or the peace, the seasonal text might be used.

There is a series of alternative endings to the service to replace everything after the sermon. The first is a 'Thanksgiving for the Word'. It needs to focus around a large copy of the Bible, the lectionary or the book of the gospels, perhaps brought in at the beginning of the liturgy and, of course, used for the readings, but now brought to the holy table. This form includes the sharing of testimonies. The second is a 'Thanksgiving for Holy Baptism', with the community gathering at the font and water poured into the font. As part of it the water may be sprinkled over the people or they may be invited to use it to sign themselves with the cross. The third is 'Thanksgiving for the Healing Ministry of the Church' and may include the laying on of hands and/or anointing with oil for healing. The fourth is a 'Thanksgiving for the Mission of the Church' and includes the possibility of the commissioning of those called and prepared to exercise particular ministries. In each case the form of service takes the place of creed, prayers and conclusion, but has these elements built into its form. There needs to be careful consideration of how these different endings might find their place in the pattern of the community's worship.

In their use of Bible, water and oil, they illustrate the need to look again at the place of symbolic action in the celebration of the office. Should the cross be brought in with ceremony at the beginning? Should the Bible or lectionary be carried in? At Evening Prayer should there be a lighting of candles if it is celebrated at dusk and the use, as the opening hymn, of versions of the hymn *Phos hilaron* ('O gladsome light . . .') as the notes suggest? Should incense burn before the altar? On a great festival, should there be a procession of the whole community around the church ending at the altar or some other focal point associated with the day's celebration and then the singing of *Te Deum Laudamus* ('A Song of the Church') just before the conclusion, as the notes suggest? All these things make the office less cerebral and recognize, in a way that we more easily recognize in the eucharist, that actions often speak louder than words.

Night Prayer

Common Worship also provides two orders of Night Prayer (traditionally called Compline), again falling within the provisions of 'A Service of the Word'. One is in traditional language, the other contemporary, but they have a common shape. It is not suitable to be the principal service of the day, but it is there for use at the end of the day (and not only on Sundays). Where there is an address at Night Prayer, it should usually precede the office, rather than follow it. It is a liturgical form of 'good night' prayer – 'I will lay me down in peace'. More talk after the words of Compline strikes the wrong note.

PART FIVE

Initiation and Pastoral Rites

22

Baptism

Rite at the heart of Christian discipleship

If the twentieth century was the century of the recovery of the meaning of
the eucharist for the Church, bringing it back into the centre of Christian
life and worship in a way that had not been the case at least in the
Reformed Churches, so that people began to understand that their
formation was all bound up with being eucharistic people, there is a
case to be made that the twenty-first century may witness a parallel
recovery of the meaning of baptism for the Church. For the process has
already begun. It is not just that there is a need to recover the richness of
multi-layered baptismal theology (though that is important), but to
recover both the sense of what it means to be part of the 'community
of the baptized' and also the liturgical forms that enable the people of
God to celebrate their baptism, to reclaim it and work out its implications
all over again. For generations people have undervalued their baptism.
They know it happened once upon a time, in most cases when they were
too young to remember it now, and they know it was the way into the
Christian Church. But it was something that was done and is now long
since past. What needs to be recovered is the sense, not that I *was*
baptized, but that I *am* baptized. What happened then committed me to
a style of living that is still being worked out, and there is a sense in which
we all need to be able to 'remember' our baptism by being able to reclaim
its promises and celebrate its meaning through the cycle of the Christian
year.

Having a clearer view of what the sacrament means and a higher
expectation of what it might mean in Christian lives might make us
more wary of 'baptism on demand' and make us more rigorous in our
policies in relation to candidates for baptism from families whose commitment to the Church is not obviously strong. And indeed there is an
inevitable debate in the contemporary Church about such things. But,

rather than making us more rigorist, it might make us more determined to share the riches of the sacrament, more determined that people should be well prepared to understand it and more determined to celebrate it with such power and conviction that it touched people deeply and challenged them to recover their own sense of being part of the community of the baptized.

This may seem a long way from where many parish clergy begin, with the knock on the door and the request to have the baby 'done', the godparents already chosen, the date expected to fit the family rather than the church community, and the numbers such that, with a fairly open policy, the child will be one of five baptized on a Sunday afternoon in a church packed with people not used to being there. The point of this chapter is to try to enable principle and pastoral reality to meet creatively. But what is on our side is that baptism, what the Church has on offer, is a gift that can change lives and, in the end, is much more exciting than simply 'having the baby done' if we can convey our conviction of what it means.

In terms of the theology of baptism we do not need to go much beyond the water that will be used generously at the celebration of baptism to find the strands of meaning. The several forms of the 'prayer over the water' in the *Common Worship* rite spell it out. Water sustains, refreshes and cleanses all life, and the water of baptism gives life, sustains growth and washes away the stain of sin. Baptism is a new birth like the breaking of waters. It is as if we enter our mother's womb and are born again. The Holy Spirit hovered over the waters at the creation and comes down now upon the candidates as they are dipped in the water. Baptism stands for dying to the old, leaving an old world on one shore, saved from drowning by the power of God, and finding ourselves in a new and promised land, like the Israelites of old, coming through the waters of the Red Sea and across the Jordan River. But above all else baptism is, as Paul says in Romans 6, a baptism into both the death and the resurrection of Christ, being conformed to him, accepting his pattern of life through death, and incorporated into him and therefore into his body, the Church. It is tomb as well as womb, but it is life more than it is death.

All this and more is celebrated in the water and in this many-layered sacrament. Yet for much of history, and in a good deal of Christian consciousness, it has been about cleansing from sin and little else, or perhaps simply a badge of membership. The Church has explored much more in recent decades the Romans 6 emphasis on the relationship between baptism and death and resurrection, making it very much an Easter sacrament, but we need also to recover some of the other emphases that belong to other seasons of the year, not least the sense of new creation and new birth.

We need to recognize that it is not possible in every church to celebrate the vast majority of baptisms within the main Sunday liturgy. Where the number of candidates is vast, or the church small and the danger is of the community being swamped by visitors, other arrangements are necessary. But the new rites, like the ASB rite before them, nevertheless regard the setting within the public liturgy (including the eucharist, but not necessarily the eucharist) as normative and desirable. There are three reasons for this.

The first is that it can make little sense to welcome a candidate into an absent community. Although baptism is not into the local Church, or even into the Church of England, but into the universal Church, that experience does need rooting in a worshipping community. When baptism is celebrated more privately, it is a loss to the candidate and family that the church community is missing, and it is a loss to the church community that it is not faced with its responsibility for the child.

A second reason is that the Church must seize the pastoral and evangelistic opportunity to draw people, who by the very nature of the occasion are more than usually open to the Spirit, into the experience of Christian worship. If we have confidence in our liturgy, and if we have planned the service clearly, when we bring them into an atmosphere of Christian worship, it ought to touch the hearts of some of them with the good news of Christ. At a private baptism, people ill-equipped to do so have to create an atmosphere of worship all of their own out of nothing. In the liturgy it is different.

The third reason is to help Christian people rediscover and to go on celebrating their own baptism, to stop regarding it primarily as something that happened once upon a time, and to see it instead as a life into which they have been called.

The direction in which the *Common Worship* rites encourage us is to identify a number of key days or seasons when we will celebrate baptism and make a lot of it. One obviously is Eastertide, but also Epiphany (particularly the Baptism of Christ on the first Sunday of the season), Pentecost, Trinity Sunday and All Saintstide. It does not include Advent (for the emphasis then is on the baptism of John, rather than on baptism into Christ) and it excludes Lent. In many parishes, more frequent celebrations of baptism will continue to be needed, but it is at least worth considering restricting the number of days, making more of the occasion and letting each celebration have its own distinctive character, using the seasonal variants in the rite that are provided.

Common Worship in its Sunday book makes provision for baptism during Sunday worship and it is to this order that we now turn. This will normally be the baptism of babies or of children not yet of confirmation age. Adults would normally be baptized by the bishop and confirmed at the same time (see chapter 23), but the possibility is nevertheless there that among the candidates will be adults, who will later be brought to the bishop for confirmation. For this reason, although in what follows reference is made to the 'font', this must be understood broadly to include the kind of baptistry in which an adult can more easily be baptized (see chapter 5).

Sunday baptism in the parish

The *Common Worship* baptism rite is a richer, fuller rite than its forerunner in the Alternative Service Book. Some have found it too rich and too full. Certainly it pulls no punches as it spells out the meaning of baptism and of Christian commitment, though it is careful in what it demands of the parents and godparents. The decision they are asked to make is specifically for the candidate, the profession of faith is made by joining with the words of the congregation, and the commission – the duties laid upon them – comes after the baptism, not before as if they are conditions to be fulfilled before baptism is administered. So the rite's intention is not to push people harder than they can go. It is nevertheless to confront the assembly with the awesomeness of the sacrament, to produce a rite that declares that God does powerful things in and through baptism. It is not a rite that can be made domestic, comfortable and cheery. It celebrates a God who acts in wonderful ways.

Its limited use has already attracted criticisms that it is both too long and too wordy. This has been met immediately by making some mandatory parts of the service optional. Careful decisions about these need to be made, and what can be omitted should alone deal with the matter of length. But the sense of a lot of quite demanding language pouring out, creating an atmosphere of wordiness, needs addressing in other ways. Two immediately come to mind. The first is that the words be broken up by the movement. This is not intended to be a static rite. There is a part of the rite likely to take place at the front of the congregation with candidates, parents and godparents gathered around. There is a procession to the font and back. It may be only of those immediately involved, but it may be of the whole community. It is a rite on the move and the movements themselves put spaces between the blocks of words. But there is also music. It is not just that hymns and chants may cover the movement to and from the font, but that some of the texts invite singing and simple musical responses, in the prayer over the water, for instance, or in the intercessions at the font. Just when the words begin to seem too much, we burst into song, and the rite is transformed.

Those with responsibility for baptizing and for arranging the baptism liturgy will do well to study the Introduction, Notes and Commentary in *Common Worship: Initiation Services*. They go well beyond the usual provision in terms of giving the rationale of the rite, and answer in detail many of the questions that arise in planning the service.

The service divides into six sections. In the first 'gathering' section, the service reads like the equivalent section of the eucharist, except that the greeting is the trinitarian form ('The grace of our Lord Jesus Christ...'), the president may insert (from the appendix) a thanksgiving for the birth of a child, the president must introduce the service in a way that stamps its baptismal character upon it (a text is provided, with seasonal variants in the appendix) and the prayers of penitence are omitted. There is also the possibility of moving the presentation of the candidates from its later point to happen immediately after the introduction. Where there is only one candidate or one family involved, this will make sense. When there are several it might involve too much movement for a very short time, for after the presentation they will immediately return to their places as the service moves on to the *Gloria* (optional), the collect and the reading of the scriptures.

The second section, 'The Liturgy of the Word', follows its usual form as far as the sermon, but in the interests of brevity there might be only two readings rather than three. A note confirms that the norm is to stay with the collect and readings appointed for the day, especially during the seasons, but there are alternatives in the appendix which can be used in ordinary time. The sermon, though it may not focus entirely on the baptism, will need to relate to it, especially as 'The Liturgy of Baptism' follows immediately.

This 'Liturgy of Baptism' begins with the presentation of candidates. Before it or as part of it the candidates, together with parents, godparents and any sponsor provided by the congregation, need to be gathered around the president, so that they are an identifiable body, but this will probably be at the front of the congregation – the chancel step in many churches – for this is not yet the point to move to the font. There is no text provided for the presentation. The president or another minister, ordained or lay (perhaps one who has prepared the families for the baptism or one who has been made a 'sponsor'), or one of the godparents presents the candidates to the congregation. At very least this involves giving the candidate's name, but sometimes might include parents' names, a child's age, and even where the family lives. A lot will depend on the number of candidates. Where there are candidates old enough to answer for themselves, they are then asked whether they wish to be baptized and they may expand their answer into saying something of their journey to faith and why they now seek baptism – 'testimony by the candidate may follow'. Such testimony may be spontaneous, or may have been prepared or written down, or may emerge from gentle questioning by the president. The president then invites both the congregation and the parents and godparents to indicate the support they will give to the candidates. All this forms part of the section called 'the presentation'.

Next comes 'the decision'. This section begins with the lighting of 'a large candle'. If at all possible, this should be the paschal candle, making the connection between baptism and the death and resurrection of Christ. The president then puts the six questions to candidates old enough to answer for themselves directly or through parents, godparents and sponsors to those too young to answer. A simpler three-question form of the decision is provided in the appendix for use 'where there are strong pastoral reasons'. The candidate's decision meets with a response in the signing with the cross and its accompanying words. This signing is not done with water (indeed we are probably not yet at the font) and such a practice has always been a confusion. The signing is one of the secondary symbols in baptism, not to be confused with the primary sign of dipping in water. The minister (and it may be a minister other than the president) may simply make the sign with his or her thumb. Or oil may be used. As a note says, 'pure olive oil, reflecting the practice of athletes preparing for a contest, may be used for the signing with the cross'. This, traditionally, is 'the oil of catechumens', one of the three oils blessed by the bishop on Maundy Thursday. The signing, whether with oil or without, need not be done only by the minister. The rubric allows the president to invite parents, godparents and sponsors to do so also. There is a pastoral decision to be made on each occasion about whether this is appropriate.

The focus now moves to the font, and ministers, candidates, families and, if space allows, the whole community move there, perhaps singing a hymn, perhaps a simple repeated chant, perhaps the 'Litany of the Resurrection' in the appendix. Once there, and the font being full of water (perhaps with a top-up at this point), the president leads the prayer over the water. This is much more than a blessing of water. It is a solemn calling down of the Holy Spirit upon the candidates. It is credal in its style, full of the theology of baptism. It is in some ways equivalent to a eucharistic prayer. There is a mainstream text, there are seasonal variants and there are responsive forms, which can be sung with a simple congregational refrain. The president should stretch out his or her hands over the water and over the candidates at the appropriate moments in the prayer.

'The profession of faith', which follows, is in the form of the Apostles' Creed, which the candidates, if old enough, and parents, godparents and sponsors say with the congregation. A simpler alternative trinitarian profession of faith is provided in the appendix, and may be used 'where there are strong pastoral reasons'.

And so to the baptism itself. Just before baptizing the president may ask a candidate old enough to answer whether this faith expressed in the creed is their faith, and they respond, either with the formula 'This is my faith' or with a more personal statement of faith. The president does not ask the candidate's name. This is not a naming ceremony and the name will have been used several times already, not least in the initial presentation.

Baptism involves as much water as circumstances allow. Dipping is the liturgical norm, even if sprinkling is more widespread. The note states:

> A threefold administration of water (whether by dipping or pouring) is a very ancient practice of the Church and is commended as testifying to the faith of the Trinity in which candidates are baptized. Nevertheless a single administration is also lawful and valid. The use of a substantial amount of water is desirable; water must at least flow on the skin of the candidate. The president may delegate the act of baptism to another lawful minister.

It might have been added that not only should the water flow on the skin of the candidate, but it is highly undesirable and symbolically inappropriate to immediately wipe it off again. Let it drip!

There is now an option, with an appropriate text, for clothing in a white robe. Where the baptism has been by dipping or immersion, this will be a necessity and there may need to be a song or chant while candidates retire to change. Yet, at a symbolic level also – being clothed with Christ – this has much to commend it.

There is also at this point an alternative place for the signing with the cross. This is the position in the Prayer Book, though the *Common Worship* rite much prefers it before baptism. If it is used at this later point, it is used with the text that follows, 'May God, who has received you by baptism . . .', and, if oil is used, it is the oil of chrism.

For this is the point where, whether there has been an anointing earlier or not, the oil of chrism may be used to signify the gift of the Spirit. The text at this point speaks of the candidate being renewed 'by his anointing Spirit'. Chrism is oil mixed with fragrant spices and, as the note says, expresses 'the blessings of the messianic era and the richness of the Holy Spirit'. If used, it needs, like the water, to be used generously. The whole question of whether to enrich (or complicate) the baptism rite with the use of oil needs careful thought, as does the place of chrism in baptism in relation to its use in confirmation. The Initiation Services commentary engages with the issues fully.

At this point all that need happen at the font has happened and there may be a return to people's usual places. On the other hand, especially if what follows is to be brief, the return may wait until after the welcome and the peace, which happen appropriately at the font. What now follows is the 'commission' – the duties of the Church, of the parents, godparents and sponsors, and, if old enough, the candidates. This can be expressed through the full text in the rite, or through similar (but probably briefer) words from the president or may be omitted altogether, although only if the issues have been addressed in the sermon.

There may now be brief prayers of intercession. One of the newly baptized, if appropriate, may lead them. This is another opportunity for music, after a lot of words, with a sung response. There are seasonal variants. All the forms assume brevity. The intercession prayers may be omitted altogether (and there will be the possibility of brief intercession later, in the eucharistic prayer). Finally, in the 'Liturgy of Baptism', there is the welcome and the peace (with its seasonal variants). The peace has a particular significance at baptism, especially with older candidates, whose reception into the body of Christ is sealed by sharing in this exchange.

If they have not already done so, everybody now returns to their places and the ministers go to the altar table and 'The Liturgy of the Eucharist' begins. It takes its usual form. As far as the eucharistic prayer is concerned, if brevity is what is now needed, Prayers D, E or H will commend themselves. If the use of the baptismal preface printed in the rite is wanted Prayers A, B or C are suitable. If brief intercession, omitted earlier, is to be included, Prayers F or G meet the need. If the return from the font is during the hymn when the gifts are prepared, it will be better today to omit an 'offertory procession' and even to find an alternative moment to take the collection.

There remains only the final section, 'The Sending Out'. The ministers need to move to where the great (paschal) candle is alight – at the chancel step or equivalent place – during the hymn. After the blessing, candles are lit for the newly baptized and given to them with the appropriate words. The dismissal is given, and it might be appropriate for the president to accompany the newly baptized (with families and candles alight) through the congregation to the door. If the candles are part of being sent out, the baptized need to move with them, rather than stay where they are and blow them out.

Baptizing in other contexts

The Initiation Services, as well as providing for baptism within the eucharist, indicate how it may be celebrated within Morning and Evening Prayer and within the provisions of 'A Service of the Word'. But, more attractive, is the baptism rite standing on its own, not as Sunday afternoon semi-private baptism, but as the principal service of the day. After all, it has all the core contents of 'A Service of the Word' and much more. It is a rich rite of word and sacrament in itself. It stands on its own as a more than sufficient Sunday service for the people of God. Of course in some churches it will be combined with the eucharist, because the eucharist is the principal service every Sunday, but, where a parish has a more diverse programme on Sunday mornings, it will make sense to make the baptism rite, without adding anything to it, the principal service on some Sundays of the year.

As for those settings where there is no alternative to the Sunday late morning or afternoon baptism when the church community is not present, the minister has to approach the rite with pastoral skill. It must not be too long; the permissions to omit or express in briefer suitable words must be used. It will benefit from music, but not necessarily from a lot of hymns very badly sung; more likely by instrumental music or even a singing group if a few musicians can be prevailed upon to come. It does not need to lose light and colour and movement because it is not in the main liturgy. If some of the regular congregation will come to share in the service, welcoming at the door, maybe providing a crèche and coming to the rescue of harassed parents, singing, carrying candles, or just upholding the liturgy by their participation and their prayer, it becomes possible to see this as an extension of the church at worship and for those who come to sense that too.

A Thanksgiving for the Gift of a Child

The one thing that 'A Thanksgiving for the Gift of a Child' is not is Christian initiation, so its presence in this chapter could mislead. But *Common Worship* prints it for Sunday use and places it in the Sunday service book before the baptism rite. The very full notes explain its several uses – to mark birth or adoption, in a private celebration at home, or at a special service in church, or as part of the Sunday liturgy. It may be used when baptism is to follow soon after, when baptism is, by the parents' wish, to be delayed until the child can make his or her own decision, or when no baptism is planned. It is a simple service of the word, with prayers of thanksgiving and blessing, and with a possibility of presenting a copy of one of the gospels. Its prayers are adaptable and, although it may be used as a complete rite, it is also a pastoral resource. Its appendix provides several prayers helpful in the pastoral care of families, parents and children. More the equivalent of the Prayer Book's 'Churching of Women' than of baptism, it ought to meet real needs and is a richer and more sensitive rite than its equivalent in ASB 1980.

23

Steps along the Baptismal Way

∿

First communion

Although there is room for other understandings, the clear message of
Church of England initiation services is that admission to the body of
Christ and all that goes with it is complete in the sacrament of baptism.
No one is half in the Church, no one is half committed, no one is simply
part of an outer circle because of their baptism. If they have been
baptized, they are part of the Church, they have been incorporated into
Christ, the Holy Spirit has been called down upon them, and, in a sense,
anything else is detail. This chapter is concerned with some of the
possible detail. Of course it turns out to be more than that, for there are
often moments of real pastoral and personal significance as people make
the Christian journey, but we should try to be clear that we are never
drawing people into anything more fundamental than what was done for
them in their baptism. We may be helping them to remember it, reclaim
it or celebrate it, but we are not in the business of changing it or adding
to it.

But, of all the things that happen after baptism, the one that comes
closest to adding something new is a moment that has sometimes been
lost in an emphasis on confirmation. This moment is the occasion of first
communion. Logically it follows, where a candidate is old enough to eat,
straight away from baptism. We emerge from the water of baptism, are
clothed in Christ and sit down to eat with the Church. But we have
inherited a pattern that delays first communion to a later stage, albeit that
stage might now precede confirmation and be at as young an age as the
bishop of the diocese permits.

How, if at all, should admission to communion be marked by a special
ceremony? In particular how should it be marked among a group of
children who have been prepared together and are to receive their first
communion together at an age earlier than confirmation? The answer will

nearly always be to mark the moment, not by any special ceremony, but by heightening the natural moments in the liturgy. Chiefly, of course, it means they will, for the first time, receive Holy Communion. That is what really counts. But almost certainly it will be right for them as a group to bring the bread, wine and water to the holy table. Immediately before, it might well have been appropriate for them to have stood with the president for the greeting of peace, the president first presenting them to the people, preferably by name. Beyond that it might be appropriate for them to lead the prayers of intercession; certainly they ought to be prayed for by name within those prayers. But that is sufficient and the one thing that is quite inappropriate is for the president to extract promises from the children. For the point of the pattern of admission to communion that the parish has adopted is one that says they are ready to receive communion before they are ready to make an adult profession of faith and commitment.

Some of this applies also in the different circumstances where older candidates have been confirmed at a service that did not culminate in the eucharist. Their first communion is on the following Sunday (probably in their own church whereas their confirmation may have been elsewhere). There might be a desire to link their first communion with their confirmation by some re-use of the candles lit and given to them at the end of the confirmation. But certainly they ought to be named and welcomed at the peace, involved possibly in the intercession prayers and certainly in the bringing up of the gifts, but again the focus should be on what really matters – receiving Holy Communion for the first time as part of the local church community.

The bishop baptizes and confirms

The Liturgical Commission's commentary on *Common Worship: Initiation Services* spells out the role of the bishop in relation to initiation:

> In an episcopally ordered church the bishop is the chief minister of the whole process of Christian initiation and is integral to its practice. This finds expression in a number of features of current practice: the requirement of episcopal confirmation (Canon B27; B15A); the canonical requirement that the bishop be given notice of an adult baptism (Canon B24.2); the final say resting with the bishop over a refusal to baptize an infant (Canon B22.2), and over any attempt to bar a baptized person from receiving communion (Canon B16).

There is important pastoral detail there that the parish priest needs to remember, but the central point is that we need to recover the sense of the bishop, not as the minister of confirmation, but of the whole business of Christian initiation and therefore of baptism. The bishop should be seen presiding over initiation – baptism, as well as confirmation and first communion – at certain key moments in the year in his cathedral and at all appropriate seasons in the churches of his diocese. Although there will be occasions when there are no candidates for baptism, this will not happen often unless some have been hastily baptized before the confirmation by the parish priest. And although there will be occasions when it makes sense for first communion to be deferred to another day (and maybe another place), again this is likely to be rare, and the norm should be the full rite of baptism, confirmation and eucharist, with the bishop presiding as the whole Christian community in that place celebrates the sacraments. And in that setting baptism must not be seen as a preliminary to confirmation, but confirmation as a pastoral rite that builds on baptism, the sacrament of Christian initiation itself.

So the bishop arrives to preside. His attitude is a key factor. He will nearly always nowadays have sent ahead of him his instructions for how the service is to be celebrated and the freedom of the parish priest to order the liturgy will have been curtailed by this. But it is proper, for it is an episcopal service, and the bishop, as much as the community among whom he is to minister, needs to be able to feel that the conditions are right for this liturgy in which the Spirit is being sought and the Christian mysteries being celebrated. The bishop may want all the candidates seated together – and that can make sense; for their preparation will often have bound them together and they are, on this occasion, a recognizable group. He may want them to sit initially with their families and friends – that can make sense; it is out of the entire community that they will be drawn and into which they will return.

A second key factor is the preparedness of the candidates. Sometimes in confirmation preparation, however thorough, the full significance of the rite is not brought out. Yet, in itself, it is a fine source of good teaching. The build-up to the great day, so that there is genuine excitement about the confirmation, heightens the whole experience. So does the involvement of the candidates as far as possible in the preparation of the liturgy.

But the most vital factor is the involvement and overcrowding presence of the whole church community. Desirable as the presence of family and friends of the candidates is, it is the presence of the local church that is required for the service to be all it could be. Whether on a Sunday or a weekday evening, whether in their own church or the cathedral or another church, the entire congregation should be helped to see its solemn duty to be present and, if the consequent squash in the church means standing room only, so much the better. What better memory of one's confirmation than that so many people came in support that there was not room for them all to sit down!

The service has five sections. The first gathers and prepares the community. Where the layout of the church would allow it to make sense, the bishop's initial greeting of the community might be at the door, with the bishop moving to his chair during the opening hymn or during the *Gloria in excelsis*. If the bishop is already at the chair, his initial introduction (which is unscripted) might, with the omission of the *Gloria*, lead straight into the silent prayer before the collect. The collect provided is a 'default text'; the assumption is that the collect will be that of the day.

The Liturgy of the Word follows. On Sundays and holy days the readings are expected to be those of the day. It is appropriate for baptized candidates for confirmation to read the first two readings; in the case of unbaptized candidates there is symbolic value in their not exercising such a ministry until later in the service. The Liturgy of the Word follows its usual shape (with a large number of candidates the pressure to reduce the readings to two will be strong) until and including the sermon.

The sermon leads immediately into the Liturgy of Initiation. At first it follows the shape and pattern of the same section as the baptism rite discussed in the previous chapter, and much of what is written there applies here and is not therefore repeated. The candidates are presented (with a clear statement of the rite for which they are presented – whether for baptism, or confirmation or both). The presentation is not to the bishop, but to the congregation. It is unscripted and the amount of personal detail will depend on the number of candidates. It might be spoken by the parish priest. Or each candidate might be presented, as the rubric mentions, by a sponsor or godparent. The bishop then asks those who are to be baptized whether they seek that sacrament, and those already baptized whether this is indeed the case and whether they seek now from their own mouth and from their own heart to affirm their faith in Jesus Christ. This is the point where testimony may follow. A note clarifies:

> If candidates are to give testimony after the preparation, it is important that this should be appropriate in length and style and not detract from the rest of the service. The bishop may, at his discretion, allow for testimony to be made at an earlier point in the service before the sermon. Testimony may be given in written form.

This last sentence presumably covers both testimony that has been prepared in a written form, but is now read, and also written testimony that might, for instance, simply be placed upon the holy table as an offering up of what has brought the candidates to this day.

The questions of 'the decision' now follow – to all the candidates. The shorter, alternative three-question version allowed at a service of baptism without confirmation is not a permitted alternative here, nor later is the alternative profession of faith. The decision leads into the signing with the cross for the candidates for baptism. The signing (with or without the oil of catechumens) may be delegated to another a minister, and sponsors may also be invited to make the sign on the candidates they have supported.

There follows the procession to the font (which may, of course, mean a baptistry for immersion), and the notes make it clear that it is a procession involving the ministers and all the candidates (not simply those to be baptized) and naturally, if space permits, the whole community follows, though it is more likely that most people simply remain in their places and turn towards the font. A note also makes it clear that, even when there are no candidates for baptism, this movement to the font should happen, so that those to be confirmed make their profession of baptismal faith at the font. So they gather, the candidates in a group around the font; those among them to be baptized in the most sensible place ready for baptism and easily identifiable to the bishop among the other candidates.

One of the 'prayers over the water' follows if there are candidates for baptism, and the whole community then makes the profession of faith. The bishop may, if numbers allow, ask each candidate to affirm individually whether this is their faith. Baptism follows. The bishop, while retaining his presidency of the rite, may delegate 'the administration of the water of baptism to another lawful minister', but, if the primacy of baptism is to be seen, it will very often be appropriate for the bishop himself to perform this part of the rite. A note makes it clear that the prayer after baptism, 'May God who has received you ...'), which at baptism without confirmation can be the moment when the oil of chrism is used, should not be accompanied by the use of oil when confirmation is to follow, for the oil has an appropriate place in the next part of the rite.

The part of the rite at the font is completed by the candidates for confirmation (but not the ones who have just been baptized) coming forward to the font and making the sign of the cross on themselves with water to recall their baptism. Or the bishop, provided with a branch (traditionally of rosemary) may sprinkle them with water from the font and may add appropriate words, such as 'Remember your baptism into Christ Jesus'.

The bishop and candidates gather 'at the place of confirmation'. This place is most likely to be at the chancel step or its equivalent, so there may be hymns, songs or chants to cover their return. But, if layout and numbers allow, the confirmation itself may very properly happen still at the font. It consists of four mandatory stages:

1. a prayer said over all the candidates by the bishop, praying that the Holy Spirit may 'rest upon them';
2. a moment when the bishop addresses each candidate by name, says 'God has called you by name and made you his own' and may at the same time anoint the candidate with the oil of chrism;
3. leading, in each case, into the moment when the bishop lays his hand on the candidate's head as he says 'Confirm, O Lord, your servant with your Holy Spirit';
4. and a congregational prayer for all the candidates together, 'Defend, O Lord, these your servants...'

The part of the congregation is to pray – the bishop may lay his hand (the rubric is clear that it is one hand, not two as in ordination), but it is not he alone, but the entire assembly, that prays for the Spirit to rest upon the candidates and for them to be confirmed with the Spirit. This is signified by their 'Amen' both to the prayer said over all the candidates collectively and to the prayer said over each individually.

The bishop will have his own view about whether he stands or sits for the laying on of hands. (The rubric gives no clear instruction, though it specifies standing at the beginning of this section, and a solemn liturgical prayer would normally be spoken standing.) Nor does it state whether the candidates are standing or kneeling. They might be standing in a line, or kneeling at the altar rail. It might be better if they were standing in a semi-circle around the bishop, moving forward to him one by one (there is no real virtue in the two-by-two tradition), whether to stand before him or to kneel as he has directed.

Two optional elements follow, the first a series of questions called the 'commission' and then prayers of intercession, using one of the forms in the baptismal rite, appropriately led by some of the newly baptized and confirmed. The Liturgy of Initiation is then completed with words of welcome when there has been baptism and, on all occasions, with the peace, when it is appropriate that the bishop greets each of the newly confirmed in turn before they move in among the congregation to greet others.

The service moves back on to familiar ground with the 'Liturgy of the Eucharist'. It is good if some of those for whom this will be their 'first communion' bring the gifts to the table. There is something to be said at this point for the newly confirmed now rejoining family and friends in the congregation and receiving communion with them rather than as a distinct group. But a lot will depend on the layout and seating arrangements; the newly confirmed do need to be a distinct group again, at least momentarily, at the end. What has been said about choices of eucharistic prayer in the previous chapter applies here also.

The service ends with the 'Sending Out', which, as in all baptism services, allows for the presentation of candles lighted from the paschal candle. It is clear that this may be included even at a service where there has been confirmation, but no baptism. It is an appropriate way to end, the bishop surrounded by the newly confirmed with their lighted candles, and a rubric indicates that he may lead them through the church. This, rather than any other point, is when the congregation may be encouraged to greet them with applause.

A note indicates that, when the service is celebrated without the Liturgy of the Eucharist, the prayers of intercession, led by the newly confirmed, are transposed until after the peace. The likely order is:

- welcome and peace;
- hymn;
- intercession prayers;
- additional prayers (provided for when there is no eucharist);
- the Lord's Prayer;
- the Sending Out (blessing, giving of light, dismissal).

In choosing the hymns and other variable material for a service of baptism, confirmation and eucharist, there is a need to bear in mind that the service always reflects to some extent the season in which it is set, but also always has at least a hint of both Easter and Pentecost, because baptism is always a paschal sacrament and Christian initiation is always about the gift of the Spirit. Red, more even that white and gold, is the liturgical colour, though except in ordinary time, the colour of the season is appropriate.

Reception into the Church of England

Common Worship: Initiation Services provide forms of service for 'Reception into the Communion of the Church of England'. This too is seen as an extension of baptism and the liturgy for it has a baptismal character and includes a procession to the font. Unless the candidate for reception is a priest, in which case the bishop must be involved in the liturgy of reception, the parish priest may preside at such a reception. Nevertheless, the normative form that is provided places the reception within the service of baptism, confirmation and eucharist at which the bishop presides. The candidates for reception take their place among the other candidates (for baptism and confirmation). They answer the same questions at the decision and they make the same profession of faith. Whether within that normative setting or in a separate service, the key elements are:

- presentation of the candidates to the people (including 'the decision');
- profession of faith at the font (made with the entire congregation);
- a declaration (through three questions and answers) of a desire to be part of the life, worship and witness of the Church of England;
- a prayer by the president that the candidate 'may continue in the life of the Spirit';
- reception by words and the taking of the hand;
- a prayer by the whole congregation;
- optional commission and intercession;
- greeting of peace.

Initiation Services sets out very clearly how this rite is integrated with baptism and confirmation.

Affirming baptismal faith

In some ways parallel to reception, but in other ways very different indeed, is 'affirmation of baptismal faith'. Here the intention is to provide a rite for those who have made a significant move forward in their Christian discipleship and wish to celebrate it liturgically. Among them may be those who had lapsed entirely from faith, even sometimes those caught up in occult activities. Certainly it will include some whose baptism was before they could remember it and whose confirmation seems to them now to have been a formality rather than a moment of illumination and growth. There are many people in today's Church who come back to faith or experience a dramatic deepening of it that needs liturgical expression. What the church is able to offer them is a rich liturgy, in which they have the opportunity to renew their baptism through the words of the decision and of the profession of faith and through signing themselves with water from the font or being sprinkled with it, a prayer by the president that they may be equipped with the gifts of the Holy Spirit and the laying of the president's hand on the candidate's head with a prayer that 'God may renew his life within you that you may confess his name' and the possibility of anointing at this point with the oil of chrism. As with the reception into the Church of England, the normative setting is a service of baptism, confirmation and eucharist, with the bishop as president, but there is also provision for a separate service, with the parish priest as president.

The core elements are:

- presentation of the candidates to the people (with optional testimony, welcome by the congregation and 'the decision');

- profession of faith at the font (made with the whole congregation);
- a declaration by those affirming with a congregational response;
- a prayer by the president that the candidate may be 'equipped with the gifts of the Holy Spirit';
- hand-laying with a prayer for renewal;
- a prayer by the whole congregation;
- optional commission and intercession;
- greeting of peace.

What the Church of England cannot offer is 're-baptism'. Those who doubt the validity of their baptism need help to see that God was at work in it, planting his Spirit, and that their new mature faith is an out-working of this. If they insist on baptism they have to go elsewhere. If we were to baptize again we would undermine our whole baptismal theology. But we can and should more readily offer this rich sacramental rite in which baptism can be reclaimed, the gift of the Spirit celebrated and Christian discipleship provided with a liturgical setting in which to leap forward.

24

Marriage

∾

The wedding service

In marriage, the bride and the bridegroom are themselves the ministers of the sacrament. The priest (or sometimes deacon) is, in a sense, the chief witness and the 'master of ceremonies', and only 'takes over', so to speak, when the couple are married, in order to pronounce God's blessing on their marriage. More than at any other service, therefore, it is right to let the participants have a say in the form that it takes, and the wise minister will not make too many rules about what will or will not be allowed to be said, sung or done. Sometimes the minister must say no to a suggestion that would make a mockery or a nonsense of the service, and occasionally needs to say 'trust me, that idea simply will not work', but in general the task is to help the people to celebrate in the way that seems to them genuine, natural and reverent. The priest is not, on this occasion, the arbiter of good taste.

The degree of involvement of the couple in the drawing up of the service will depend a good deal on their understanding of even the most simple idea of Christian worship. Every priest knows the blank faces that can meet even the suggestion that the couple might choose the hymns. But it is not always like that. To involve them as far as possible in the decisions is good. They can be assisted in their involvement – they can be sent away from one interview with a collection of twenty suitable hymns and invited to come back with a short list of four or five from which priest and couple together will make the final choice; similarly with the twenty obvious passages of scripture. After another interview they might go off with copies of the various sets of intercession prayers, to choose which they prefer and to suggest inserts into it, even when they would never avail themselves of the freedom to create their own prayers. On the other hand they should not be so involved that they begin to feel a degree of responsibility for the smooth running of the service. The chief pastoral need is to help them to relax and to feel assured that the service is in safe hands.

Their first choice, of course, is in terms of the rite. Do they want the service from the Book of Common Prayer ('brute beasts', 'incontinence and all'), the 1928/Series One service that most people mean when they talk of 'the old service', or the *Common Worship* service? Of course they need help to see that this is partly about language, but also about a variety of models of marriage. They need help to see that the issue of the bride obeying or not obeying is part of a serious question about how the couple understands the nature of marriage. Certainly to look with the couple at the 'preface' in each of the three rites opens up key questions about contemporary attitudes to marriage and helps, not only to enable them to choose the marriage rite, but to prepare for their marriage beyond the great day.

In what follows the assumption is made that we are dealing with *Common Worship: Marriage Service*, though much of it applies whatever rite is being used.

The service has what has sometimes been called a 'eucharistic shape'. This has been misunderstood to mean that the Church regards the eucharist as the proper setting for the marriage service. But this would be foolish in our contemporary culture, though it is good when a communicant couple do celebrate their marriage in such a context, and both the Prayer Book and *Common Worship* do urge communicant newly married couples to receive Holy Communion together as soon as possible after their marriage. But the eucharistic shape is simply an out-working of the principle that the sequence, consisting of Gathering, Liturgy of the Word, Special Rite (in this case Marriage), Prayers, provides the most satisfactory shape for the liturgy. In the case of marriage, this represents for many people a radical change from previous practice, which has been to have the preface, declaration, vows and blessing of the marriage straight away at the beginning, before any reading, sermon or extended time of prayer, and from a belief that somehow this shape must be best, for a bride and groom cannot relax and enjoy the service until the nerve-wracking promises are over. The *Common Worship* service rejects that quite firmly and believes that through the usual Gathering and Liturgy of the Word stages of the service the couple and indeed the whole congregation are led naturally by the liturgy and the minister to the moment when, with initial nervousness well behind them, they can make their vows and have their marriage blessed as the service moves towards its climax. (But it does, by a note, concede that the readings and the sermon, or the sermon alone, may be moved to a late point in the service after the blessing of the marriage.)

The service brings 'gathering' and 'word' together in a first half it calls the 'Introduction'. The priest meets the bride at the door. The notes allow bride and bridegroom to enter together. Where a couple have long been living together, that reflects reality. But much more often the bride will enter accompanied by her father or another (not necessarily male) member of her family and the notes allow all these options.

With the bride and groom standing before the minister, the service encourages 'the welcome', consisting of trinitarian greeting, sentence of scripture and communal prayer, before the first hymn. After it the minister reads the preface. There are two possible texts (the second close, but not identical, to that in the ASB 1980 service, in the appendix). Then come 'the declarations', intentionally moved away from the vows in order to be seen as part of the preliminaries. The minister asks both congregation and couple whether there is any legal impediment to their marriage, and then asks bridegroom and bride in turn whether they will take the other, and they each answer 'I will'. The minister then asks the congregation whether they will support and uphold the marriage and needs to make sure the answer is a strong and affirmative 'We will'. With the preliminaries over and the scene set, so to speak, the minister invites everybody to pray and the collect is said.

We have now reached the Liturgy of the Word, at very least a Bible reading (from a large selection) and the sermon, but sometimes a fuller form, involving probably two readings with a psalm (four are indicated), a song, an anthem or a hymn between them, as well as the sermon. If at all possible the readings will be by family members or friends. The bride and groom need to be able to sit down together and the notes specifically recommend chairs for them. In the rehearsal the minister will also have sorted out where bridesmaids, best man and others are to sit. Here the focus moves off the couple and on to the scriptures, and this helps the process whereby they can relax. The sermon gives the minister the opportunity to communicate something about marriage and about the gospel in a less formal way than the words of the liturgy. Care needs to be taken not simply to reiterate what the preface has said. Clergy doing many weddings have to guard against saying the same thing on every occasion, sounding less and less fresh on each successive occasion, and one way of avoiding this is always to make the couple choose the readings and then to preach on their choice, however much the central message does not need to change. The sermon is the last part of the 'Introduction'. By the end of it people need to be ready for the moment that the vows are made, though first there may be a hymn or other piece of music while the bride and groom and those who attend them come to stand again before the minister.

The second part of the service, 'The Marriage', begins optionally with the minister asking 'Who brings this woman to be married to this man?'

However much a 'giving away' (though the wording here is different) is part of an outdated picture of marriage, this is a ceremony to which families naturally hold. The response is by action, not words (there is no 'I do'), and the bride's father (or, as the note says, 'mother, or another member of her family or a friend representing the family') gives the bride's right hand to the minister who puts it in the bridegroom's right hand. The minister then invites them to make their vows. They should do this, holding hands in the way the rubrics order, and facing one another (full on, not half facing the minister). The words of the vows may be in the form in the main text or in the Prayer Book words (which may also be used earlier at the 'declaration') or in a form that allows the bride to say that she will 'obey' (both these alternatives are in the appendix). They may say them line by line after the minister, or off by heart (with the minister as a kind of prompter) or they may read them, though this ought to be discouraged if it means that they do not face one another.

There follows 'the giving of the rings'. The minister blesses the rings (again there is an alternative text in the appendix). The bridegroom places a ring on the fourth finger of the bride's left hand. The minister needs to be careful not to 'feed' the words to be said until the ring is safely on. The bridegroom, again repeating after the minister or with the minister as prompter, speaks the appropriate words to the bride. The same then happens in reverse. There is also provision for both bride and groom to say the words together and also for slightly varying words to be used if only one ring is given. Addressing the congregation, the minister pronounces them married and, joining the right hands of the couple, says 'Those whom God has joined together let no one put asunder'.

'The blessing of the marriage' is the next stage of the rite. In earlier rites it has been almost lost, a single prayer among other prayers. Yet this ought to be one of the high points of the service. In a sense it is the Church's response to all the couple have said to one another. There is an extended blessing prayer (with a series of alternatives in the appendix, some of which involve the congregation in the text). Although this prayer, with its alternatives, is optional, without it the single and very short mandatory blessing that follows is insufficient to make this section all it is intended to be. This is a solemn moment, with the minister praying with arms outstretched over the couple, and it brings to an end this central phase of the rite.

The order now provides for the registration of the marriage. The law requires the registers to be filled in and signed immediately after the solemnization of the marriage, but a note interprets this as meaning one of three points:

1. after the blessing of the marriage, the preferred place and where the registration is indicated in the text;
2. earlier, after the proclamation of the marriage, but before the blessing of the marriage, thus highlighting the latter further by separating it from the marriage itself;
3. at the end of the service.

Only if it comes at the end of the service will the practice of going out into the vestry or a side chapel to sign the registers make sense, and this practice needs discouraging. It is perfectly appropriate for the signing to be in the body of the church. It is completed much more expeditiously without the need for people to disappear for a while, and the music that normally covers this part of the service is less likely to be spoilt by chatter when the congregation has action to focus on. By far the better option is for the registration to be during the service, not after, and in the sight of the people, not hidden away.

After it there may be a hymn, or this may be the moment for a psalm, or if there has been an anthem of some kind, long enough to cover the registration, the prayers may follow immediately. Before them the minister may lead the newly married couple to the altar step. It is all that is left in most weddings of the first journey of the newly married to the altar to receive the sacrament. Even without that at the end of it, for their first walk together to be 'to the altar of God' is a good thing. The prayers, which the rubric indicates move from thanksgiving to prayer for spiritual growth, for faithfulness, joy, love, forgiveness and healing, and then for children, family and friends, may follow a mainstream text, or a number of appendix alternatives, or may be in the form of free prayer or with a text prepared by the couple with the help of the minister. The prayers do not need necessarily to be led by the presiding minister.

There follows the Lord's Prayer, a final hymn if that did not happen before the prayers, and the blessing of the entire congregation. With the registration of the marriage much earlier, the service is able to end on this note of prayer and blessing and then, as the music strikes up, the newly married couple move through the church and through the congregation to the door and the inevitable photographs.

The minister needs to have decided long before about issues such as photography, confetti and collection. There is nothing worse than a wedding that begins with a series of prohibitions and an appeal for money. If something has to be said about these, it is best printed in the service book, but there is a case for keeping prohibitions to a minimum. The Church can so easily appear killjoy and churlish about such matters as photographs and confetti, and the rules that do have to be set need to be expressed in as positive and friendly a manner as possible. There is also a

185

need to put into the hands of the congregation something better than the usual four-sided wedding service sheet, with nothing on it but the hymns. Each church needs either its own booklet or to ensure that what the couple produce in the way of a service sheet includes both the outline order and the key texts the congregation will need if they are to be encouraged to join in the service.

When a minister from another Christian denomination is invited to assist at a wedding, there are clear procedures and permissions set out in Canon B43 and reflected in a full note. For legal reasons it is a Church of England minister who must 'establish the absence of impediment, direct the exchange of vows, declare the existence of the marriage, say the final blessing and sign the registers'. Where there is a 'mixed marriage' the bishop may permit some variations to the form of service, as are included in the 'Order for the Marriage of Christians from Different Churches', which has been approved by the General Synod, but is not printed out in *Common Worship*.

A wedding within the eucharist

The *Common Worship* marriage provision sets out how the marriage service may be set within the eucharist. It is very straightforward, not least because of the eucharistic shape of the marriage rite. Prayers of penitence may precede the preface, the entire 'Liturgy of the Sacrament' and 'Dismissal' may follow the prayers. The readings must include a gospel reading. Special texts are provided for the prayers of penitence, the gospel acclamation, the introduction to the peace, the preparation of the table and the gifts, the eucharistic preface, the prayer after communion and a solemn blessing at the dismissal, but most of these texts are optional even when the marriage is celebrated within the eucharist.

At the peace it is appropriate for the newly married couple to greet one another and for each of them to greet, not only his or her own family, but also each other's families. The couple then follow the priest to the altar step where they appropriately present the bread and wine for the eucharist. They remain standing or kneeling before the altar, and a note allows the blessing of the couple to be moved from its earlier place to be between the Lord's Prayer and the breaking of the bread, a traditional point for it where it brings the blessing of the marriage and the reception of communion as close as possible together. After receiving, the couple need to be able to go to sit down if there is to be a general communion; and there ought to be if at all possible. The old custom of communion for the couple only is not normally justifiable, though there can be special pastoral reasons. For instance, if one of the partners comes from a totally unchurched family, there might be a concern at the divisiveness of a general communion. In the end a pastoral decision has to be made, but for a couple to receive communion with family and friends on their wedding day is a good way of expressing the new life they begin in the community.

Where the wedding is set within the eucharist, it is all the more important there be a clear presidency. It is not ideal for one person to officiate up to the peace and another to take over at that point. But the president, having begun the service with the greeting, might delegate much of it until the blessing of the marriage, including the declarations, the vows and the proclamation, though these three at least must be delegated to a single lawful minister, who must also sign the registers.

After a civil marriage

Church of England practice in relation to the marriage in church of those with partners from a previous and dissolved marriage has been going through a period of change. Even without a formal shift of policy nationally, an increasing number of clergy have believed it right under certain circumstances to solemnize a marriage where at least one partner has a former spouse still living. Sometimes the pastoral case seems very strong. But there exists also *Services of Prayer and Dedication* (1985), the principal, though not exclusive use of which is for those who have entered into a civil marriage. At a certain level, it is difficult to see the difference if the key contribution of the minister in both marriage and service of dedication is to call down God's blessing upon the couple.

In relation to a Service of Prayer and Dedication (officially so called, rather than the 'blessing of a civil marriage', though clearly blessing is part of its text), the two factors that need to be held in a proper balance are, on the one hand, to make it clear that this is a different service, despite the renewal of vows and the blessing of the couple, by gently insisting that the couple walk in together as husband and wife, that the rings are already on their fingers before they are blessed and in other ways to be real about what is happening, yet, on the other hand, to be warm and welcoming, affirming and celebratory. If the Church is going to offer this ministry it needs to do it well, with sensitivity and without apology. Although the service allows for public expression of penitence (by everyone, not just the couple), it is better that there be penitence for past failure at the point of failure, or at least in a private pastoral setting before the new marriage, rather than have it intruding on the day of fresh beginning.

The Service of Prayer and Dedication, now fifteen years old, is in some ways a thin service. That is partly because of the desire to produce something that cannot be confused with the Marriage Service. But it also reflects the approach of the early ASB years and in some ways needs supplementing from more recent resources. Chief among these will be the prayers and collects of the *Common Worship: Marriage Service* which, for this and for many other occasions related to marriage and family life, is a real treasury of resource material.

25

Healing and Reconciliation in Church

The ministry of healing

In the New Testament, in Mark's Gospel, for instance, when the twelve are sent out to preach and to anoint, or in the Letter of James, where the elders are called to anoint and to pray, there is a community setting. People are put into a right relationship with the community and, through the community, with God. The ministry of healing has its proper place in the public liturgy of the Church. Where it happens in home or hospital, that is an extension of a ministry that is corporate and public.

The symbols used in the ministry of healing are reminders of the corporate nature of our faith and of our belonging to the body of Christ. Olive oil, an ancient and soothing balm, is suggestive of the wholeness of the new life to be found in being a member of Christ and his body. The laying on of hands, an ancient sign of blessing, commissioning and empowering, evokes and acknowledges the Holy Spirit at work in us as members of the community of the Spirit. In anointing with the laying on of hands we have both symbol and proclamation of belonging to the community of Christ's presence, sharing in suffering, bringing new life. This ministry is not a private prescription, a magical potion or a wonder drug, to be used in emergency if all else fails. Rather, behind it lies the belief that wholeness of life requires right relationships with God and each other in the Christian community, that what makes us the individuals we are is, not only our physical bodies and our minds, but the extension of ourselves into relationship with another, with the community and with the world. Sickness distorts this relationship, puts us at dis-ease. This dis-ease needs more than clinical cures to bring us back to wholeness. Acknowledgement of this reality is the first step to healing our dis-ease. The ministry of healing enables Christians to do this, to put themselves into a right relationship with God and the community, and to say to God 'Your will be done'

It is against this background that the local church needs to appreciate, teach and practice the ministry of healing. The healing works that Jesus did were signs of the kingdom already present and growing in the world, signs of the ultimate transformation of humankind, and in the ministry of healing the Church is proclaiming and sharing in those signs and that vision.

It is a mistake to look for so-called 'results' of the healing ministry in a clinical sense, for that is to attempt to confine God's work to our own immediate horizons. Nevertheless, that being said and that needing to be taught, many can testify to the reality of the Church's healing ministry. There are countless examples of those enabled to grow through pain and suffering to become people of great spiritual stature, of those given the confidence that enables the doctors to do their work so much more effectively, of those enabled to die well, who could not previously face that step with openness, of those patients and relatives whose bitterness with life, with God and with each other has been healed and transformed, of those who, despite handicaps, have received the courage and grace to live life to the full, of those who come out of the depths of despair and guilt weeping for joy and relief at the assurance of a fresh start, and there are those who, after painful physical illness, unexpectedly and in a way doctors cannot explain, get better. All these are examples of healing. We must never define it too narrowly and we must never allow it to be on the edge of church life when it is so near to the heart of the gospel of wholeness and reconciliation.

There are a number of public liturgical contexts in which this ministry can be celebrated. But the eucharist is the richest of these theologically. For every eucharist is, in a sense, a sacrament of healing. The Prayer Book communion rite, with its 'We do not presume...', taken up in poetry such as George Herbert's 'Love bade me welcome...', makes this point tellingly. It would be a loss if, in all the renewed emphasis on the laying on of hands and anointing, that were lost. The eucharist is *par excellence* the healing sacrament. Where special rites for the ministry of healing are incorporated into the service, they are best placed before the Liturgy of the Sacrament, so that everything is brought to completion in sharing in the eucharist.

But who does the ministering? The gift of healing is given to the Church, not to the ordained ministry alone. The role of the priest in this ministry is one of liturgical and organizational presidency. If the priest alone lays on hands that is because the priest acts here, as at other sacramental moments, for the community, the community that plays its part by upholding those receiving this ministry by prayer. Equally if lay people share with the priest in the laying on of hands, it is a recognition that the whole Church is involved in the healing ministry.

The president may of course delegate the laying on of hands to others. Two different models may lie behind this, though they can overlap. One simply emphasizes the community – people lay on hands as representative of the entire congregation that meanwhile is praying. The other is more interested in 'gifts' – particular people lay on hands because God has given them healing gifts (and they may be the professional gifts of doctors and those who work in hospitals, hospices and general medical practices). The two models can go together, but theologically a church needs to have sorted out how it understands the way this ministry is celebrated. In the Church of England the canons, while allowing anyone to take part in the laying on of hands, restrict anointing to ordained ministers, though there can be no absolute logic to that, particularly if those anointing use the oil that has been blessed by the bishop or a priest.

Just as significant as who lays hands and who anoints is the question of who counsels. People will sometimes want to receive the laying on of hands without a word before or after with anyone, but the offer should always be there – to talk to someone before receiving the ministry of healing or to follow it up, and here skill and training is required for clergy and lay people involved alike.

The key issue is not so much how the liturgy and its personnel is ordered, but that the ministry of healing should form part of the regular liturgical life of each community. Whether on a weekly, monthly or quarterly basis, there needs to be an occasion when this ministry is offered and seen to be very much at the heart of the Church's sacramental life. The laying on of hands at a quiet service one lunchtime or weekday evening may, in some communities, be absolutely right, but in some others it ought to be part of the Sunday programme.

Common Worship provides a series of services and resources for 'Wholeness and Healing'. In time this is to be followed with provision for 'Reconciliation', but work on this is to a different timescale. Meanwhile the gaps are plugged, and much good liturgical material for a whole range of needs in terms of healing and reconciliation is to be found in *Pastoral Prayers*, published in 1996, a modern-day equivalent to the priest's *Vade Mecum* and an invaluable resource in church and at the bedside in ministering to the sick.

Common Worship: Wholeness and Healing

The *Common Worship* provision is in five parts, all of it provided 'to recognize the links between prayer for healing and the wider celebration in the church of reconciliation and renewal in the gospel of Jesus Christ'

One part is the provision for Holy Communion at home or in hospital (and this is considered in chapter 28).

Another comprises prayers for protection and deliverance. These are for use with those suffering from a sense of disturbance or unrest. But a note emphasizes that to go beyond these prayers, and to exercise a ministry of exorcism and deliverance, is a ministry restricted to priests acting with the specific authority of the bishop to do so.

A third element is a series of helpful pastoral guidelines on 'prayers for individuals in public worship'. These are intended more for the inclusion of such prayers in the week-by-week regular worshipping life of a congregation than for a special healing service. They allow for the possibility of prayer with the laying on of hands for:

- people who do not explain their particular need;
- people who have explained briefly to those who are ministering to them the nature of their need;
- people whose need is briefly shared with the whole congregation.

The notes suggest that such prayer ministry may take place:

- as part of the prayers of intercession;
- during the distribution of communion;
- at the end of the service.

What is being described is established practice in a number of churches, but unfamiliar to the majority. A degree of official recognition of this style of ministry is intended not only to give it some additional authority, but also to encourage more churches to draw it into their worship. An important note encourages the earlier position in the service for this ministry because 'it is important that the gift and promise of communion is not overshadowed by prayer for individual needs'.

The fourth part of the provision is 'A Celebration of Wholeness and Healing', especially suitable for a diocesan or deanery occasion. It is not intended for regular parish use, but for a great gathering, possibly with the bishop as the president, possibly in an extended celebration over a number of hours, with long periods of silence and lengthy periods of ministry in terms of healing and reconciliation. It has a eucharistic shape, but with the prayers of intercession and penitence together after the Liturgy of the Word, it includes the blessing of oil, the laying on of hands and anointing, and assumes a setting within the eucharist itself, while allowing for a service without communion. Its texts are a useful resource beyond the service for which they are designed, and its 'Sending Out' includes a brief gospel passage, a liturgical device that can helpfully be employed on other occasions too.

The final provision, the most important for the ongoing parish ministry of healing, is 'The Laying on of Hands with Prayer and Anointing at Holy Communion'. Here is a service for regular parish use, following a familiar order, but with special texts to focus on the work of wholeness and healing. The Gathering includes a *Kyrie eleison* form of penitence. The Liturgy of the Word includes a fine litany of healing for use at the intercession, though this section of the service will usually need opening up first into a time of prayer for the sick, particularly for those who are not present to receive the laying on of hands. There follows the provision for the laying on of hands and also for anointing (with a prayer for the blessing of oil if this has not happened previously). The service continues with the peace, and there are special texts for it, for the eucharistic preface, the post communion and the blessing. It is not a spectacularly different service, but intentionally so, for this ministry needs to be embedded in the parish's regular liturgical life, attended by those who will not very often come forward to receive the laying on of hands, but who understand that their part in the rite is to pray for those who do, always holding in mind that every person in the service, including those who minister, is always in need of the healing touch of Christ.

Reconciling the penitent

The power to absolve sin, like the authority to anoint, is given to the Church, rather than to the ordained ministry. That is the biblical emphasis. In pronouncing absolution, the bishop or the priest speaks in the name of the Church and reconciles the sinner with the Church as well as proclaiming the sinner's reconciliation with God. Confession and absolution is, therefore, for all the privacy that naturally protects it, an act of the community, and importantly so if we are not to lose the corporate dimension to our talk of sin and evil in our world.

'Going to confession' has never been part of the regular practice of the very large majority of Anglicans. The Prayer Book encourages it where there is a conscience that cannot otherwise cope, and provides, in the Visitation of the Sick, an absolution text that has been something of a landmark for catholic Anglicans, but which has also been the cause of difficulty in previous efforts to take an authorized text through the General Synod. There has been a change in the use of this sacrament in the last generation. It has, with many clergy and penitents, been shorn of its 'confessional' setting and much of its formality, and more often than not has become part of a more complex encounter that involves spiritual

direction and sometimes counselling. Something of what it has traditionally done for people has been taken over by some of the liturgical
provision of the ministry of healing. Some of the things that are whispered
to a minister before the laying on of hands for healing are not far from the
mention of particular sins that traditionally have been part of confession
before priestly absolution. Indeed, whereas in the past the 'sign' at the
absolution would have been the sign of the cross, now it is recognized
that this is a moment for the minister to lay hands on the penitent or to
extend hands over the penitent, the same sign as in healing.

We are dealing here with the overlap between healing and reconciliation, between sickness and sin. It is an area fraught with difficulty, for at
all costs we need to avoid conveying the impression that sin is the cause of
sickness. But the connections need nevertheless to be taken seriously.
Sometimes when people come asking for healing, they need to be
encouraged to confess their sins. Sometimes when people come burdened
with guilt, they need to be offered healing. In almost any liturgy that
concerns human wholeness, penitence (even if it is only part of the
preliminary and the preparation) and absolution will have a place.

What are needed for the ministry of reconciliation in today's Church
are confident well-trained flexible ministers, able to discern when the
emphasis needs to be on forgiveness and when on healing, and when a
formal church setting and a precise liturgical form, the penitent kneeling,
will meet that person's need and when something more like a dialogue in
armchairs in the study will meet the need. But whatever the setting, and
whatever the form (*Pastoral Prayers* provides a formal but flexible
liturgical form), the reconciliation of a penitent is always part of the
ministry of the whole Church.

26

Funeral Rites

Commending and comforting

A Christian funeral has several purposes. To achieve them all in an hour's
liturgy in church is difficult, let alone in twenty minutes at a crematorium.
A series of less formal and in some cases more domestic rites before and
after may help. A minister well trained to be thoroughly professional both
pastorally and liturgically is crucial. And a clear but flexible liturgy is
necessary too. A Christian funeral seeks to bring a community together:

- to honour a life;
- to commend the dead to God;
- to give space for grief and yet to move people on;
- to express the love and compassion of God to the bereaved;
- to proclaim the gospel message of Christ's death and resurrection;
- to warn of the inevitability of death and to encourage them to walk
  in this life with an eye to eternity;
- to take leave of the body and to say farewell;
- to dispose of the body reverently.

To speak of bringing a community together raises an immediate question,
for the nature of the typical funeral community has changed. The norm in
the past has been a gathering of people who know one another and who
are familiar with the tenets of the Christian faith in relation to death and
afterlife and with the forms of Christian worship, including the funeral
rite. They have gathered in the parish church, a building into which they
have regularly come, the setting of all Christian celebrations and rites of
passage, a place more associated with life than death, and they have been
led by a minister whom they know and to whom they relate. More often
than not, they have been remembering someone they saw soon before he
or she died, or they were even present at the death if it was not sudden, or

had seen the body in the period between death and funeral. They had, as an extended family or a community, begun the grieving process before ever the funeral service began.

Instead today the most typical funeral is a gathering of people, many of whom are strangers to one another, to the teachings of the Church and to the forms of its worship. They gather in the crematorium, a place they associate only with death, and are led by a minister whom only a few of them have met and then perhaps for only a short time. They are remembering someone whom some of them have not seen for a time, from whose death they were distanced, and for whom they have had little time to grieve till now. That is the setting in which the minister has to create a sense of community so that all the purposes of the funeral may have some chance of being fulfilled.

In the Church of England three funeral rites are available – that in the Book of Common Prayer, the modified version of that in the Prayer Book of 1928 given legal authority as 'Series One', and the form in *Common Worship*. This last is the form on which this chapter focuses, though many of the points apply to all three rites. Funeral rites are difficult to devise in the Church of England because of divisions about prayer for those who have died. A minority find themselves unable to pray for the departed, simply on the grounds that it is too late to do so; death is the moment when God decides. The majority see prayer for the departed as a natural expression of affection and care within the communion of saints. But the majority has not imposed on the minority texts that it cannot accept at key moments in the liturgy. Sometimes the richer provision of prayers that commend and entrust the dead need to be sought out in supplementary material and sometimes among the prayers for the dying, rather than the dead.

For the funeral liturgy can be understood as a ritual recapturing of the moment of death for those who were not there. The funeral becomes the moment of farewell for most people and so texts designed to be said as the person dies are appropriate also at the funeral. The prayer, 'Go forth upon your journey from this world . . .', belongs properly as a person dies, but it has long been a feature of funeral liturgy, and that has been a wise instinct with broader application.

One of the key changes in contemporary funeral liturgy has been a recognition that we need to recover the rituals of farewell for a generation that has lost them and yet knows that actions so often speak louder than words, never more so than in the emotionally charged mood of a funeral. Thus old 'secular' customs need recovering – members of the family carrying the coffin, earth thrown into the ground on top of the coffin at an interment – but also Christian symbols need to be renewed – the coffin draped in a pall (preferably white, rather than purple), the coffin sprinkled with the water of baptism, the paschal candle carried in front of the coffin or placed near it during the funeral. And, as far as possible, these signs and symbols need to be something people do, rather than simply watch, so that they may participate fully even when words would be choked by tears.

Part of that recovery is a stronger sense of the paschal nature of a Christian funeral. Grief has its rightful place and we must never encourage that brave but mistaken desire to rule out mourning and to fight back all the tears. But sorrow is for what those who are left have lost and is bound up with our sense of the fragility of human life. However quietly and sensitively it is expressed, a Christian funeral is a celebration (and that is a proper word to use in this context) of the death and resurrection of the Lord. The prayers proclaim it and the reading(s) may do so too. The sprinkling with baptismal water makes the connection also, as does the paschal candle burning by the coffin. At least one of the hymns should have the same message too.

All this points to the desirability of a longer liturgy than we have been used to and longer than is suitable in a crematorium or cemetery chapel. We should always try to ensure that people know that this is on offer, a full service in the parish church, whatever may follow elsewhere. The reasons why people do not often opt for a church funeral are complex, but part of why is that a church funeral is not sufficiently different to justify something more difficult, expensive and time consuming to arrange. We need to let it be known, by good practice, what we can offer, while still doing all in our power to make the twenty-minute service in the crematorium as helpful as possible.

There needs to be a new flexibility also about the relationship of church service, cremation and interment. In the Christian tradition the return to the earth is significant – 'dust to dust, ashes to ashes'. That may be achieved through the burial of the body, but, when the body is disposed of by cremation, the significant final moment is not the consigning to the fire, but the return of the ashes to the ground. That is why the tradition frowns on 'scattering' ashes; they are to be interred. Logically this points to the words of committal happening at the interment of ashes, not at the crematorium, but this cannot be a hard and fast rule, for the committal does need to be when the close mourners can all be assembled.

Similarly there are questions about whether the committal can be at the church door (especially if there would otherwise be a thirty-mile drive for the mourners to the nearest crematorium) or whether the body can be burnt before the funeral, with no focus at the funeral or simply the casket of ashes. There are no absolutely right answers here; nevertheless there is little doubt that the body in the coffin is better present as the mourners take their leave, and an interring in the ground is a more satisfactory way of completing a process than seeing a hearse drive off into the distance.

We need to be wary also of the private funeral followed later by the public memorial service. There is a place for memorial services, but they seldom, if long delayed, serve the grieving process satisfactorily and are no substitute for attendance at the funeral. In a whole series of instances we must not conspire with people's desire to avoid the moment of farewell; however much they dread it, it is part of the grieving and healing process.

The service in church

In this section the *Common Worship Funeral Service* is examined as it might be celebrated in a parish church without undue constraints of time. In a later section consideration is given to how the service needs to be celebrated under pressure of time in a crematorium or cemetery chapel.

The service has six sections – Gathering, Readings and Sermon, Prayers, Commendation and Farewell, Committal and Dismissal.

The Gathering is the part of the service in which the minister has very speedily to bind the mourners into a community and set the mood of the service. The constituent parts of this section are:

- the reception of the coffin (if it is not already in the church);
- one or more sentences of scripture may be said;
- a greeting and introduction to the service (with a set text but freedom to use other words);
- an optional prayer for strength for the mourners;
- a hymn may be sung;
- a brief tribute may be made;
- optional prayers of penitence;
- invitation to pray, silent prayer and the collect.

All that is mandatory is the greeting, introduction and time of prayer leading into the collect, but in a full service some of the further material will be valued. The reception of the body may be very simple – the minister goes to the door and leads it in silence to its place in the church. It is nearly always preferable for the mourners to move into the church and take their places before the coffin is brought in, but their own sense of what is right and proper needs to be respected. However, the reception can include:

- words as the coffin is received at the door (the text is in the appendix);
- a sprinkling at the door (again with a text provided, but there are other later points for the sprinkling);
- the sentences of scripture as the coffin is brought in;

- the coffin led in by a minister carrying the paschal candle which then remains burning near the coffin;
- a pall placed over the coffin by family, friends or other members of the congregation (with texts provided);
- 'suitable symbols of the life and faith of the departed person' placed on or near the coffin (texts are provided for placing a Bible or a cross); this may happen a little later after the opening prayer or hymn.

This is a long list and clearly some degree of selectivity is required, but it is a pity to exclude all those that involve action and symbols, for words, especially this early in the service, may hardly get through to the congregation. Immense care is needed in relation to the 'suitable symbols of the life and faith of the departed person'. For some a Bible and a cross may be a natural choice, but what of a pack of cards, a beer tankard or a teddy bear? Each church needs a clear and consistent policy, not too narrow, for these things can help personalize and give authenticity, but avoiding the unsuitable and the bizarre.

Too many stages to the 'reception' would delay too long the minister's greeting and introduction. These lead naturally into a prayer for strength for the mourners (there is a choice of texts) and, if there is to be singing, a hymn follows naturally at this point. There is then provision for a 'tribute' about which a note says:

> Remembering and honouring the life of the person who has died, and the evidence of God's grace and work in them should be done in the earlier part of the service, after the opening prayer, though if occasion demands it may be woven into the sermon or come immediately before the Commendation. It may be done in conjunction with the placing of symbols, and may be spoken by a family member or by the minister using information provided by the family. It is preferable not to interrupt the flow of the Reading(s) and Sermon with a tribute of this kind.

This is a strong and prescriptive note. It is designed to ensure that the sermon, when we reach it, is about the Christian faith, rather than turned into a panegyric. It is also intended to ensure that the sermon is delivered by the minister, for if there is to be a tribute by family or friend it is a separate exercise at this earlier point. Yet it may be argued that if the minister is entrusted with the tribute, as will very often be the case, the weaving into the sermon may be exactly what is needed.

The optional prayers of penitence follow. These could be simply the words of the *Kyrie eleison*, but could also be a longer form, with invitation, silence, confession and absolution. Penitence is always a proper element in a funeral, both because the deceased stands under the judgement of God, but also because the mourners often carry a burden of guilt and regret that needs to be named and unburdened. However, when these prayers of penitence seem too much, it may be noted that the later prayers in the rite provide another opportunity.

Finally in this section comes the collect. It is a mandatory element of the rite, but it may be transposed to the end of the later prayers, and this may be appropriate if otherwise it followed immediately after the 'opening prayer'. The opening prayer is about the mourners, the collect about the whole church in general and the departed in particular.

The second section is the 'Readings and Sermon'. It is good if readings can be read by lay people, but not necessarily by close relatives for whom this might be testing. A choice of about forty biblical readings is given and there is an encouragement to have Psalm 23 or another psalm. The minimum here is one reading from scripture. Where other, non-biblical, readings are wanted as well, this may not be the best moment for them. They may be better as a kind of epilogue near the end of the service.

The sermon has already been mentioned. A note insists that its purpose is 'to proclaim the gospel in the context of the death of this particular person'. That is clearly right, but this may also be the proper place for the minister to weave something of the story of the person who has died. The minister needs to understand in a funeral, and especially in any tribute and sermon, the role he or she has as spokesperson. They speak for God to people who are hurting and fragile, and need to do so with a sure combination of sensitivity and confidence. But they also speak for the congregation. They have been trusted with articulating what the mourners are thinking. They are charged with saying enough to allow people to have their own thoughts and do their own remembering. The minister has to get inside their minds and say words for them. It is a demanding role, speaking for them from inside their grief and speaking to them from outside in the name of God and of the Church. When it is well done, it is a superbly effective piece of Christian ministry.

'The Prayers' follow. A normal sequence is indicated:

- thanksgiving for the life of the departed;
- prayer for those who mourn;
- prayers of penitence (if not used already);
- prayer for readiness to live in the light of eternity.

There is a text in the main rite that reflects this structure and allows for some interpolation of personal material. The Lord's Prayer follows (unless it is to be kept to say after the committal) and the collect is said now if it was not used earlier. This may be the point for another hymn.

The fourth section is 'The Commendation and Farewell'. The minister stands at the coffin and there is an encouragement, where appropriate, to gather the mourners around it too. Silence leads into a prayer of commendation. There is one in the text, together with several in an appendix, including ones that call to mind the moment of death, and texts particularly for a child and for a baby. This is an alternative moment for the sprinkling of the water of baptism and the minister may invite the principal mourners to sprinkle too. One of the commendations, 'Give rest, O Christ, to your servant...' (the *Kontakion* from the Russian Liturgy), could be sung during the sprinkling, but there are other suitable songs and chants.

The fifth section is the 'Committal', but, if that is to be in another place, the dismissal might follow immediately. If the Committal follows straight away in the churchyard, the coffin is now led out of the church to the graveside. The Committal, whether now or in a later separate service elsewhere, consists of:

- optional sentences of scripture (probably only if this is a separate service);
- one of two texts that recall the transitory nature of life (the second of which is 'In the midst of life we are in death...');
- the Prayer of Committal.

There are three forms of this prayer. The first is for the burial of a body. The second is not technically a committal, but

> now, in preparation for burial,
> we give his/her body to be cremated

in a prayer that consigns the body to the flames while keeping the formal committal for a later time when the ashes will be interred. A third form is a committal at the crematorium, when no interment of ashes is to follow soon after.

Finally there is the 'Dismissal', the entire text of which is optional and will depend on pastoral circumstances. But the Lord's Prayer may be said here, rather than earlier, the *Nunc Dimittis* may be used and there is a collection of prayers, including 'God be in my head', some of which are congregational. Either *Nunc Dimittis* or 'God be in my head' might be sung. There are four ending prayers, one of which is a blessing.

There is a separate form of service for the funeral of a child, with suggested resources differing according to the age of the child. The basic service follows the same form, even though the texts vary, prayers of penitence are not included, white is the usual liturgical colour and an important note challenges an all too common assumption about the unsuitability of bringing children to a funeral when it states that 'the

201

presence of young children at a child's funeral should be welcomed and their needs should be borne in mind'. Although this refers principally to the text and the address, they also have needs in terms of 'doing something'. It may be sprinkling the coffin or it may be lighting candles from the paschal flame.

A funeral eucharist

The *Common Worship* provisions also print in full a funeral service within the eucharist. Although this will obviously not be the norm, there is no better way of saying farewell to a Christian person than within the eucharist, where we are conscious both of the merits of the death and resurrection of Christ and also of the communion of saints. The fact that the main rite has a eucharistic structure makes the joining of the two very natural. The Liturgy of the Sacrament is inserted between the Prayers and the Commendation.

Although the possibility of the eucharist at the funeral is desirable, there is also the possibility of the eucharist before the funeral, with the coffin brought into the church the night before the funeral and the eucharist being celebrated that evening or next morning. This is a sensible way forward when there are many coming to the funeral who would find the eucharistic context difficult. But it remains something of a second best. A funeral eucharist is a powerful Easter liturgy.

The twenty-minute funeral

However much we may want to encourage longer and richer funeral liturgies, we look foolish if our funeral provisions cannot be used satisfactorily in the limited setting of the crematorium chapel where the requirement may be a service of about twenty minutes. Although there are other ways of ordering the service within this timescale, the following provides a suitable model:

- a single sentence of scripture ('I am the resurrection...');
- greeting and introduction;
- opening prayer for the mourners;
- a psalm (sung in a metrical version or said) or a hymn;
- scripture reading;
- brief sermon (incorporating the tribute);
- the prayers as set, including penitence, concluding with the Lord's Prayer and the collect;
- another hymn (optional; perhaps only two or three verses);

- commendation (with silent sprinkling by the minister only);
- committal;
- blessing.

If the layout and numbers allow, the congregation might, even in the crematorium, be gathered around the coffin for the commendation and committal. More time would always make for a better service, but here is a format that will meet the purposes of the service in a way that is pastoral and liturgical.

The less faithful and the unchurched

There is sometimes anxiety among clergy and others who officiate at funerals about the inappropriateness of the Christian funeral service for someone whose faith was never known and whose connection with the Church was tenuous or non-existent. The fundamental thing that has to be said is that the Church cannot offer anything but the Christian funeral service. To have two versions, one for the faithful and one for the less faithful, would be to make the Church a judge. We need to use the liturgy with confidence, knowing that God himself is the judge. But we do need to exercise the many options in the rite intelligently. Some prayers are more suitable than others for those whose faith was hidden or weak. There is a rich resource of prayers and we can choose well. The minister also has the opportunity to engage a little with the issue in the sermon, so that the rite has integrity. ('N found the Christian faith very hard to accept . . . nevertheless in the words of this service we entrust him to the God in whom the Church believes . . .' or appropriate words along these lines.)

There is one objective question relating to the status of the deceased. Had he or she been baptized? It is not a question that clergy always ask, but it is appropriate to do so, for some of the texts have a baptismal character and need amendment if the deceased was not baptized, and certainly the use of the sprinkling of water, as a recalling of baptism, is quite inappropriate in such a case.

Staged rites

This chapter has focused on the main funeral liturgy, whether in church or elsewhere. But grieving is a process and *Common Worship* provides a rich treasury of simple services and resources for use through the continuum from the time of dying to the burial of ashes (whether this is the setting for the committal or not) and even beyond that in memorial services (for which a sample service is provided) and annual commemorations. Some of this is domestic liturgy – at the time of death, on hearing of someone's death, on the night before the funeral, on arriving home after it. In any one case the minister will use only one or two of the many possibilities, but we need to encourage people to turn to these resources even when there is no minister and no formal liturgical gathering. Especially with church families, the minister should take the opportunity to talk through with them which stages they might like to mark by prayer together.

27

Welcome, Blessing and Commission

Welcoming a new priest or deacon

When a new parish priest is instituted there is a diocesan form of service. But there are many occasions when new clergy arrive in the parish without an episcopal service. It may be a new deacon ordained in the cathedral, a priest licensed in the bishop's chapel, or a newly retired priest with permission to officiate in the parish. The parish very properly wants to give a welcome, probably at the eucharist. The occasion is not one of commissioning. The bishop has done that already. It is an occasion of welcome, acceptance and the pledge of support. The constituent parts of such a welcome might be:

- The parish priest presents the new minister to the people;
- The people extend their welcome and promise their prayerful support;
- Symbols of ministry among them are presented by lay people;
- The new minister greets the people;
- The new minister exercises his/her new ministry as the liturgy proceeds.

There are three areas where the minister has a clear role – teaching, pastoral care and the sacramental ministry. For a priest these might be represented by a Bible, the oil of healing and chalice and paten. In an ordination, Bible and sometimes chalice and paten are given by the bishop, but here by the people as an indication that they will accept these ministries among them. For a deacon the gifts might be different – jug and bowl and towel as a sign of service, for instance.

It is also important that in the words that accompany the giving of symbols the picture of ministry that is given is one of sharing, both the sharing among the ordained ministers in the parish, but also among the whole Christian body. Texts like these, for instance:

> We give you this sign.
> Be among us as a preacher and teacher.
> Share with us the task of discerning God's word in our day.
> Help us proclaim it boldly in our community.

> We give you this sign.
> Be among us as a pastor and counsellor.
> Share with us the task of serving our neighbours
> Help us spread God's love in our community.

> We give you this sign.
> Be among us as a deacon and servant.
> Share with our clergy their duties and their joys.
> Help us worship in spirit and in truth.

Ministries and tasks

Should there be a commissioning for people exercising particular ministries within the congregation? This has already been discussed in chapter 3 where the conclusion was that such commissioning should be minimal and, when it does happen, should relate to the fundamental baptismal calling. But one of the reasons why there must not be too rigid a policy is that it would not take seriously enough the need for those who go out from the Church to minister in its name to have some form of validation to make their ministry acceptable. An argument can be made for a distinction between gifts and functions within the body, for which there is no commissioning, and ministries on behalf of the Church to the wider community beyond, for which some simple commission that gives authority is appropriate.

When there is to be a commissioning at the eucharist, the procedure can be quite simple. Prayers for those to be commissioned are offered in the prayers of intercession. After the distribution or post communion prayer, those to be commissioned come to stand before the priest. The priest:

- spells out very simply the task they are to do;
- asks them whether they believe they are called to do it and whether they will undertake it sensitively and faithfully, and they reply;
- asks the remainder of the congregation whether it is their will that these people should exercise this ministry and whether they will

support them with their prayers, and the people respond graciously and warmly;

- blesses those to be commissioned for their new work and sends
them out in the power of Jesus Christ and in the name of the
Church.

Gifts

There are occasions when gifts are given to the church – a new Bible, a
chalice, an embroidered kneeler – and have to be used for the first time.
How is the gift to be dedicated or blessed? The most satisfactory answer is
by use. Its holiness does not depend on words said over it or water
sprinkled upon it. Its holiness may depend in part on the loving labour
that has gone into it or the costly sacrifice that has bought it, but mainly
its holiness is in proportion to the reverence attached to it as part of the
'holy things' of the Church's worship. But where some outward sign is
required, it is appropriate for the gift to be brought to the altar, at the
same time as bread and wine and the collection of money, carried by the
donor unless it is anonymous, or, if it has been made locally, by the
person who has made it. It is then placed on or near the altar.

If words are needed, then there needs to be thanksgiving for the
generosity of the donor and the skill of the artist or craftsman, a
remembrance of anyone in whose memory it may be given, and the
calling down of a blessing. Some people worry about the blessing of
inanimate objects, but the religion of the incarnation takes seriously the
part the material plays in conveying God's gifts to his creatures. Our
prayer is really that the gift may, by God's grace, be a blessing to us. In
praying that we recognize that, however much we, naturally, focus on the
gift, God's grace will be focused on us. The prayer might be along these
lines:

> Blessed are you, O Lord our God,
> from you comes all that is good.
> We praise you for this gift,
> for the generosity of those who have given it
> and the skill of those who have made it.
> Make it useful in the service of your Church.
> And now send down your blessing upon us
> as in you name we bless and dedicate this gift
> (in thankful memory of *N* and)
> to your praise and glory,
> Father, Son and Holy Spirit.
> **Blessed be God for ever.**

A sprinkling with water would also signify a claiming for Christ.

There will of course be larger gifts that require a more significant dedication – new windows, a new bell, a restored organ – and an altar is always consecrated by the bishop.

28

Liturgy in the Home

Blessing a house

The minister is sometimes asked to bless a home. Usually this is when the house is new, but it may also be requested when a new family moves into a new house. This is entirely appropriate, for it is the family that makes the house a home and the prayers of blessing should be as much a blessing of those who live in it as of the house itself. There is a long tradition of going from room to room, saying in each a prayer suitable to that room's function, and sprinkling it with water. *Pastoral Prayers* provides a fine set of prayers. It is also appropriate that, where there are to be any religious symbols in the house, whether crucifix, icon or other picture, they should be put in place as part of the blessing of the house. It is also appropriate to bless the house by celebrating the eucharist within it, with the family inviting their Christian neighbours and those who will enjoy the hospitality of the house to be present and to share in a party afterwards. Where the eucharist can be round the dining table, all the better, the readings chosen and read by members of the family.

The home and the Christian year

The Promise of His Glory introduces a section of Advent prayers to be used at home with the words:

> Prayer in the home has played an important part in both Jewish and Christian tradition and can deeply enrich our grasp of the grace of God made known to us in Jesus Christ. Imaginative patterns of domestic prayer need not be limited to homes with young children.

That is well said, but it has to be added that in most parishes little is done to encourage communal prayer at home. The parish does have opportunities here. If there is an Advent wreath in church, let the families be encouraged to have one at home. If the prayer that greets the lighting of the new candle each week appears on the Sunday notice sheet, people can be encouraged to use it again when they light the candle at home. If people take home a cross of palm on Palm Sunday, they can be encouraged to place it somewhere significant in their home through Holy Week with appropriate words. If they bring home candles at Candlemas and after the Easter Liturgy, they can be encouraged to relight the candles at home or even to find a way of bringing the light from the church to their home without it going out. And through seasonal graces for use at meal times (*The Promise of His Glory* gives four) the Christian year can be marked in simple ways at home. This is just the beginning, but it is worth beginning to reclaim something that is a present-day equivalent of the 'family prayers' of the past that have been almost entirely lost.

Holy Communion for the housebound

The *Common Worship* Wholeness and Healing provision authorizes two ways of ensuring that the sick and housebound receive Holy Communion. One is by the priest presiding at a celebration of the eucharist in their home, and all four forms of the eucharistic rite are reproduced in simple and shorter versions for this purpose.

When someone is ill or housebound over a long period of time, they will be helped by the occasional full celebration. But the other model is better as the norm. It is the bringing to the sick or housebound of the sacrament consecrated at the main eucharist of the week. Near the beginning of the rite of 'distribution of communion to those not present at the celebration' the minister says:

> The Church of God, of which we are members, has taken bread and wine and given thanks over them according to our Lord's command. These holy gifts are now offered to us that, with faith and thanksgiving, we may share in the communion of the body and blood of Christ.

Through this way of reception the communicant is joined to the community and drawn into the celebration at which they would be present if health allowed. The ideal is that at the principal eucharist of Sunday, at the same time as the bread is broken for the congregation to share, some should be set aside, with consecrated wine also, to be taken to the housebound either straight away or at the end of the service. This will nearly always be undertaken by lay communion ministers who go from the service to the sick person's house and share with them the simple authorized service. But if the visit to the home is delayed to a later time or day in the week (perhaps so that the parish priest may be involved in this ministry) and the consecrated elements are reserved in an aumbry, this is still 'extended communion' and a holding of the sick person within the fellowship of the worshipping community. Those who will receive in this way from the Sunday eucharist should always be prayed for in the intercessions at that service to strengthen that sense of incorporation. And the renewing of the sacrament in the aumbry should be done quite openly at that main service so that people may be put in mind of those who receive at home.

Those who are to take the sacrament to the housebound need to be carefully instructed, not only in the reverent conduct of the service in the home, but also in the need to develop a genuine pastoral relationship with those to whom they take the sacrament. The communion minister should go straight from the service and, on arrival, should not delay long in 'chat' before beginning the home liturgy, though sometimes a pastoral conversation with the communicant about his or her condition, fears, anxieties or joys, which can be gathered up in brief intercessions, will be helpful. How much of the authorized service needs to be used will depend partly on the health of the housebound person and partly on the extent to which he or she will have 'read the service' while the eucharist has been going on in church. The rite assumes communion in both kinds, 'but where necessary may be received in one kind, whether of bread, or, where the communicant cannot receive solid food, wine'. The liturgy over, the minister should hardly ever leave without a time of conversation with the housebound person, and very often with the family, who frequently are carrying a strain in giving care. Before leaving the minister should consume any of the sacrament that remains unless it is being returned immediately to the aumbry in the church.

Ministry to the seriously ill and dying

There is much more to pastoral care of those who are ill and those who are near to death than simply a liturgical ministry. But prayer and worship do have an important place and, the more sick the person is, the more likely that familiar liturgical words and actions will help and conversation and counselling fail.

In ministry to a sick person likely to recover, liturgical ministry is an extension of that ministry of wholeness and healing that is celebrated in the church and that is described in chapter 25. The minister needs to ensure that, through the stages of the illness the sick person:

- hears the scriptures read and is given the opportunity to pray with others on a regular basis;
- is encouraged to confess their sins and to receive absolution;

211

- has the opportunity to receive Holy Communion regularly;
- is given the time to talk through anxieties and questions of faith and even to reflect on their mortality;
- receives the laying on of hands with prayer as often as seems helpful;
- is offered the ministry of anointing, after careful teaching that this is for the healing and strengthening of the Holy Spirit rather than in preparation for death, if possible at a turning point in the illness;
- is made aware of the regular prayer of the church community for their return to health.

Several of these elements may happen on one occasion, but illness is hardly ever pastorally neat and things often happen in an unexpected order. There may be more than one person involved in visiting the sick person at home (and it is even more complicated if they are in hospital). It is important that they communicate with one another and that there is an overall plan to ensure that the proper ministry is given.

In relation to the dying, much of the same still applies. There are few death-bed scenes where a person makes a confession and an act of faith, is anointed, receives Holy Communion and dies as the priest says words of commendation and farewell. But there are many people who, in the days and weeks before they die, experience many of these things, though sometimes in a different order. When people are near to death, the need for the occasional not too hurried visit with time for pastoral conversation gives way to a new need for more frequent shorter visits, when the minister does not converse but prays out loud, using familiar words that the dying person will know and may possibly try to say, and also sits sometimes in silence and holds their hand. In the course of a series of such brief visits the wise pastor will judge the moment to use prayers of penitence or an affirmation of faith or when to give communion or to lay hands or to anoint. It is more by instinct than by a rule book. The key thing is that, as far as both prayers and touch are concerned, it must carry on even when the person appears to be unconscious. The priest never knows what is getting through and how the power of God is at work.

Though the chief need for the words is that they should be familiar – that core of liturgical text discussed in chapter 2 – there is also the need for the words to ring true. If we anoint a dying person, we may speak of healing, but not of recovery, and we need to have the courage to speak of the healing of death. If we speak of strength, we need to have the courage to say that it is strength for a journey from this world. All around a dying person are people who dare not tell the truth. The priest must tell the truth, with gentleness in an almost matter of fact way, and kindle faith and confidence for the journey.

PART SIX

The Christian Year

29

Advent

༄

Beginning with the end

Part Six of this book looks at the principal seasons of the Christian year in turn. It does so in the light of what has already been written in chapter 7 about the potential of the cycle of the Church's feasts and seasons to deepen our Christian experience and to conform us to Christ's pattern. *Common Worship* provision will be complete when it includes a Book of Times and Seasons, a reworking and refining of the seasonal material already made available to the Church in *Patterns for Worship, Lent, Holy Week, Easter, The Promise of His Glory* and *Enriching the Christian Year*, all of which enable the seasons, with their different moods and flavours, to be enriched by words and actions distinctive to that season. (For more detailed consideration of the seasons, and especially for some account of their history, readers should turn to *Welcoming the Light of Christ* and *Waiting for the Risen Christ*, commentaries on the Church of England provision by Kenneth Stevenson and the present writer.)

The Christian year begins on the First Sunday of Advent. On that day the Sunday lectionary moves into a new 'year' – A, B or C. The annual cycle has come back to its beginning. The season of Advent is between 22 and 28 days in length, depending on the day of the week when Christmas Day falls. It always has four Sundays, though the last of them is sometimes Christmas Eve. It is a difficult season to sustain, for there is always the pressure to anticipate Christmas, but in terms of structure the season has two parts. The first runs until 16 December, the second is a kind of countdown to Christmas, beginning on 17 December, and from that date the lectionary provision is not only by calendar date, rather than day of the week, but also engages in the gospel of the day with the passages in the first chapter of Matthew and Luke that bring us to the birth of Jesus.

Advent is essentially about preparing for the Lord's coming. As such it

215

can easily degenerate into a season of getting ready for Christmas. Yet the coming to which the season points is, as far as the tradition is concerned, principally about the second coming at the end of time, and a primary Advent theme is judgement. The Advent hymns that people love to sing, with their 'Come, Lord, come', are looking to that coming of Christ at the end of time, rather than to the coming of Christmas. But it is not only the modern mind that sees in Advent a pathway to Christmas. The liturgy of the season has always allowed these two strata to lie together and the two themes to interact. What is wrong with the contemporary approach is that it focuses so much on preparing to celebrate the first coming that it has no thought for the second. Yet, for all the difficulty of much eschatological thought to the modern mind, a Christianity that does not engage with the theology of the end is not true to the gospel that Jesus proclaimed and will not begin to understand him. At least until 16 December we have to ensure there is engagement with those fundamental Advent issues. In the second shorter part of Advent, from 17 December, there is something of a change. The second coming theme does not disappear, but it fades a little into the background as the Church tunes in to Christmas.

The mood of the season – well picked up in the hymnody for these weeks – is a curious amalgam of hope, penitence, expectancy and joy. The key to it lies in the fact that a season that looks for the return of the Lord to judge will always have a sober and solemn flavour to it and a call to penitence, so that we may have confidence to stand before him when he comes, and yet the scriptures do not so much fear the return of the Lord, as yearn for it, and the Church awaits him with joy. Sober joy and heightening expectation are the marks of the season, whichever coming it focuses on, and the cry of the Church '*Marana tha*' ('The Lord is coming'). Though part of preparation will always be penitence, Advent has never been a penitential season in quite the way that Lent is. A long tradition omits the *Gloria* at the eucharist, but there is no banishment of *alleluias* as there is in Lent.

The calendar keeps saints' days to a minimum during Advent in order that the spirit of the season is not undermined. Sometimes St Andrew's Day slips into an early Advent. But December has few saints except those that have Advent associations – Nicholas, the origin of Santa Claus, the Conception of Mary, with the annunciation story as its gospel, and Lucy, whose name means light and whose feast falls on almost the darkest day of the year. The Prayer Book keeps St Thomas on 21 December, but it is almost bound to be neglected there and cannot be kept on a Sunday, and so the alternative date of 3 July is better.

An Advent liturgy

On the first Sunday of Advent itself there is no distinctive liturgical rite to mark the new liturgical year, though the change of colour, the use of the Advent seasonal material and the choice of music will indicate a contrast with the previous week. However, there has built up over the last few decades in many churches a custom of a special Advent service exploring some of the Advent themes, usually in the evening, often involving candlelight and engaging with the 'darkness and light' theme, in a big church frequently involving movement, and more often than not advertised as an 'Advent Carol Service'.

Such services have a variety of forms, though there are common features. For few of them is 'Advent Carol Service' the most helpful name, for carol singing in the popular sense is one thing that will not happen. Cathedrals can speak of 'The Advent Procession', but that implies space and movement. 'The Advent Liturgy' is a possibility, but in some places would sound too grand. *The Promise of His Glory* provided ideas about the shape of such a liturgy as well as a series of sequences of themes and readings. Something along these lines might meet the need:

- the blessing and sharing of light;
- an opening responsory;
- greeting, introduction and opening prayer;
- sequence of music and readings;
- the gospel reading;
- prayers of intercession;
- Our Father;
- the blessing;
- a final responsory.

This is only the bare bones of the rite. Although 'darkness and light' is an obvious theme, it can be overdone and, even when there is the use of light moving through the church, other themes can be explored. There may be non-biblical readings that people want to include, but in this of all seasons the Old Testament provides an unsurpassed treasury of readings. Whatever the theme that is followed, the gospel reading can provide the opportunity to signal the approach of Christmas with the use of some part of the first chapter of Luke. The key, of course, is the music; not just that it has an Advent flavour, but that the choices accord with the sequence of readings. In a service such as this, well advertised, there is real opportunity to offer a popular service at the beginning of the Church's year that may well draw in people not seen every week and which will certainly open up the hearts of Christian people for what is to come in the following weeks through Advent to Christmas and Epiphany.

The Advent wreath

With its origins in Germany and its associations in Scandinavia with St Lucy's Day, the Advent ring, wreath or crown (variously called) with its greenery and five (sometimes four) candles has established itself in England, both in churches and at home. A series of themes has been attached to its candles and a variety of forms provided for lighting them during the liturgy on the four Sundays of Advent and on Christmas Day. *The Promise of His Glory* identifies the candles with those who prepared for the coming of Christ:

Advent 1   The Patriarchs
Advent 2   The Prophets
Advent 3   The Baptist
Advent 4   The Virgin

The identification is with the Lord himself on Christmas Day. Three prayers are provided for each day, the first formal and liturgical in the style of a 'blessing of light', the second a narrative and didactic prayer, the third short and congregational.

Each church needs to decide where in the church the wreath should be and therefore its size. Very often a church has a wreath of domestic proportions that makes very little statement in a large building. A church might consider a hanging wreath or a specially made candlestick standing in its own space, and the liturgy on the Sundays in Advent might begin or end with everyone moving to that space for the lighting of the additional candle. Another custom worth considering is the use of purple candles in Advent, in line with the liturgical colour of the season, and then a change to red or white candles at Christmas, all of them burning for the principal services until Candlemas.

The Advent antiphons

The countdown to Christmas, beginning on 17 December, is marked partly by the choice of gospel reading from the first chapter of Matthew and Luke, but also by an antiphon, which practically becomes the name of the day, addressing Christ in a series of Old Testament titles and inviting him to come without delay. They are familiar because of their incorporation in the hymn 'O come, O come, Emmanuel', but their origin is as an antiphon before and after the Song of Mary at Evening Prayer. The new weekday lectionary allocates psalms and readings at Evening Prayer through those seven days to complement the antiphon, so it is appropriately used then, but can also form the pre-gospel acclamation at the eucharist or be adapted for use in a variety of ways. *The Promise of His Glory* builds an Advent penitential rite around the antiphons.

The sequence runs thus:

Date	Gospel	Antiphon	
17 Dec.	Matthew 1.1–17	*O Sapientia*	O Wisdom
18 Dec.	Matthew 1.18–24	*O Adonai*	O Lord of Lords
19 Dec.	Luke 1.5–25	*O Radix Jesse*	O Root of Jesse
20 Dec.	Luke 1.26–38	*O Clavis David*	O Key of David
21 Dec.	Luke 1.39–45	*O Oriens*	O Morning Star
22 Dec.	Luke 1.46–56	*O Rex Gentium*	O King of the nations
23 Dec.	Luke 1.57–66	*O Emmanuel*	O Emmanuel
24 Dec.	Luke 1.67–79		

(There are versions of the antiphons that introduce an additional antiphon addressed to Mary, *O virgo virginum*, on 23 December, pushing all the others back a day, but this is best ignored.)

Anticipating Christmas

There is a major pastoral and liturgical issue in most parishes about the extent to which Christmas celebrations should be allowed to begin in Advent. On the one hand there is so much of importance to celebrate among the Advent themes that it is a loss if they are squeezed out. On the other hand here is the one time in the Christian year when over a sustained period of days people on the edge of the church community, and even outside it, are engaging with a major Christian story and truth, and it is foolishness not to grasp the opportunity. We have to learn to live creatively with the tension – to relax into a school nativity play in the church one afternoon, but then return to the spirit of Advent for Evening Prayer, in a city-centre church into shoppers singing carols one lunchtime and celebrating a eucharist with John the Baptist as the focus at noon next day. We need to do this confidently and without a sense of unease. The pastoral and evangelistic opportunities are simply too great to be missed.

But we need to have our set of criteria nevertheless. They will differ from place to place. But we might want to say that, for the regular services, no carols until the afternoon or evening of Advent 4, no tree or crib in the church till 17 December, no baby in the crib till Christmas Eve, and no 'O come all ye faithful', John 1.1–14 or white vestments till

219

the midnight mass. Where we do have some guidelines like these, it is never to be 'spoilsport', but in order to hold some things back to heighten the anticipation and to ensure that when we come to Christmas night and Christmas morning there is a real sense of climax.

30

Christmas to Candlemas

Forty incarnation days

Even if it sometimes seems that in the commercial world Christmas ends on 24 December, most people still hold on to the idea of the 'twelve days of Christmas' which bring us to the feast of the Epiphany on 6 January. It is at this point that people become less clear what is happening to the liturgical year. *Common Worship* is clear that at that stage we enter a second phase of the celebration of the incarnation in a season called Epiphany that will take us on until the forty days from Christmas Day bring us to the Presentation of Christ in the Temple, often known as 'Candlemas'. So we have forty days, part Christmas, part Epiphany, but all reflecting on the coming of Jesus Christ into the world and the revelation of his glory through a number of key events at the beginning of his life or his ministry.

The origins of these seasons is, of course, complex, for in the feast of the Epiphany we are dealing with both an Eastern alternative date for the Western Christmas and also a second feast in the West with an emphasis other than the story of the Lord's birth. But that emphasis is not, in the tradition, narrowly about the story of the magi, but more broadly about the revelation of Christ's nature and glory, and particularly in three moments, of which the visit of the magi is one, but only alongside the baptism of the Lord and the turning of water into wine at Cana. Other stories also become associated with this season – the twelve-year-old Jesus in the temple and the calling of the first disciples, for instance, so that there is rich provision of gospel material to explore through the weeks of January.

An early decision to establish the timetable of the season has to be made in relation to the celebration of both the Epiphany and Candlemas. Epiphany is 6 January, but in any year when there is a second Sunday of Christmas (i.e. a Sunday between 1 and 5 January), it may be moved to that Sunday, but not to the following Sunday where it would clash with the important celebration of the Baptism of Christ. Similarly, Candlemas, properly on 2 February (the fortieth day from Christmas Day), may be kept instead on the Sunday between 28 January and 3 February. There is also a decision to be made about the 'Christmas saints'. St Stephen, St John and the Holy Innocents, if they fall on the First Sunday of Christmas, may be celebrated then or may be moved to the next free weekday. The argument for keeping them on the Sunday is strong – 'on the feast of Stephen' the celebration of the first martyr makes a telling point in relation to the birth of the Saviour, John has key insights in relation to the incarnation, and the story of the holy innocents prevents a decline into sentimentality.

The integrity and unity of the forty-day period can be affirmed in a number of ways through the liturgy. The liturgical colour is white throughout (with gold optionally for the three principal feasts and the Baptism). Although the Christmas decorations will no doubt be put away after the feast of the Epiphany, the crib should remain until Candlemas and be used at points during the season as a focus for prayer, and, if the Advent wreath has turned into a Christmas candlestand, this also can appropriately be kept in use until Candlemas and become the source of light for the Candlemas candles. It is through the lectionary and through the choice of music that the forty days are most obviously allowed both to develop with each new story, but also to hold on to the seasonal identity, and some (not all) of the carols of Christmas and Epiphany remain appropriate all the way till Candlemas.

Celebrating Christmas

There are important questions to be addressed in relation to Christmas services, for the aim will be to attract as many people as possible into services that will meet their need and present the gospel to them. But the local church will not want to overstretch itself, divide its numbers too much or end up with nobody on Christmas Day. There are probably five major elements to the Christmas celebrations in most churches:

- Carol service;
- Crib service, sometimes with nativity play, preparing families, especially children, for Christmas;
- Christingle service;
- Christmas midnight mass;
- Christmas morning (whether eucharist or not).

Each has its own style and to some extent its own 'target' congregation. But especially in a small community to hold all these within two or three days will overstretch the church and leave some of the services poorly attended. For instance, a family carol service or a crib service at dusk on Christmas Eve may fill the church, but leave it half empty at midnight and again next morning, and something has gone wrong when attendance on Christmas Eve is greater than in the middle of the night and on Christmas Day itself. The reality is that most people will not come more than once in any twenty-four hours, so the services need to be spaced appropriately. There is no one pattern that applies everywhere, but either carol service or crib service could be candidates for the Fourth Sunday of Advent, some services in town centres might be timed in relation to work and shopping, and the Christingle might well move back to the beginning of Advent or forward to the New Year or to Epiphany.

What of the shape and content of the Carol Service? The King's College Cambridge model of nine lessons and carols has an enormous hold in many places, with the lessons read by representatives of different groups within the church (or, better, groups within the wider community). The strength of the King's approach is in the firm use of scripture and in the insistence that the service tells the story in a logical sequence (all the better if the carols are chosen with care to fit the readings). The weakness is in the way that scripture is used and the integrity of the different authors somewhat violated in the search for a coherent story, in the difficulty of finding appropriate carols and songs to accompany the many Old Testament passages, in the inflexibility of the form and in the brevity and formality of the element of prayer. In reaction to this some carol services, especially school ones, have departed entirely from this style, reduced the scriptural content so much that the story is hardly told and added in much new material more about Christmas customs in many lands than about the birth of Jesus. Some fresh thinking is needed. Perhaps the core elements of a carol service should be:

- greeting, introduction and opening prayer;
- a reading from the Old Testament;
- a reading from the New Testament reflecting on the meaning of the Christmas story (e.g. Galatians 4.4–7, Hebrews 1.1–5 or 1 John 4.7–14);
- a reading from the gospels;
- prayers of intercession and thanksgiving, perhaps focused at the crib;
- The Lord's Prayer;
- homily;
- blessing;
- a variety of hymns, carols and songs.

223

In the past we have usually thought a sermon unnecessary; the story tells itself. But the truth is that today, even if people still know the story, they have little clue to its meaning for their lives. We miss an opportunity if there is not a short sermon at every carol service. This outline of core elements ought to apply not only to the parish's own carol service, but to those for schools and organizations coming to the church for their own carol service. Input by the minister into these services is important to ensure the core elements are present and that the service has shape and direction, and so that, in among everything else, the story is told and the meaning unfolded.

The Promise of His Glory has provided the Church with special service forms for a Crib Service (it assumes a time on Christmas Eve), a Christingle Service (and here allows the possibility of giving it an Advent, Christmas, Epiphany or Candlemas flavour), for the eucharist of Christmas (whether celebrated at night or in the morning) and for a family service on Christmas Day. All of these can be used almost as they stand or used as resource material. The Christmas midnight service, though it needs to be within the provisions of the eucharistic rites, calls for special treatment also. The special elements might include:

- a procession to the crib to bless it at the beginning of the rite;
- special prayers of penitence focused at the crib;
- a carol with an Old Testament flavour in place of the psalm;
- the special intercession text printed in both *Patterns of Worship* and *The Promise of His Glory*;
- the extended gospel acclamation found in the *Promise* service;
- the use of one of the eucharistic prayers that can include the extended Christmas preface in *Common Worship* – Prayers A, B and E;
- a more generous use of carols through the service than the normal number of hymns in the eucharist;
- the solemn blessing printed in both *Pattern* and *Promise*;
- the reading of Luke 2.1–14 at the gospel point, but a procession to the door at the end to read John 1.1–14, symbolically proclaiming the birth of Christ and its meaning to the world.

The new year

1 January is the Naming of Jesus, following the gospel account that he was circumcised and given his name on the eighth day. It is also New Year's Day and the coincidence is entirely appropriate, for the Church needs to name each new year for Jesus. Until the midnight mass of

Christmas Eve took over as the principal occasion of a night service, there had been a strong tradition in the Church of England as elsewhere of the 'Watch Night Service' on New Year's Eve. This has disappeared in most churches, though sometimes there is a short liturgy in churches where the church bells are to ring the new year in. Liturgical provision at the end of 1999 for the new century and millennium may have given new ideas and enthusiasm for new year liturgy. This would be a good thing, for the Church, however much it may regard the new calendar year as a secular observance, is ill-advised to ignore an occasion when there are people wanting to see a spiritual element celebrated. At very least there ought surely to be a service in every church on New Year's Eve or Day. The eucharist of the Naming of Jesus at midday might be appropriate, with new year material from *The Promise of His Glory* or re-use of some of the material produced in the millennium *New Start* books.

Celebrating Epiphany

The use of the seasonal material of the Epiphany right through the season has been underlined already, but what of the feast day itself (whether on 6 January or on a Sunday in the days before)? As a principal feast it requires a celebration of the eucharist; that might very well be supplemented by a parish Epiphany party. *The Promise of His Glory* provides special texts and among them three acclamations for the presentation of the gifts of the magi. After the greeting of peace there might be a procession of the three gifts to the altar, each received and acclaimed using the texts provided. It is better if the gifts, once presented, can be used. If the 'gold' is the chalice or flagon for the eucharist, that can immediately be put into use. The incense can burn before the altar – and it does not need a thurible or even a custom of using incense in worship regularly for this to be appropriate at Epiphany. The 'myrrh' is more of a problem. If it really is myrrh, it can be placed on the altar, but has no use. Nevertheless, myrrh as an ointment of healing – the acclamation speaks of 'medicine to heal our sickness and the leaves of the tree of life for the healing of the nations' – suggests the possibility of the use of the oil of healing and even a rite of anointing later in the service. Where a procession of these three gifts is not appropriate, there might be a procession of the figures of the magi to the crib, but this is not as satisfactory.

The Baptism of Christ is celebrated on the first Sunday of Epiphany (except in that rare year when 6 January is a Sunday and then, for that one year only, the Baptism is kept on the Monday). Obviously more general Epiphany themes will be present, but the day does have a clear focus. It is an obvious day for a baptism within the liturgy. *The Promise of His Glory* provides material for use on this day and part of it is a gathering at the font, a prayer over the water and the renewal of baptismal commitment. To do this on this feast day, with its seasonal associations with new creation and new birth, is to celebrate a different aspect of baptism from the death and resurrection emphasis that is natural at Easter.

The Promise of His Glory also provides a more extensive Epiphany Liturgy that holds together the three major Epiphany themes – the magi, the Baptism and the miracle at Cana. With incense, water and wine as the signs of these three wonders, and with processions to the crib, the font and the altar, there is the basis for an exciting liturgy on the move. The *Promise* text is wordy and needs lightening with Epiphany hymns and carols, but, celebrated on a Sunday in the Epiphany season, it has a lot to teach and much to engender thankfulness for the revelation of Christ's glory.

Celebrating Candlemas

The *Common Worship* calendar makes the Presentation of Christ in the Temple a principal feast and pivotal to the shape of the Christian year. Because it has not been that, certainly in the minds of most church people, there is work to be done in establishing its place. There is a case for moving it to the Sunday between 28 January and 3 February, though a rite that involves candlelight can be more effective in the evening than at a morning service. This is a many-layered feast, with its rich gospel story, and not every layer can be brought out on every occasion. There is:

- the theme of presentation;
- the purification of Mary;
- the witness of old Simeon and Anna, the old order welcoming the new;
- the theme of light as Simeon speaks of the one who will be the light to enlighten the nations;
- the theme of judgement as the Lord comes suddenly to his temple (with echoes of the prophet Malachi);
- the bitter-sweet nature of the feast, with Simeon's talk of the child 'destined for the fall and rising of many' and of the sword that will pierce Mary's soul too.

Candlemas is a key day in three ways. It completes the forty days of Christmas and Epiphany, it celebrates this story rich in its layers of meaning and it is a pivotal day – bitter-sweet when, having looked back a last time to Christmas, we turn towards Lent and the passion.

The Promise of His Glory has provided rites and resources (including a complete Candlemas eucharist) and the *Common Worship* eucharist also has proper material for the day. The elements that might be brought into a service (or perhaps in some places spread through two services, one morning and one evening) are:

- the blessing of light and the holding of candles at least for the reading of the gospel (Luke 2.22–40);
- the use of the crib as a focus of prayer for the last time;
- a procession of candles, whether at the beginning, or part-way through or at the end of the service;
- the singing of the Song of Simeon (*Nunc Dimittis*), if necessary in a metrical version;
- the reading of John 1.1–14 at the end of the liturgy, a recovery on this one day of the old catholic practice of reading this at the end of every eucharist, but here marking the end of the incarnation season;
- a text, possibly at the font, that takes leave of Epiphany and turns towards Lent and Easter (*The Promise of His Glory* gives such a text).

Whether on 2 February or on the nearest Sunday, Evening Prayer of the Presentation marks the end. The white and gold vestments are put away (it is green tomorrow) and the crib is taken down. It will be 'ordinary time' from next morning until that gives way to Lent.

31

Lent and Holy Week

∾

Forty days to Easter

The purpose of Lent is to prepare people for the annual celebration of the death and resurrection of the Lord. It was not originally and is still not intended to be a re-enactment of the forty days in the desert at the beginning of his ministry and, significantly, the gospel that recounts that story, which is only one among the readings for Lent, is not that appointed for the first day of the season. The thrust forward to Easter is always present in Lent. It is not a static season, but a dynamic one as it moves resolutely towards the cross and the resurrection. The Lent hymn, 'Forty days and forty nights . . .', for all that it leads us off on a false trail by its opening lines, at least recognizes at the end that where we are heading is to 'appear at the eternal Eastertide'. Behind the mood of the season lies the experience of the two specific groups for whom the season was first developed. One of these was the group of those who had been excommunicated because of grievous sin. For them the emphasis was on penitence. The other was the group of catechumens preparing for their baptism at Easter. For them, their long period of learning almost complete, the emphasis was on spiritual growth as they entered as deeply as they could into the mystery of Christ's passion and resurrection. This background gives us the flavour of Lent. It is a time for penitence, but also for growth, and both in order to enter more deeply into the mystery of Christ. Yet George Herbert called Lent a 'feast' and one of the eucharistic prefaces for Lent speaks of preparing 'with joyful hearts and minds'. For the Christian the exercise of discipline and of turning to the cross, though it may mean sorrow for sin, is always a joyful acceptance of the goodness and forgiveness of God. So there is no place for liturgy that is depressing, dreary and dull; austere, but never dull.

In terms of the shape of the season, a word needs to be said about Passiontide. Lent does not give way after four and a half weeks to

Passiontide. Lent continues until it is caught up in the celebration of the Lord's death from Maundy Thursday through till Easter Day. But what happens on the Fifth Sunday of Lent is that Lent changes gear and goes a little deeper into the mystery of the cross; different hymns and lections become appropriate and *Common Worship* provides a new set of seasonal material. Passiontide has begun, but Lent continues. Despite quite a lot of common usage, neither the Prayer Book nor *Common Worship* calls the Fifth Sunday of Lent 'Passion Sunday'. The reason is clear. Of all Sundays of the year the Sunday of the passion is the final Sunday of Lent, Palm Sunday. (Indeed in the Roman Catholic Church that Sunday is called 'Passion Sunday'.) Nevertheless, on the Fifth Sunday of Lent, as passiontide material is used, the Church moves closer to Christ's death as it prepares for the Sunday of the passion and the days of Holy Week.

The idea of 'giving things up' seriously for Lent is out of fashion, although, at the level of sugar and sweets, it has become common. It can be a superficial exercise and a form of escapism from harder questions about real self-denial. But the giving up of certain things in the liturgy during Lent is a prerequisite to a dramatic and exciting Easter. Traditionally this has meant the omissions of all the *alleluias* in the liturgy (including those in the hymns) and of *Gloria in excelsis*, vestments of a solemn colour, whether purple or Lenten sackcloth, and the banishment of flowers from the church. All this is for the good, and it needs to be matched by a carefulness on the part of those who choose the hymns and other music. The air of austere simplicity should give the liturgy its distinctive flavour through Lent in order that the return of all these things may give Easter a glorious ring. What is not sometimes given up is always taken for granted.

It is this idea that has led in many churches to the custom of covering crosses, crucifixes, statues, etc. during Passiontide or, in some places, throughout the whole of Lent. Again this adds to the mood that the liturgy creates. But the intention is not so much cross-covering as the covering of the excessively ornamental, decorated or jewelled. One ought to be able to make out the shape of the cross through the covering. Banners may also be removed from the church through this period. All returns at Easter in a blaze of glory.

Ash Wednesday

The first day of Lent is the principal day of penitence in the Christian year. Although penitence continues to be a feature throughout the season, it remains there only as a consequence of an emphasis on discipline and growth. But Ash Wednesday majors on penitence, for we have to face the need for it and then to express it first if Lent is indeed to be a growing time.

The Prayer Book gives us the Commination Service and thereby commits us to a special liturgy of penitence on this day. *Lent, Holy Week, Easter* has given us the contemporary liturgy for Ash Wednesday and *Patterns for Worship* supplements it with a solemn blessing. The service assumes a eucharistic context, but where circumstances require it can be a word service with lay leadership. For pastoral reasons its use may also be postponed until the First Sunday of Lent. The heart of the service is an extended Liturgy of Penitence as a response to the Liturgy of the Word and leading on into the greeting of peace.

The key elements in the rite, beyond the ordinary, are:

- words of introduction that invite the people to 'the observance of a holy Lent';
- the use of Psalm 51, whether after the Old Testament reading or at the imposition of ashes;
- the litany (or the ten commandments);
- a significant period of silence for self-examination, leading into the confession;
- the blessing and imposition of ashes;
- absolution or another concluding prayer.

Hymns need to be of penitence, of resolution and, as throughout Lent, many hymns of the Spirit that we associate with Pentecost are appropriate in this season of trying to be open to the prompting of God ('Come down, O Love divine ... till earthly passions turn to dust and ashes in its heat consuming').

The call to penitence, the significant time of silence and the form of the confession all mark this out as a special rite for a special day, but the imposition of ashes is a telling sign both of penitence and of mortality. The Christian begins Lent by once again receiving the mark of the cross, in dust because of human fallenness, but nevertheless it is the cross, put back where it belongs as the Lent journey to the cross of Christ begins.

Mothering Sunday

The Fourth Sunday of Lent has long meant a mid-Lent slight relaxation of the Lenten rigours before redoubling efforts as Passiontide draws near. It is also Mothering Sunday, and holds together thoughts of the Church as 'mother' (the Prayer Book epistle for the day speaks of 'Jerusalem as the mother of us all'), of Mary the mother of the Lord (on a day usually near to the Feast of the Annunciation) and of our own mothers. The

Common Worship lectionary provides collect, post communion and readings for Mothering Sunday. The collect intentionally holds the Mothering Sunday themes together with the cross, so that the spirit of Lent is not lost, and one of the gospel readings offered is the passage where Mary stands at the foot of the cross. *Enriching the Christian Year* provides additional texts.

Here is one of those days when Christian practice (Mothering Sunday) and popular culture (Mothers' Day) meet, and we are foolish if we do not go with it and make something of it. But it needs treating with sensitivity, especially in the sermon and the intercession prayers, for not every woman has a child, not everyone's experience of motherhood and mothering has been happy, and some mothers have died. Not every family is happy and not everyone lives in a family. All these things need to be remembered.

As to a special moment in the service when something is blessed and given – a posy of flowers, a piece of simnel cake, a card – we need to be clear who is giving to whom. Is the church providing a gift for each child to give to mother, or a gift from the church to every mother, or a gift from mother Church to everyone? The last is the most inclusive if the numbers will allow.

Planning Holy Week

Holy Week is not only the most important week of the Christian year; it is also the week with the greatest potential for leading Christian people into a deeper experience of life and faith. This has been discussed already in chapter 7. The minister is right to challenge people (well before Holy Week, not at the last minute) to take it with the utmost seriousness and to clear their diaries for one week of the year of engagements that get in the way. They will need an attractive leaflet setting out the arrangements for the week; in some parishes they will need to know about parallel children's work and crèche provision if adults are to take part in the liturgy. They also need to know what really matters among all that is on offer.

The liturgy of Holy Week is like a symphony with its different movements or a drama with its several acts. One can gain something from being attentive to one movement or one act, but, if at all possible, one needs to be present for the whole work. In terms of Holy Week the crucial movements or acts are these:

- the liturgy of Palm Sunday morning;
- the eucharist of the Last Supper on Maundy Thursday evening;
- the liturgy of Good Friday (ideally in the early afternoon);

231

- the Easter liturgy (whether in the night, or at dawn or in the morning).

There may be other services on those days, indeed there probably ought to be if possible, for no one time can suit everybody. There may be services on the other days. Monday, Tuesday and Wednesday of Holy Week might be marked by an evening service consisting of brief eucharist, address, silence and Night Prayer. There may be musical offerings at points in the week. There might be an *agape*. But people need to be able to see what really matters, to be encouraged to take that with the utmost seriousness and not, by coming to too many less central liturgies early in the week, to have had enough before the four-movement symphony is over.

Palm Sunday

Palm Sunday is a day when the liturgy has two quite distinct parts, both very important. A parish should not opt for one and neglect the other. One is a Commemoration of the Entry into Jerusalem, essentially a liturgy of palms. The other is a move into the passion, for this is the Sunday of the passion, the reading of Matthew, Mark or Luke's account of the passion is central and, if possible, the response to it is in the eucharist where 'we show forth the Lord's death till he come'. A Palm Sunday service that does only the first, and neglects the second, sends people home still bubbling with *hosannas*, when by then the word 'crucify' should ring in their ears as they begin a week in which they need to reflect on a Lord moving towards his cross. And even a shorter service, such as an 8 o'clock communion, should try to encompass both elements in a way – the palms and then the passion.

Lent, Holy Week, Easter provides the rite. Ideally the first part is celebrated somewhere outside the church where the eucharist will be – another church, the village green, the school car-park, the church hall, at very least the church gate. The people gather. They either bring branches to carry or some industrious members of the church have been cutting down these (with permission) and bring them so that each may have one. They may receive palm crosses too, to be blessed at the same time, but these are more in the way of mementoes to take home afterwards. There is a greeting and an introduction, the palm gospel and then the procession to the church. Singing as they go, they set off, the more extrovert waving their palms, the music probably hopelessly out of time with one another, but no great matter, moving slowly enough for all to keep up. Someone will have suggested a donkey (and the case for it is that it may pull in the crowds), but the idea will probably have been resisted, for a donkey tends to become the focus, and the focus of this celebration must be Christ, hidden among his people. It is a subtle experience as they walk, for at one level it is like a carnival, but below that is the sense of beginning to walk with Christ the journey of the week to the cross.

As they enter the church, throwing down their branches at the door, the atmosphere changes. All the atmosphere of carnival is left behind. They will sing a mood-changing hymn, such as 'Ride on, ride on in majesty', pray and then settle down to the scriptures and principally the passion – sung or read, sometimes with parts for everybody, sometimes heard silently while only a few speak the words – leading into silence, may be a brief homily, special intercessions and then on into the Liturgy of the Sacrament, with the sense of the passion stronger than ever. The palm they take away at the end has been made into a cross and that reflects what the liturgy has done too.

Maundy Thursday

The Eucharist of the Last Supper clearly belongs in the evening and there is a tradition that there is no other celebration on that day. If there is a pastoral need for one, it is better in the mid-afternoon than in the morning, if it is to capture the special atmosphere of today.

The Maundy Thursday liturgy needs to be sufficiently like what happens week by week for the connection to be made between this holy night and every celebration (and that is an argument for not having an *agape* and eucharist in the church hall on this night or for other major departures from usual practice), but sufficiently different to allow the distinctive events of this night to come into prominence. Like Palm Sunday, this is another liturgy that moves people on – it begins with the supper, strong on fellowship and, even on this night, with hints of celebration (by tradition the *Gloria* returns to catch the mood), but ends with the garden, the watch, the desertion of disciples and the darkness.

Lent, Holy Week, Easter has once again provided the rite and the texts, though its provision at the end is not as clear it might be. The *Common Worship* eucharist provides other material. The key distinctive elements to the rite are:

- after the sermon, a commemoration of the washing of the disciples' feet;
- a special sense of 'this very night in which he was betrayed' in the Liturgy of the Sacrament with texts to enhance that sense;

233

- after the distribution, the beginning of a watch, possibly with the consecrated bread and wine for use tomorrow as the focus;
- the stripping bare of the altar and sanctuary;
- the departure of the people, whether after keeping watch for a while or not, in darkness and silence without blessing or dismissal.

None of this is mandatory, but all of it contributes to the power of the liturgy to bring us very close to the Lord. Foot-washing is messy and many (like Peter in the gospel story) do not at first see the point, but it is a wonderfully humbling experience both for the president to wash the feet of some members of the congregation and for them to have their feet washed. The stripping of the altar and the sanctuary as the lights are put out moves the congregation on from supper to betrayal dramatically and ensures they go home aware that the passion has indeed begun. A watch, either communally for a short time, or by people coming and going (perhaps backed up by a rota) for a longer time (probably till midnight) is a profound experience for many, kneeling in a silent shadowy darkened church as if in the garden of Gethsemane, engaging with what it means to 'watch with Christ'. Where the liturgy has been well planned and is then celebrated with love and longing to identify with Christ, there is no night like it in all the year.

Good Friday

Finding the right pattern of services for Good Friday is difficult. As many people as possible ought to be enabled to share in the main service of the day. Traditionally and appropriately that happens at the time that the Lord hung on the cross – either an extended service of three hours from noon till 3 o'clock or a shorter one for an hour till 3 o'clock. But perhaps, in communities where large numbers of people now work on Good Friday, it should instead be in the early evening. There is also the need to provide for children. This may be achieved by a children's project and liturgy parallel with the adult worship, but that is not always possible. And if the main service has been in the period until 3 o'clock, there is a need for some service in the evening for those who cannot come at any other time.

Patterns of services on Good Friday in the past have included family services, Litany and Ante Communion, ecumenical processions of witness, three-hour preaching services, devotional services and Stainer's *Crucifixion*, with no clear liturgy of Good Friday used right across the land. *Lent, Holy Week, Easter* has however provided such a service. It has three mandatory sections and one optional:

- the Liturgy of the Word (including the key texts – Isaiah 52.13—53.end, Psalm 22 and John's account of the passion);
- the Liturgy of the Cross (involving the bringing in of a great cross and devotional anthems and prayers with the cross as the focus);
- the Solemn Prayers (a series of biddings, times of silence and collects, usually offered at the foot of the cross);
- optionally either Holy Communion from elements consecrated on Maundy Thursday night or the entire Liturgy of the Sacrament.

In retrospect it is strange that for so long we celebrated Good Friday with services that were liturgically weak and which did not include the substantial passages of scripture that so clearly belong to this day. And 'celebrate' is indeed the right word, for on Good Friday it is John's account of the passion (as opposed to the synoptic accounts on Palm Sunday) that is read and, for John, the cross is always victory and accomplishment. The liturgy of Good Friday, with its red vestments and its large cross carried in high and dominating the liturgy, is, for all its austere simplicity and its silences, a celebration of the victory of the Crucified.

Perhaps just as strange is the Anglican tradition of abstinence from Holy Communion, whereas Roman Catholics since their reforms do receive on that day and, in the Free Churches, Good Friday has often been a key day for communion. It is almost an accident of history, for in the tradition reception of Holy Communion on Good Friday is not from a celebration of the eucharist, but from the sacrament reserved the night before. In a Church that for several centuries had no reservation of the sacrament, there could therefore be no communion. But Paul's words in 1 Corinthians 11 are apposite here – 'Every time we eat the bread and drink the cup, we show forth the Lord's death until he comes' – and there is an important sense in which we need to get out of our seats, to stop gazing at the cross and instead to receive the broken body and the wine that has been poured out as a sign that we share with Christ in his passion.

The Day of Waiting

Easter Eve is an a-liturgical day. Morning and Evening Prayer may be said, though very austerely, without 'Glory to the Father...' wherever it usually occurs, and with much silence. There may be feverish activity in the church preparing it for Easter, but for the liturgy it is a day of reticence and waiting. If there is a great liturgy in the darkness of the evening or the night, it is not an Easter Eve service, but the beginning of the feast of Easter itself.

32

The Great Fifty Days of Easter

∾

From Easter Day to Pentecost

Easter Day begins a period of unparalleled joy and celebration in the Christian year which extends through fifty days until the Day of Pentecost. Along the way it takes in, on the fortieth day, the feast of the Ascension. To understand this season as a unity – the Great Fifty Days – is novel for some Anglicans, who have seen Easter as just a week (or an 'octave') of celebration of the resurrection, followed by a sense that Easter is over and done, but with two short seasons coming along a little later, first Ascensiontide and then Whitsuntide. The Prayer Book calendar gives some encouragement to that view. *Common Worship* understands it differently. It returns to an older tradition whereby the three great Easter mysteries – the resurrection, the ascension and the giving of the Spirit – are held together, celebrated in one joyful season, where, rather than moving from one to another, the Church adds new layers as the weeks go by. On Easter Day there is the empty tomb and on the succeeding Sundays stories and other passages of scripture that reveal the resurrection until, like a jigsaw, there are only two pieces still to be put in place – the ascension and the giving of the Spirit. When they have been added, the picture is complete and on the evening of Pentecost, the last day of Easter, the season comes to an end.

For that reason the Sundays through this period are very definitely 'Sundays *of* Easter, not 'Sundays *after*', even though that may create a confusion for those using the Prayer Book calendar too, for there the Sundays are 'after' and therefore the numbering is different – the First Sunday *after* Easter is the Second Sunday *of* Easter.

It sometimes seems that in the Church of England we find it easier to sustain the austere discipline of Lenten liturgy than we do to sustain for fifty days a period of joy and celebration that ought to thrill and excite. Eastertide is one long sustained season of praise. That needs to be reflected in choices of hymns and other music, with no collapse into a false 'ordinary time' around the middle of the season. And as well as the usual seasonal provision in terms of invitation to confession, gospel acclamation, introduction to the peace, eucharistic prefaces and blessing in *Common Worship*, there are a number of elements that give the season its unity and its distinctiveness. These include:

- the Easter acclamation ('Alleluia. Christ is risen . . .') printed in the eucharistic rite but for use on many occasions beyond that;
- the Easter invitation to communion ('Alleluia. Christ our passover . . .');
- the generous use of *alleluias* throughout worship, especially in hymns and songs, contrasting with their absence in Lent;
- the reading of the Acts of the Apostles in place of the Old Testament in the Sunday Principal Service Lectionary and as the first reading at the eucharist each day;
- the paschal candle burning in a prominent place at every service;
- an Easter garden with an empty tomb;
- the Easter dismissal ('Go in the peace of Christ. Alleluia. Alleluia . . .').

As marks of the season these are effective only if they are signs of a church full of resurrection life and Easter joy.

The Easter Liturgy

It is one of the most extraordinary facts of liturgical life that the scholars insist that the key to understanding the Church's worship and the occasion that is at the very heart of it is the great liturgy of Easter, with its vigil, its service of light and its celebration of both baptism and the eucharist. Yet in anything like its richest liturgical form it is never celebrated in the majority of churches. There is a long process of liturgical formation to follow if this is to be changed, and those who have experienced the Easter Liturgy celebrated in its full form would never want to settle for anything less. It is through this liturgy that we are able to see most clearly the salvation of God at work in human history, to engage with the victory of light over darkness and life over death, to make the connections between our baptism and the experience of Christ, going down into death but bursting from the tomb, and to know the deep communion of being reunited with our risen Lord. The Easter Liturgy is about all those profound truths.

If it is that good, every Christian needs to have the chance to share in it and the key pastoral question is how to commend it and to offer it at a time when people will come. The fact that they share in it is much more important than that it happens at the 'correct' time. Not that there is any agreement about that. For some it belongs in the night, ideally around midnight. For others, however many hours before it may begin, it ends with the dawn very early on Easter morning. Yet if people will not come in great numbers at midnight or at dawn, it is better to hold it at some other time than have them missing. It might be after dark on Saturday night, for we do not need to be purist about whether it is after midnight; we do not know when the resurrection took place, only that the tomb was empty at first light. It might be at the normal Sunday morning time, though what is lost then is the element of darkness, which for both the vigil and the service of light is clearly helpful. What *Lent, Holy Week, Easter* advised was that, although the entire sequence was a unity and dividing it into two parts – one on Saturday night and the other on Sunday morning – was not ideal, if it did happen only the vigil part of the liturgy should be detached from the rest; service of light, proclamation of the resurrection, baptism and eucharist all need to be held together. It is a pastoral decision when to celebrate this liturgy, but there ought to be no question of whether to celebrate it.

It is a service of darkness and light, of waiting and of fulfilment, of powerful words, of music, silence, movement and symbol, an 'all-age service' if ever there was one. Here there is only space to set out its principal stages. *Lent, Holy Week, Easter* has provided the detailed rite. Making it come alive in the parish requires much work, all of it well worthwhile. The stages of the liturgy are:

- a vigil of Old Testament readings (always including the account of the exodus), with silence, prayer and singing, the possibility of drama and of other non-biblical readings, either for a short vigil of three or four readings, or for a longer vigil through the hours of the evening or the night;
- the service of light, with the paschal candle lit from a fire, the candle carried through the church, candles lit for everyone, and a proclamation of the resurrection in a song of praise (*Exsultet*);
- the Liturgy of the Word, including Romans 6.3–11 ('Do you not know that when you were baptized into Christ Jesus you were baptized into his death...?') and the gospel account of the empty tomb;
- the Liturgy of Baptism, with all gathered at the font for baptism, confirmation if the bishop is present, and the renewal of baptismal vows;
- the Liturgy of the Sacrament, the proper climax of the rite in which the worshippers are reunited with the risen Lord;
- the Dismissal, with cascades of *alleluias*.

But this is a flexible rite. The first two sections may be the other way round, with the service of light right at the beginning and the congregation gathered outside around a bonfire before entering the church for the vigil. Or the vigil first in another building and then all gathered round the fire before entering the church to proclaim the resurrection. Or the Liturgy of the Word might disappear in favour of Romans 6 read at the font and the gospel saved to be read at the door at the very end as part of the Dismissal. Every parish needs to find its way of making this great liturgy its own.

When the Easter Liturgy has been celebrated in the night and at dawn, there is the possibility of using some of its material again in a later eucharist. It might begin with the Easter acclamation at the door and a procession led by the paschal candle, and there might be a renewal of baptismal vows with water brought from the font to sprinkle the congregation. For children in the liturgy there might be a procession to the Easter garden and, at the end, a lighting of candles from the paschal flame in order to take home the light of the risen Lord. Later in the day, if there is an evening service, there could be the use of the 'Litany of the Resurrection' from *Common Worship* and the service might end with a procession of the whole congregation, led by the paschal candle, and with a pause for prayer (a 'station') at both the Easter garden and the font, before the solemn blessing that *Patterns for Worship* provides.

Rogation Days

The three days before the Ascension are called 'Rogation Days' and the Sunday before, the Sixth Sunday of Easter, is frequently known as Rogation Sunday. Traditionally they are days of prayer for a good harvest, and this has often been broadened to be a time of prayer for the world of work. Christian Aid Week is usually at the same time. The *Common Worship: Calendar, Lectionary and Collects* makes provision of three different collects, a post communion and readings for the Rogation Days. There is no specific provision for the Sunday, but Easter themes of new life and growth very easily dovetail with concern for the farming community, for the harvest and for the hungry of the world. There is a need for imaginative new Rogationtide liturgy. There is a need for a service that celebrates realistically the mutual dependence of town and village, commerce and agriculture, employment and leisure, a service that would help people to understand their environment and be discerning about the changes that are occurring in relation to it. Whether at Rogationtide, Lammastide or Harvest, these are vital issue about which

Christians should think and pray, whether they live in urban or rural communities.

Ascension Day

For Ascension Day, one of the nine principal feasts, *Common Worship* provides a set of proper material for use on this one day and *Patterns for Worship* supplements it with acclamations and a solemn blessing. There is no special liturgical ceremony associated with Ascension Day. The putting out of the paschal candle after the gospel, part of the older Roman ceremonial, is quite wrong; the candle burns at all services until Pentecost evening as one of the expressions of the unity of the season. For it to remain alight on Ascension Day also signals that the ascension does not change the fact that 'I am with you to the end of time'.

Ascension Day might be the occasion in the life of the parish for a celebration of gifts and ministries. For these are, as the Letter to the Ephesians teaches, the gifts of the ascended Christ. But equally such a celebration might be focused on the Day of Pentecost.

Pentecost

There is no Whitsun season in *Common Worship*, but there is an important note: 'The nine days after Ascension Day until Pentecost are days of prayer and preparation to celebrate the outpouring of the Spirit.'

In effect, therefore, there is a Pentecost sub-season in the last ten days of Easter. The crucial change from the Prayer Book calendar is that this period leads up to the day of Pentecost, rather than follows it. Just as the disciples in the Acts of the Apostles return from the ascension and spend their time in watchful prayer, waiting for what the Lord has promised, so the Church observes the days between Ascension Day and Pentecost by praying 'Come, Holy Spirit, renew'. Hymns, songs and prayers of the Spirit are appropriate through this period, the lectionary reflects this emphasis and the *Common Worship* proper material for Pentecost is also ordered for the nine days before, so that we arrive at the Day of Pentecost with a real sense of openness to the Spirit whose presence that day celebrates.

The Day of Pentecost itself is, in a sense, a double feast. It has its own focus in the outpouring of the Spirit, but it is also the last day of Eastertide. The liturgy should reflect that. *Patterns for Worship* supplements the available texts with acclamations, intercession and solemn blessing of the Spirit, but the Easter material is still present for the last time. This may be the day for a celebration of the renewal gifts and ministries in the local church, with the possibility of a liturgy of anointing. Easter needs to end on a note of proclamation, people ready to take the gospel out with confidence. The liturgy might end at the open door, indicating the interaction of the Church and the world as the Spirit blows where he wills and as the Church is anointed to preach the gospel to the whole creation. Pentecost, and therefore Eastertide, needs to end on a strong note.

Next day it will once again be 'ordinary time'. The liturgical colour will be green. The paschal candle will be moved to the font. For the rest of the year its primary use is in those rites that most obviously relate to Easter, at baptisms and at funerals.

33

The Kingdom of Christ and of his Saints

All Saints' Day

All Saints' Day (1 November) is a principal feast day. In order that it may be widely celebrated, *Common Worship* permits it to be kept on the Sunday falling between 30 October and 5 November – All Saints' Sunday – and, if this happens, allows nevertheless a 'secondary celebration' on 1 November. For this reason it provides a second set of readings for use at such a celebration.

The desire to give All Saints' Day more prominence than in the recent past is, at least in part, a desire to counter something of the modern foolishness of 'Hallowe'en', where a Christian celebration – Hallowe'en is of course the eve of All Hallows Day, i.e. All Saints' Day – has been hijacked for a secular celebration that is at best devoid of meaning and at worst dangerously close to the world of the occult. The Church needs to counter a culture of ghosts, witches and broomsticks with its own celebration of the good purposes of God, the communion of saints and the promise of eternal life.

The Promise of His Glory has provided the eucharistic rite for All Saints' Day and *Common Worship* also makes provision. The rite includes a responsory at the beginning, a fine intercession and a solemn blessing, and, as a separate provision, there is a 'Thanksgiving for the Holy Ones of God' that celebrates, along with the saints of the universal Church, the heroes of the English and Anglican traditions.

There may be a desire for a service on the evening of 31 October itself to counter some of the darker practices of that night. Such a form could take a variety of forms, but a possible outline, drawing all the texts from *The Promise of His Glory*, might be:

- blessing and sharing of light (with All Saints text);
- greeting, introduction and opening prayer;
- sequence of All Saints readings with suitable music and with silence;
- canticle: *Te Deum Laudamus*;
- gospel reading: Matthew 5.1–11;
- thanksgiving for the holy ones of God;
- Lord's Prayer;
- solemn blessing.

But something much less formal might be preferred, especially if children are involved, providing a Hallowmass party for them, rather than the kind of Hallowe'en celebrations to which they might be invited.

All Souls' Day

All Souls' Day, more fully and correctly called 'The Commemoration of the Faithful Departed', is on 2 November, but transferred to the following day if 2 November is a Sunday. Logic also suggests that if All Saints' Day may be moved, All Souls' Day ought to be able to moved to a pastorally convenient day close to All Saints' Day.

Anglican theology carefully avoids a categorization of the departed in ways we cannot justify, so that on one day we might celebrate the saints in glory and on the other pray for less saintly souls yet to reach the full bliss of heaven. We simply cannot know about such things. All the Christian dead are with the Lord and all of us with them are bound together 'in one communion and fellowship'. That is as far as we can say. So All Souls' Day, even if it emerges from a theology of categorization, has become for us much more the 'shadow side' of what we celebrate on All Saints' Day. There is a natural human fear and fragility in the face of death, an anxiety about our eternal destiny, an ongoing sense of our loss of those who have died, our desire to do some remembering of those who were dear to us as much as of the great saints of the Church, and our need to pray as well as to praise. All these elements come at All Saintstide from a different angle than the equally proper joyful celebration of the glories of the saints in light.

In some smaller communities All Saints and All Souls simply have to be held together in one celebration and theologically that is fine. Liturgically it is asking a lot and, where they can be separate, twin, services there is much to be gained. *The Promise of His Glory* has provided for All Souls both a eucharistic and a non-eucharistic liturgy to remember the departed. At the heart of both is the 'Commemoration'. The eucharistic order places it after the distribution, both to be a climax to the service, but also to avoid any sense, that some would find difficult, of a *requiem* offered for the souls of the departed. Yet the most natural place for such a commemoration is after the intercessions and before the peace, so that our sense of communion with all God's people, living and departed, is brought to completion in the eucharistic prayer and the sharing of the consecrated bread and wine that anticipate the heavenly banquet. On the other hand, held in the evening on a day when the morning has focused on All Saints, the non-eucharistic order, more like a vigil, will serve well.

The key elements of the 'Commemoration' are the reading of names of the departed, the keeping of silence and some rich prayer texts. A note introduces the possibility of the lighting of candles, and this is highly desirable, first of all because this is one of those occasions when actions are more satisfactory than words, but also because this may avoid a very long list of names, restricting these to those who have died in the last year, and allowing everyone to remember all their other departed silently as they light their candles. But it takes time for a large congregation to light candles and music needs to be planned accordingly.

This may be the occasion in the year (though a Sunday of Eastertide is another possibility) when a church may specifically invite to a service all those to whom the parish has ministered in the previous year at the time of a bereavement. It is a good pastoral opportunity and there is much evidence that people find such a service a significant help in the grieving process.

Between All Saints and All Souls

Common Worship calls the Sundays between 30 October and Advent 'Sundays before Advent'. All Saints' Day marks a shift, and its theme of the kingdom of Christ and of his saints colours the weeks of November. It falls short of being a season – 'before Advent' implies something less than that, and this is still 'ordinary time', but the lectionary engages with the theme, as do the collects and post communions. A note explains that 'the period between All Saints' Day and the First Sunday of Advent is observed as a time to celebrate and reflect upon the reign of Christ in earth and heaven.'

Common Worship provides a new set of material for the eucharist, as if this were a season, and there may be a change of liturgical colour to red, the colour of kingship. There is a degree of choice here. Much can be made of this sense of 'all but a season' by those who want to make this period distinctive and coherent. Those who want to continue with a sense of a 'green season' of ordinary time can do so, though some of the prayers and readings will go on gently signalling the kingdom theme.

Remembrance Sunday

One of those Sundays before Advent will be Remembrance Sunday, the Sunday nearest to 11 November. This makes it normally the Third Sunday before Advent and the collect and post communion for that Sunday have Remembrance Sunday in mind. When, as happens in some years, Remembrance Sunday is on the Second Sunday before Advent, a note allows the collect and post communion of the two Sundays to be reversed.

The desire to remember those who have died in war, especially in the great world conflicts of the twentieth century, shows no sign of fading as a new century begins. Clearly the focus changes little by little as there are fewer of those who fought in these conflicts. There is more concern for other conflicts and a desire to make this a day of prayer for peace, but the remembering remains important. What has happened in recent years has been a desire to return to the old Armistice Day observance by which all comes to a halt at 11 o'clock on 11 November, whatever day of the week this may be, and there is a silence of two minutes. Although this may be admirable and certainly reaches people who do not share in Remembrance Sunday services, there is a danger the Church needs to watch. For it takes the remembrance away from Sunday and from the church, makes it more privatized than communal, and observes it in a setting detached from Christian worship and preaching.

For this, as well as for other reasons, a church does well to be welcoming to those who want to use the church on Remembrance Sunday to commemorate the dead and to pray for peace. The war memorial, whether inside or outside the church, is a proper focus for remembering. It may be a matter of incorporating a commemoration into a normal service, or of holding a special service, or of being flexible enough to change service times to meet the desire for a commemoration at 11 o'clock. *The Promise of His Glory* reproduces the ecumenical form of service for this day since 1968. Remembrance Sunday may not be a part of the universal Christian calendar, but it is important in the life of this country and many of its people, and a church is foolish not to engage with it graciously and creatively.

Christ the King

The Sunday next before Advent is designated by the *Common Worship* calendar as the feast of Christ the King, bringing the Church of England into line with many other churches that have adopted this twentieth-century feast, variously under the title of 'Christ the King', 'the Kingship of Christ' or 'the Reign of Christ'. It brings the themes that have been present through the month of November to a natural climax and, on the last Sunday of the Christian year, brings the focus very firmly back on to the figure of the Lord himself. (Those who will regret that, with this new emphasis, it is less likely to be known by the popular name 'Stir Up Sunday' will be glad that the collect that gave it that name is retained as the post communion prayer of the day and may be used as the collect at Morning and Evening Prayer through the week.)

The *Common Worship* material for the period through from All Saints' Day is entirely suitable for this feast day, as is much Ascension Day liturgical material and hymnody. Those who somewhat regret that the old Ascension season has disappeared in the new emphasis on preparing for Pentecost can take comfort in the fact that in the feast of Christ the King its concerns are celebrated as the climax of the year.

Of course with Advent only a week away, a celebration of Christ in the assembly of the saints in heaven is not far from a commemoration of the Christ who returns to the earth as judge. As any cycle should do, the end is leading naturally into the new beginning.

34

High Points and Holy Days

Sanctorale and Temporale

The Christian year has, as has been shown already, two distinct parts, the seasons before and after Christmas Day and Easter Day, and 'ordinary time'. Technically this picture of the year is called the *temporale*. The calendar of saints and some other holy days that fall on fixed dates, technically the *sanctorale*, cut right across this, and these days occur throughout the Christian year. Although it is ordered that principal holy days be kept and that festivals will feature in daily worship at least in Morning and Evening Prayer, for the rest of the calendar of saints local decision making prevails. But there is encouragement not to let too many saints days cut across the distinctive character of a season; there is less at stake in 'ordinary time'. Similarly, where there are local celebrations and festivals to be allocated a date or even a Sunday, the encouragement is to locate them in the period of ordinary time.

Among local celebrations may be local saints and Christian heroes. *Common Worship* encourages 'diocesan and other local provision' to supplement the national calendar, for nearly always the recognition of sainthood has begun in the community where a saint lived and died and some of the local saints of our history can still matter to us centuries on.

In choosing dates for local celebrations of different kinds, it is useful to bear in mind that, notwithstanding what has been said before, there are three Sundays of ordinary time that, because of their collect, post communion and readings, do have one strong and important theme. The first two are before Lent. The Second Sunday before Lent is, in effect, a 'creation Sunday' and the Sunday next before Lent focuses on the transfiguration of Jesus. There is a kind of sequence from creation through transfiguration into the season that engages with redemption. At the end of October, on the Last Sunday after Trinity comes 'Bible

247

Sunday', relocated from December so that the character of Advent is not interrupted on its second Sunday.

The Annunciation

The cinderella among the nine principal feasts is likely to be the Annunciation of our Lord. Falling on 25 March, it is transferred to the Monday if 25 March is a Sunday and to the ninth day of Easter if 25 March falls in Holy Week or Easter Week. So there is never the possibility of a Sunday celebration of it. Yet it is an important feast, nine months before Christmas, full of subtlety as the Church thinks 'out of season' about the incarnation. When it does so in Lent it is always with an interaction with the figure of the woman at the foot of the cross and when it is in Easter with the figure of the same woman gathered in the upper room among the disciples awaiting the gift of the Spirit at Pentecost. The collect engages with this relationship: 'that as we have known the incarnation of your Son Jesus Christ by the message of an angel, so by his cross and passion we may be brought to the glory of his resurrection...'

Although sometimes called 'Lady Day', this is a feast of the Lord himself. It is worth trying to make something of it. Its status as a principal feast assumes a celebration of the eucharist, and *Common Worship* provides a set of proper material for this service.

Trinity Sunday

A week after Pentecost comes Trinity Sunday. People sometimes talk of the 'Trinity season', but there is no such season. It is simply that this day gives its name to all the Sundays through the long summer and autumn period of ordinary time. But there is a principal feast, just a single day, in honour of the holy and undivided Trinity, always on a Sunday, always a joyful celebration of the unity of the God to whom we pray as Father through the Son in the power of the Spirit. *Common Worship* provides for the feast and *Patterns for Worship* supplements it with acclamations and solemn blessings.

Patronal Festival

There are only a very few churches without a 'dedication', in most cases to a saint, but in some cases to a 'mystery' (Holy Cross, Holy Trinity, etc.) or to the Lord himself (St Saviour, Christ Church, Emmanuel). In most churches it is clear on what day or date the patronal festival is. In a few cases this is not so. Churches dedicated in honour of Jesus Christ himself may opt for the Naming of Jesus on 1 January or the Transfiguration on 6 August, but both have the disadvantage of being holiday dates, and probably preferable is Christ the King on the Sunday next before Advent. Churches dedicated in honour of the Blessed Virgin Mary have 15 August, which is her main festival, but may move it for pastoral reasons to 8 September (the Birth of Mary) or celebrate it on 31 May (the Visit of Mary to Elizabeth) or 8 December (the Conception of Mary).

Common Worship indicates that the patronal festival is to be kept as either a festival or a principal feast. If it is kept as a principal feast, then

> it may be transferred to the nearest Sunday, unless that day is already a principal feast or one of the following days: The First Sunday of Advent, The Baptism of Christ, The First Sunday of Lent, The Fifth Sunday of Lent or Palm Sunday.

So, as a principal feast, the patronal festival can be kept on a Sunday even in Advent, in some parts of Lent and in Eastertide. Where it is not already a festival, the minister chooses psalms and readings from the eucharistic 'commons' to provide for all the services of the feast.

It is easy for a whole number of different days in the parish's year to end up being about the same thing. Somehow the patronal festival, the feast of dedication, Stewardship Sunday and other occasions too all come down to a similar re-dedication of the congregation. If all these occasions are to say something distinct, and not to be mere reverberations of one another, it needs to be drawn out that the distinctive focus of the patronal festival is on the patron saint. 'Who is this saint? What is to be learnt from his/her life? What kind of flavour can it give to this community to be under the name and patronage of Saint N?' Questions such as these give the patronal festival a point of its own.

Dedication Festival

Some of the same things need to be said about the dedication festival, also called the 'feast of dedication'. People sometimes confuse the dedication festival with the patronal festival, but whereas the one is about the church's patron saint, the other is about the church building itself. The *Common Worship* rules state that:

> The dedication festival of a church is the anniversary of its dedication or consecration. This is kept either as a festival or as a principal feast. When the date of dedication is unknown, the dedication festival may be observed on the first Sunday in October, or on the Last Sunday after Trinity, or on a suitable date chosen locally.

Common Worship provides collect, post communion and readings on the three-year cycle, but for the time being one has to turn to *Enriching the Christian Year* for other liturgical material. Like the patronal festival, as a principal feast the dedication festival can be celebrated on a Sunday, with the few exceptions listed above.

The distinctive theme of the feast of dedication is its celebration of the church building. Of course it is true that 'the church is the people' and the building is but a tool in the task they undertake. But an incarnational religion does not despise places where God's presence is sought and where, in response to prayer, he chooses to make himself known. The feast of dedication is the day for thanksgiving for the place of the church building in the community's life. It may well also be the opportunity for questioning or reassessing that place. But there is room in the Christian year for a liturgy about bricks and mortar, and the feast of dedication should not be spiritualized into something else, but given an imaginative liturgy that celebrates, through the wood, the glass and the stone, and the altar, the lectern and the font, the God whose 'house' people claim it to be.

Harvest Thanksgiving

Harvest Thanksgiving is not a fixed date. *Common Worship* recognizes that it will normally be celebrated on a Sunday and allows its collect, post communion prayer and readings (on a three-year cycle) to replace those of the day, unless that day is a festival (such as Michaelmas). Late September and early October is the preferred time, though in reality this is late; the harvest has usually been gathered in several weeks before.

There is a case for broadening the harvest, for recognizing that in the kind of society in which we live our interdependence involves the world of industry and commerce as much as of agriculture, and is as much concerned with world trade as with local production of food. Harvest Thanksgiving must not be the occasion for a kind of rural 'make believe'. On the other hand there is something to be said, in our complex world, for giving thanks for the basics, for the things we grow in the ground, for the weather conditions that make for growth, for the real necessities, and something of the simple thankfulness of an old-fashioned harvest can make sure these are not lost. Bringing gifts to the altar bought at the supermarket to be sold later for Christian Aid or taken to the housebound is good. Bringing gifts that one has grown oneself is better still, even if they are not prize-winning marrows.

There is a real concern that our liturgy should engage with issues of creation and the environment and some criticism that our liturgical texts are still light on these, though there is good harvest provision in *Patterns for Worship*. But at least the Church now has three well-spaced Sunday celebrations when in different ways we can pray for the relationship between humankind and the wider creation – the Second Sunday before Lent with its creation theme, the Sixth Sunday of Easter with its rogation emphasis, and in the autumn Harvest Thanksgiving.

When the bishop comes

The visit of the bishop of the diocese, or one of his suffragan bishops, is a high point in the year in any parish, whether he comes to baptize, confirm and preside at the eucharist or for some other purpose. The entire Christian community should be urged to be present, not in order to impress the bishop, but because the bishop is the symbol of unity among all Christians, and those in communion with him should be present to make him welcome.

He may need to be invited. Of course he ought to feel that he can invite himself, but there is on the part of some bishops an understandable reluctance to do so. A parish does not need to have candidates for confirmation before it can feel it can invite the bishop. He may come simply to preside at the eucharist. He may come to baptize. There is no closed season for inviting bishops. Of course the bishop of the diocese may well be in his cathedral on certain key days, though not necessarily so, and the suffragan bishop has no cathedral in which to be. A bishop belongs on Sundays and feast days among his people presiding at their liturgy.

As has been said already (in chapter 14), the bishop within his diocese is the normative president of the sacraments. When he comes to the parish he is not sidelined in the sanctuary, but presides over the worship; it is one of his key contacts with the people among whom he is set as 'shepherd'. His right to preside should also serve as a warning about the wrong sort of welcome. It is good to welcome the bishop and to make sure he is 'at home'. But that is exactly where he is, somewhere he ought to experience a sense of belonging. He is a not a visitor. It is not so much 'We welcome the Bishop of N', as if he belonged elsewhere, but 'Welcome, Bishop N, our chief pastor and teacher'.

Perhaps the most important principle for a parish to remember, when planning for a visit by the bishop, is not to overdo things, not to pull out stops that have not worked for years. Just as the wise parish will want the bishop to be natural and relaxed, and to try to avoid fussing him with unimportant details – let him do the liturgy his way; it might be quite refreshing – so the bishop will want to find a community that enjoys worship and is natural and relaxed about it. Let him be to the community the pastor that he wants to be.

Ember Days

Ember Days are the days traditionally kept as a time for prayer for those to be ordained and, slightly more broadly, for vocations to ordained ministry. The traditional dates have been the Wednesdays, Fridays and Saturdays within the weeks before the Third Sunday of Advent, the Second Sunday of Lent and the Sundays nearest 29 June and 29 September. With the virtual disappearance of Advent and Lent ordinations, and in some dioceses none at Michaelmas either, the Ember Days may be thought to have lost some of their point. *Common Worship* responds in two ways. First of all it lays down that they should be observed, under the bishop's direction, in the week before an ordination as days of prayer for those to be made deacon or priest. Thus the traditional dates should be moved locally, so that the reality is that the churches of the diocese are praying by name for the candidates in the week of their retreat leading to their ordination. Second, it states that 'Ember Days may also be kept even when there is no ordination in the diocese as more general days of prayer for those who serve the Church in its various ministries, both ordained and lay, and for vocations.' This broadening out is much to be welcomed and it may be hoped that, as a result, these days may once again be valued in the daily praying life of the Church.

Coming by invitation

Some of the high points in the parish year will, however, be in those special services for particular groups that are either 'targeted' by the church community – those married in the church in the last ten years, for instance – or else arranged in collaboration with local organizations or community groups. Forms of service will vary enormously, though, as has been discussed, 'A Service of the Word' provides the core for a whole variety of styles. But one of the elements that these occasions have in common is that people do not simply read about the service or hear it advertised on the local radio. They receive an invitation, whether from an organization or from the church or from the two together. They arrive, clutching the invitation. It is the invitation that has given them the courage to come and it has been the easier because they have not had to come alone, so to speak, but as part of a group to which they belong. Invitation services of one sort or another are a crucial part of the ministry of the church today. Of course the invitation only gets people through the door. It is the liturgy that must then draw them deeper into the Church's life and enable them to get a first grasp on the heel of heaven.

Epilogue:

Liturgy for the World

❧

When trying to get the detail right so that the liturgy may make people more open to the Spirit, it is easy to lose sight of the broader picture. It is to that broader picture that we must now return.

The celebration of the liturgy is always a bringing to God of needs far beyond those of the congregation, however large or small, that is gathered together in one place. It is always for the community, and it is, in a sense, always for the whole creation. In every offering of penitence, prayer and praise, the world is drawn to God.

The individual praying of every Christian ought to have that dimension that looks beyond self, and the celebration of the Church's daily office, its corporate prayer, morning and evening, has the same quality, and through the intercession, which is its classic climax, brings to God prayer that is always on behalf of a much wider constituency than those who share its recitation.

And then there is the eucharist. In the eucharist we come, with our spiritual hunger, to the Maker and Sustainer of the creation, and are fed with the bread of life. We ritualize and celebrate God's response to human need. We bring to God his world, and in our communion we taste and see how he satisfies.

In the eucharist we call down the Spirit who touches and transforms, not only bread and wine, but people and relationships. The Spirit makes people holy, equips them with gifts of many kinds and flows between them, healing and renewing their relationships one with another. We pray, 'pour out your Holy Spirit as we bring before you these gifts of your creation'. We focus the renewing power of the Spirit in the eucharist, but know that to be a sign that the Spirit, who hovered over the waters at the creation, fills the whole universe, and is at work in every human soul and in the relationships between them, especially where love, peace and healing are flowing from one to another.

In the eucharist we celebrate how God is at work in the world of

253

matter. Our eyes are on bread and wine, fruits of the creation, and even they, as Francis of Assisi knew, sing his praises. Yet it is not the creation's praising, for all its loveliness, that is at the heart of our worship. It is not what they do, but what God does. God, who is holy indeed, the source of all holiness, by the power of his Spirit makes holy the gifts of his creation. It is in that sense that as they celebrate the eucharist, with bread and wine upon the table, Christians can hold on to a cosmic view of the whole creation, with all its goodness and its pain, being put in touch with heaven and renewed by the Spirit of God.

All these overlapping images – of hunger being satisfied, of the Spirit at work in people and between them, of the creation made holy – emerge from the eucharist. Yet they are not trapped within it, but are images of God's working wherever hands and hearts are engaging with him in prayer and worship. They come very close to the heart of the matter. But not quite.

At the heart of the matter, in liturgy as in the life of faith, is the cross. In every prayer we pray is the Crucified One pleading with the Father. Over every Christian celebration hangs the cross of Christ. In every eucharist there is set forth the sacrifice that takes away the sins of the world and reconciles the human race to God.

So, in coming with the world on their hearts to offer their prayers and praises, to share in the liturgy and, supremely, to celebrate the eucharist, Christian people are recognizing the world's need for redemption, and bringing it, as far as they are able, to the cross where that redemption is found. The liturgy is always a setting for the sanctification of the creation. Everywhere and every time it is caught up in the redemption of the world.

Bibliography

Books referred to in the text, in alphabetical order of title:

Celebrate the Christian Story. Michael Perham. SPCK, 1997.

Celebrating Common Prayer. Mowbray, 1992.

Common Worship: Calendar, Lectionary and Collects. Church House Publishing, 1997.

Common Worship: Initiation Services. Church House Publishing, 1998.

Common Worship: Pastoral Rites. Church House Publishing, 2000.

Common Worship: Services and Prayers for the Church of England. Church House Publishing, 2000.

Enriching the Christian Year. Michael Perham (ed.). SPCK, 1993.

Faith in the City: The Report of the Archbishop of Canterbury's Commission on Urban Priority Areas. Church House Publishing, 1985.

In Tune with Heaven: The Report of the Archbishops' Commission on Church Music. Church House Publishing/Hodder & Stoughton, 1992.

Lent, Holy Week, Easter: Services and Prayers. Church House Publishing/Cambridge University Press/SPCK, 1986.

New Start: Worship Resources for the Millennium, Books One and Two, New Start 2000 Ltd, 1999.

Pastoral Prayers. Richard Deadman, Jeremy Fletcher, Janet Hudson and Stephen Oliver. Mowbray, 1996.

Patterns for Worship. Church House Publishing, 1989, 1995.

Psalm Praise. Marshall Pickering.

Public Worship with Communion by Extension. General Synod of the Church of England (GS 1230B), 2000.

Services of Prayer and Dedication after Civil Marriage. Church House Publishing, 1985.

The Promise of His Glory: Services and Prayers for the Season from All Saints to Candlemas. Mowbray/Church House Publishing, 1991.

The Revised Common Lectionary. Canterbury Press, 1992.

BIBLIOGRAPHY

Waiting for the Risen Christ: A Commentary on Lent, Holy Week, Easter: Services and Prayers. Michael Perham and Kenneth Stevenson. SPCK, 1986.

Welcoming the Light of Christ: A Commentary on The Promise of His Glory. Michael Perham and Kenneth Stevenson. SPCK, 1991.

Index

There are no entries in this index for Jesus Christ, The Church of England, Common Worship, worship, eucharist, prayer, scriptures, parish church, officiant, president, priest, reader, reading or hymn and song because references to them occur throughout the text.

Absolution 31, 36, 59, 108, 116, 117, 143, 157, 193–4, 199, 211, 230
acclamations 20, 34, 107, 108, 114, 120, 133–4, 240, 248
address *see* sermon
admission of children to communion 86–7, 172–3
Advent 56, 57, 58, 60, 61, 71, 72, 95, 108, 117, 123, 145, 157, 158, 165, 215–20, 223, 224. 246, 248, 249, 252
Advent antiphons 218–19
Advent Liturgy, an 217–18
Advent, Sundays before 57, 58, 75, 244–5
Advent wreath 209, 218, 222
Aelred of Rievaulx, St 59
'Affirmations of Faith' 123, 143, 144, 145–6, 156
affirming baptismal faith 179–80
Agape 232, 233
Agnus Dei see Lamb of God
all-age worship 11–12, 35–6, 74, 76, 80, 82, 86–91, 147, 223, 234, 238
alleluia 7–8, 61, 120, 140, 216, 229, 237, 238

All Saints' Day 57, 58, 59, 61, 75, 96, 123, 165, 242–3, 244, 246
All Souls' Day 61, 243–4
altar 23, 24, 38, 40–4, 45, 48, 49, 86, 93–94, 127, 128–31, 159, 170, 175, 185, 186, 207, 208, 225, 226, 234, 250
Alternative Service Book, 1980 vii, 11, 13, 15, 16, 58, 63, 65, 66–7, 70, 74, 84, 104, 1–5, 106, 114, 115, 116, 122, 125, 130, 133, 134, 136, 149–150, 152, 165, 166, 171, 183, 188
alternative worship 90–1
angels 5, 19
Annunciation 59, 230, 248
anointing 159, 189–93, 212, 240 *See also* oil
Ascension 57, 59, 61, 236, 239, 240, 246
ashes, interment of 197, 203
Ash Wednesday 56, 59, 61, 75, 115, 145, 147, 229–30
Augustine of Hippo, St 22
aumbry 211

baptism vii, 7, 11, 27, 35, 36, 38–9, 46, 49, 68, 86, 96, 130, 159, 163–71, 172–6, 178, 197, 201, 203, 206, 228, 237–9, 241, 251

baptismal vows, renewal of 85, 176, 179–80, 226, 238

Baptism of Christ 39, 57, 59, 72, 145, 158, 165, 221–22, 225–6, 249

baptistry see font

Basil, Liturgy of St 134

beatitudes 108

Benedictus see Zechariah, Song of

Benson, Edward 55

bells 26, 83, 152, 208, 225

Benedicite 157

Bible 39–40, 64, 69–76, 112, 119–23, 144, 150, 152, 159, 199, 205, 247–8

bishop 6, 27, 36–7, 39, 44, 69, 94, 110, 116, 165–6, 168, 172, 173–8, 191, 192, 193, 205, 208, 238, 251, 252

blessing 6, 31, 54, 56, 108, 109, 121, 137, 139–40, 145, 159, 178, 184, 185, 186, 193, 203, 207, 209, 217, 223, 234, 237

bread 9, 23, 26, 28, 40, 42, 48, 49, 51, 98, 103–104, 112, 128–38, 186, 210, 211, 234, 235, 244, 253–4

breaking of bread 31, 48, 49, 67, 129, 134–5, 148, 210

body, human 33, 47–8, 49–51, 53–4, 189–91, 195

Body of Christ 25–7, 33, 49, 98, 111–12, 127–8, 134–5, 137, 164, 170, 172, 189, 206, 235

Book of Common Prayer 10, 11, 13–16, 20, 23, 37, 52, 55, 56, 62–7, 69, 70, 74, 82, 83, 104, 105–6, 114, 116, 121, 122, 125, 127, 131, 136, 149–50, 152, 153, 156, 169, 171, 182, 184, 190, 193, 196, 229, 230, 236, 240

'Book of Times and Seasons' 56, 109, 139–44, 215

building, church 10–11, 35–46, 48, 50, 80–1, 84, 99, 218, 249–50

burial see funeral services

Candlemas 55, 56, 57, 58, 59, 61, 75, 96, 145, 210, 221–2, 224, 226–7

candles 41, 3, 47, 49, 55, 61, 90, 157, 159, 168, 170, 171, 172, 178, 197, 202, 210, 217, 218, 226–7, 238–9, 243, 244

Canterbury, Archbishop of 14

canticle 119, 149, 152, 153, 157, 158

cantor 132

carol service 55, 143

cathedrals 37, 39, 45, 54, 58, 83, 149, 151, 174, 205, 217, 251

Celebrating Common Prayer viii, 56, 150, 152

celebration 7–8, 63, 156, 253–4

'Celebration of Wholeness and Healing' 192–3

chair 37, 43, 44–5, 93, 175

child, funeral of a 201–2

children 80, 86–91, 116, 122, 133–4, 209–10, 231, 234, 243

choir 19, 26, 44, 49, 89, 112, 140, 157 see also music

chrism, oil of see oil

Christian year 39, 46, 55–61, 75–6, 209–10, 215–51

Christingle 147, 222, 224

Christmas 45, 55, 56, 57, 59, 61, 72, 96, 123, 147, 157, 215–216, 218, 219–220, 221–7, 247

Christ the King 59, 245–6, 249

civil marriages, blessing of 187–8

cleansing of vessels 34

collect 21–2, 31, 54, 55, 59, 66, 108, 112, 117–18, 125, 144, 145–6, 153, 154, 167, 175, 183, 198, 200, 202, 231, 239, 244, 245, 246, 248, 249, 251

collection 49, 128–30, 150

colours, liturgical 61, 95–6, 178, 202, 217, 218, 219, 222, 227, 229, 235, 244

'Comfortable Words' 108
commemorations 59–60
common prayer 10–16, 143
communion *see* distribution
communion assistants 28
community, sense of 4–5
Compline *see* Night Prayer
concelebration 37, 94
confession *see* penitence
confirmation 96, 166, 172, 173–8,
    238, 251
congregation 19–21, 48, 114, 118,
    125, 132–4, 147, 174–5, 191,
    195–6, 206, 253
Corpus Christi 59
Cranmer, Thomas 11, 65, 71, 97, 105,
    139, 152, 153
creation 96, 104, 124, 134, 157, 226,
    241, 247–8, 250–1, 253–4
credence table 44, 129
creed 52, 67, 85, 108, 122–123, 144,
    145–6, 156, 158, 168
cremation 196, 197, 201
crib 45, 222–4, 225, 226–7
cross 11, 41, 43, 50, 103, 104, 112,
    116–17, 129, 134–5, 140, 159, 168,
    169, 176, 194, 199, 209, 228, 230,
    231, 232, 233, 234–5, 248, 254

daily prayer 83–85, 145, 149–55, 253
dance 50, 93
deacon 27, 30–7, 92, 94, 116, 120–1,
    124, 128, 129, 132, 140, 181,
    205–6, 252
dead, prayer for the 195–6, 243–4
Dedication Festival 59, 96, 249–50
deliverance, ministry of 192
dialogue 20, 51–3, 129, 131, 133–4
Didache, The 130
Dismissal 34, 46, 52, 67, 128, 139–
    140, 145, 148, 170, 278, 186, 198,
    201, 234, 237, 238
distribution of Holy Communion 20,
    22, 26, 27, 28, 34, 45, 108, 135–8,
    192, 206, 210–11, 234, 235
diversity, path of 10–16

doctrine, liturgy and 13, 62, 63, 92
drama 7, 26, 28, 48, 93, 231–2, 238
dying, ministry to the 15, 196, 203,
    211–12

'early service' 23, 63, 74, 77, 84, 122,
    132
Easter 9, 39, 45, 55, 56, 57, 58, 59,
    60, 61, 73, 95, 96, 114, 123, 136,
    140, 157, 164, 165, 178, 197, 210,
    227, 228–9, 232, 235, 236–41, 244,
    247, 248, 249
'Easter Anthems' 157
Easter Eve 235
Easter Liturgy, the 235, 237–9
ecclesiology 14
ecumenism 14, 56, 66–7, 71–3, 104,
    105, 123, 134, 186, 234, 245
Elizabeth of Hungary, St 59
Ember Days 252
Enriching the Christian Year 55, 215,
    231, 249–50
Epiphany 39, 47, 57, 58, 59, 60, 157,
    165, 218, 221–2, 224, 225–6, 227
eucharistic prayer 13, 16, 20, 31, 49,
    52, 54, 61, 66, 87, 88–89, 98, 104,
    105, 110, 122, 129, 130, 131–4,
    148, 168, 170, 177, 224, 244
evangelism 4–5, 165, 219
Evening Prayer 6, 10, 32, 36, 51, 58,
    59, 63, 77, 80, 81, 82, 83–5, 93,
    114, 116, 143–5, 149–55, 156–60,
    170, 218–19, 227, 235, 246, 247
evening worship 61, 82 *see also* Evening
    Prayer
Evensong *see* Evening Prayer
Exsultet 238
extended communion 28, 109–10,
    210–11

Faith in the City 12
family likeness 14
family service *see* all-age worship
fellowship and wonder 3–5, 97–9, 147
festivals 59, 117, 123, 247, 249
first communion 171–3, 177

flowers 26, 27, 51, 61, 147, 229, 231
font 38–9, 45–6, 85, 93, 166–71, 176,
  178, 179, 180, 226, 227, 238–9,
  241, 250
fraction *see* breaking of bread
Free Churches 112, 135
freedom and order 5–7, 10–16, 53–54,
  107–8, 126, 143–48, 151
funeral services vii, 21, 32, 35, 36, 96,
  195–204, 241
furnishings 38–46, 147

Gathering 31, 32, 36, 111–18, 144,
  148, 167, 182, 193, 198
gender viii, 25, 28–9, 67
George, St 59
gesture 3, 33, 41, 47–54, 87, 132
gifts 5, 9, 21, 25, 41, 90, 129, 147,
  173, 177, 191, 205, 207–8, 225,
  231, 240, 250, 253
Gloria in excelsis 6, 52, 61, 117, 144,
  167, 175, 216, 229, 233
Good Friday 55, 57, 59, 61, 109, 231,
  234–5
gospel acclamation 56, 186, 224, 237
gospel canticle 152–4, 158
gospel reading 23, 27, 34, 35, 49, 52,
  55, 70–71, 74, 85, 90, 106, 208,
  120–1, 148, 186, 192, 217, 223,
  224, 227, 231, 232, 232, 239, 243
gospels, book of the 34, 112, 159
greeting 21, 31, 53, 107, 108, 112,
  113–114, 128, 144, 145–6, 148,
  150, 153, 175, 183, 187, 202, 217,
  223, 232, 243

Harvest Thanksgiving 41, 147, 239,
  250–1
healing 159, 189–94, 198, 210–12,
  225, 253
heaven 3–5, 8, 19, 54, 103–4, 252,
  254
Herbert, George 190, 228
Hippolytus 133
Holy Cross Day 59

holy days *see* Principal Holy Days,
  Festivals and Lesser Festivals
Holy Innocents 222
Holy Spirit 3, 5–7, 8, 12, 74, 77, 96,
  104, 114, 131–4, 164, 165, 168,
  169, 172, 174, 177, 179, 180, 189,
  212, 230, 236, 240–241, 248,
  253–4
Holy Week 9, 57, 58, 60, 96, 210,
  229, 231–5, 248
home 189, 192, 209–12
homily *see* sermon
house, blessing of a 209
housebound 210–11
Humble Access, Prayer of 66, 105,
  106, 136

inauguration of ministries 205–7
incense 51, 159, 225, 226
inclusive language 67
initiation vii, 169, 171, 173–80 *see also*
  baptism and confirmation
intercession 7, 8–9, 21, 27, 34, 60, 66,
  90, 104, 108, 118, 124–6, 134,
  145–6, 147, 150, 153, 156, 158,
  166, 170, 173, 177, 178, 179, 180,
  181, 192, 193, 206, 211, 217, 223,
  224, 231, 233, 240, 242, 244, 253
In Tune with Heaven 89
invitation to communion 136, 148,
  237

John the Baptist, St 218, 219
John the Evangelist, St 222
Joint Liturgical Group 72
Joseph, St 59
Jubilate 157
Justin Martyr, St 30, 127

Kingdom, Sundays of the 56, 244
Kyrie eleison 82, 106, 116, 117, 144,
  193, 199

Lamb of God 82, 104, 106, 128, 135
language 11, 20, 47–8, 62–8, 87,
  104–5, 150
law *see* freedom and order

laying on of hands 50, 54, 159, 177, 179, 189–194, 212
lay ministers 6, 19–21, 25–9, 30–6, 80, 112, 116, 120–1, 124, 151, 190–1, 210, 230
lectern 24, 38, 39–40, 43, 45, 46, 69, 76, 93, 112, 119, 120, 150
lectionary vii, 16, 57, 59, 69–76, 84, 88, 112, 119, 144–5, 153–4, 158, 159, 215, 218, 222, 229, 231, 240
Lent 6, 57, 58, 60, 61, 73, 96, 108, 117, 120, 123, 137, 145, 147, 157, 165, 216, 226, 227, 228–35, 236–7, 248, 249, 252
Lent, Holy Week, Easter 55, 215, 230, 232–5, 238
Lent, Sundays before 58, 72, 247–8, 250
lesser festivals 59
life, liturgy and 8–9, 60–1
light, blessing of *see* candles
litany 125, 153, 193, 230, 234
Liturgical Commission vii, viii, 12, 13, 16, 56, 64, 66, 107, 150, 173
liturgical revision 10–16, 62–3, 65–7, 97, 104, 106–7
Lord's Prayer 67, 105, 108, 128, 134, 145, 146, 150, 153, 159, 178, 185, 200, 201, 202, 217, 223, 243
Lucy, St 216, 218
Luwum, Janani 59

Magnificat see Mary, Song of
Marana tha 216
Marriage Service 11, 21, 35, 68, 181–7
Mary Magdalene, St 59
Mary, Song of 15, 153, 158, 218
Mary, the Blessed Virgin 59, 67, 96, 216, 218, 226, 230, 248, 249
Maundy Thursday 55, 59, 96, 109, 168, 229, 231, 233–4, 235
memorial services 143, 198, 204, 244
memory 14–16, 62–6
Michaelmas 250, 252
ministries 19–21, 25–9, 30–7, 89–90, 107, 159, 189–191, 205–7, 240

mission vii, 4–5, 12, 80, 82, 159
Morning Prayer 10, 32, 36, 59, 74, 80, 81, 83–85, 93, 114, 116, 143–5, 149–55, 156–60, 170, 235, 246, 247
Mothering Sunday 58, 147, 230–1
Murray, Gregory 65
music 10, 50, 61, 65, 87, 88–9, 113, 132, 149, 158, 166, 170, 171, 183, 185, 217, 222, 232, 237, 238, 243
see also choir
mystery 87, 97–9, 147, 236

Naming of Jesus 224–5, 249
New Revised Standard Version 15
New Year 223, 224–5
Nicholas, St 216
Night Prayer 82, 153, 160, 232
notices 112, 114
Nunc Dimittis see Simeon, Song of

offertory 9, 48, 128–31, 170
oil 159, 168, 169, 176, 177, 179, 189–193, 205, 225
open prayer 126, 153, 157
ordinary time 56, 57–8, 73, 75, 96, 120, 157, 241, 244, 247
ordination 13, 96, 177, 252
organ 121, 151, 208

Palestrina, Giovanni 65
Palm Sunday 96, 145, 147, 158, 210, 229, 231, 232–33, 249
Parochial Church Council 79, 94
participation 19–21, 25–9, 47–53, 132–4, 147
paschal candle 45, 168, 170, 178, 197, 199, 202, 237, 238–9, 240, 241
Passiontide 228–9, 230, 231–5
Pastoral Prayers 191, 194, 209
Patronal Festival 59, 248–9
Patterns for Worship viii, 12, 76, 114, 125, 139–40, 143, 144, 147, 215, 224, 230, 239, 240, 250
Paul, St 26, 60, 123, 164, 235, 238
peace, the 4, 22, 31, 34, 50, 52, 56,

82, 97–8, 105, 108, 109, 127–8,
145, 148, 159, 170, 177, 178, 179,
180, 186, 193, 237, 244
penitence 7, 11, 16, 34, 446, 48, 52,
56, 61, 82, 103–4, 105, 106, 108,
114–17, 143, 144, 145, 147, 140,
156, 157, 167, 186, 187, 192, 193–
4, 198, 199–200, 202, 211, 219,
224, 228–30, 237, 253
Pentecost 39, 56, 57, 59, 61, 77, 96,
123, 136, 140, 165, 178, 230, 236,
240–1, 246, 248
Phillips, J.B. 15
Phos Hilaron 159
pilgrimage 45–6, 112
post communion 22, 59, 66, 105, 108,
138, 186, 193, 206, 231, 239, 244,
245, 246, 249, 251
posture 20, 22, 24, 33, 34, 41, 48,
51–3, 61, 107, 132, 147
Prayer Book of 1928 10,182, 196
prayers at the preparation of the table
130, 186
praying the liturgy 21–5, 33–4, 50, 54,
117–18, 124, 132
preaching *see* sermon
preface of eucharistic prayer 55, 56,
105, 106, 109, 122, 132–4, 186,
193, 224, 228, 237
preparation 107, 108, 144
preparation of the table 34, 108, 128–
31
Presentation of Christ *see* Candlemas
presidency 30–4, 41, 53–4, 118, 147,
187, 190–1, 251
principal feasts and holy days 55, 56,
58–9, 108, 117, 122, 123, 145,
225, 227, 240, 242, 247, 248, 249,
250
principal service lectionary 71–2, 74,
158, 237
procession 45–6, 112, 129, 140, 159,
166, 176, 178, 217, 224, 225, 227,
232, 239
Promise of His Glory, The viii, 55, 56,

76, 209, 210, 215. 217, 218, 219,
224–7, 242–3, 245
psalmody 51, 59, 84, 106, 119–20,
144, 145–6, 149, 150, 152, 153,
158, 200, 202, 230
pulpit 38, 39–40, 46, 93
Purity, Collect for 15, 114

Reader 10, 30–6
Reception into the Church of England
178–9
reconciliation, sacrament of 191,
193–4, 211
Reformation 51, 63, 92, 105–6, 163
Remembrance Sunday 58, 145
renewal 5–7, 8, 9, 12, 47, 65, 97, 180,
192, 253
reserved sacrament 109, 210–11, 235
Revised Common Lectionary, the 71–3,
88
Rogation Days 239, 250
Roman Catholic Church 10, 13–14,
19–20, 34, 47, 52, 56, 71–3, 78, 84,
88, 94, 95–6, 104, 112, 114, 128,
130, 133, 150, 229, 235
rural communities 79–80, 98

Sacrament, Liturgy of the 127–40,
148, 186, 190, 202, 232, 235, 238
Sanctus 4–5, 20, 53, 133–4
saints 4, 57, 96, 202, 216, 242–3, 246,
247–8, 249
sacrifice 129, 254
sanctorale 247–8
seasonal material 12, 55–61, 105,
108–9, 120, 125, 128, 132–4, 159,
165, 210, 215–51
second service lectionary 74
senses *see* body, human
sermon 4, 22, 34, 53, 74–5, 121–2,
144, 145, 156, 167, 170, 175, 182,
183, 198, 199, 202, 223–4, 231,
233
servers 26–8, 90, 95
Service of Prayer and Dedication *see*
Civil Marriage, Blessing of

'Service of the Word, A' viii, 36, 143–8, 149–50, 156–60, 170–71, 252

service planning 6–7, 145–7

shape 5–7, 16, 143–8, 175, 182

sick, ministry to the 189–93, 210–12

silence 3, 21, 23–5, 50, 107, 108, 116, 117, 119, 125, 137, 138, 147, 154, 157, 175, 192, 198, 200, 230, 233, 234, 238, 243, 244

Simeon, Song of 153, 201, 226–7

solemn blessing 139–40, 186, 224, 230, 239, 240, 242, 243

space 38–46

spirituality 8–9, 12, 14–15

Stephen, St 222

structure see shape

subdeacon 27

summary of the law 106, 108

Sumner, Mary 59

Sunday 4, 25–6, 36, 45, 55, 57–8, 59, 60, 61, 71, 77–82, 84, 111, 112, 116, 117, 121, 122–3, 135, 143, 145, 149, 156–60, 164, 165–71, 173, 174, 191, 210–11, 221, 225, 226, 227, 236, 239, 242, 247, 248, 249, 250, 251

supplementary consecration 108, 137

symbolism 47–54, 103–4, 112, 196–7, 205, 238

table see altar

Taizé 51, 65, 83, 150, 158

taking of the bread and wine 128–31

teaching 4–5, 147 see also sermon

temporale 247

ten commandments 106, 108, 230

Te Deum laudamus 153, 159, 243

testimony 159, 167–8, 175

thanksgiving 7, 110, 131–4, 145, 146, 147, 150, 157, 159, 207, 223

Thanksgiving for the gift of a child 167, 171

Thanksgiving for the Holy Ones of God 242, 243

theme 12, 74–5, 146

third service lectionary 74

Thirty-Nine Articles 13

Thomas, St 216

time of day 61

transfiguration 59, 72, 247, 249

Trinity Sunday 58, 75, 145, 158, 165, 248

Trinity, Sundays after 58, 123, 247, 249

Veni Creator 108

Venite 144, 157

vesture 10, 11, 33, 92–6, 229, 235

vigil 51, 108, 237–9, 242, 244

water 11, 38–9, 49, 130, 159, 164–70, 172, 179, 197, 198, 201, 203, 207–8, 226, 253

wedding see Marriage Service

welcome to new ministries see inauguration of new ministries

weekday worship 58, 59, 71, 83–5, 117, 146, 148, 174, 218

Wesley, John 82

Whitsunday see Pentecost

wine 23, 26, 28, 40, 42, 48, 49, 51, 98, 103–4, 112, 128–31, 131–8, 186, 210, 211, 226, 234, 235, 244, 253–4

Word, Liturgy of the 31, 32, 35, 36, 39–40, 46, 69–76, 117, 119–126, 127, 148, 156, 175, 182, 183, 192, 193, 230, 235 see also 'Service of the Word, A'

world 8–9, 45, 103–4, 127, 190, 250–1, 253–4

young people 8, 27–28, 80, 86–91 see also Children

Zechariah, Song of 152–3, 158

The Society for Promoting Christian Knowledge (SPCK) was founded in 1698. Its mission statement is:

To promote Christian knowledge by

- **Communicating the Christian faith in its rich diversity**
- **Helping people to understand the Christian faith and to develop their personal faith; and**
- **Equipping Christians for mission and ministry**

SPCK Worldwide serves the Church through Christian literature and communication projects in 100 countries, and provides books for those training for ministry in many parts of the developing world. This worldwide service depends upon the generosity of others and all gifts are spent wholly on ministry programmes, without deductions.

SPCK Bookshops support the life of the Christian community by making available a full range of Christian literature and other resources, providing support for those training for ministry, and assisting bookstalls and book agents throughout the UK.

SPCK Publishing produces Christian books and resources, covering a wide range of inspirational, pastoral, practical and academic subjects. Authors are drawn from many different Christian traditions, and publications aim to meet the needs of a wide variety of readers in the UK and throughout the world.

The Society does not necessarily endorse the individual views contained in its publications, but hopes they stimulate readers to think about and further develop their Christian faith.

For information about the Society, visit our website at *www.spck.org.uk*, or write to:
SPCK, Holy Trinity Church, Marylebone Road,
London NW1 4DU, United Kingdom.